Dictionary of Globalization

Dictionary of Globalization

Andrew Jones

polity

First published in 2006 by Polity Press
Reprinted in 2008

Polity Press
65 Bridge Street
Cambridge CB2 1UR, UK

Polity Press
350 Main Street
Malden, MA 02148, USA

ISBN-10: 0-7456-3440-0
ISBN-13: 978-07456-3440-1
ISBN-10: 0-7456-3441-9 (pb)
ISBN-13: 978-07456-3441-8 (pb)

A catalogue record for this book is available from the British Library.

Typeset in 11 on 13 pt Scala
by SNP Best-set Typesetter Ltd, Hong Kong
Printed and bound in United States by Odyssey Press Inc., Gonic, New Hampshire

The publisher has used its best endeavours to ensure that the URLs for external websites referred to in this book are correct and active at the time of going to press. However, the publisher has no responsibility for the websites and can make no guarantee that a site will remain live or that the content is or will remain appropriate.

Every effort has been made to trace all copyright holders, but if any have been inadvertently overlooked the publishers will be pleased to include any necessary credits in any subsequent reprint or edition.

For further information on Polity, visit our website: <www.polity.co.uk>

Contents

Defining Globalization: A Guide on How to Use this Book

1   Defining the indefinable? An introduction

The idea of producing a dictionary of globalization may seem a strange undertaking. The concept is, after all, just one word. Yet many social scientific commentators have argued that globalization – as a concept – has become what the sociologist Raymond Williams calls a *keyword*. Within academic thought, its significance is such that it is already at the head of a developing discipline called 'globalization studies'. More importantly, however, beyond academic and policy discussions it is now everywhere in daily life: in newspapers, on television, in advertisements and even in rock music lyrics. And what is perhaps most remarkable is the *speed* with which this has happened. This word, that hardly a soul outside the academic world used fifteen years ago, supposedly captures one of the most important changes occurring in every society in every country on the planet, and no one can escape its influence. Everyone has heard of it.

This important word is a new arrival in most major languages, and over the last decade globalization has also rapidly become the headline target for new forms of worldwide political resistance. The emergence of one (or many) anti-globalization movements, along with the associated protests around the world in recent years, has already created a highly polarized and contentious debate about the validity, significance and implications of this phenomenon. I am regularly asked when speaking on this topic whether or not I am 'for' or 'against' globalization, as if such a choice were as easy as deciding which team I supported in a sports match. Such questions are far removed from the academic usage of this concept, and they betray another problem in contemporary understandings of the word: few people have a clear or consistent view of its precise meaning. As Zygmunt Bauman argues, globalization has become in this way one of the 'words of our time' used in numerous different contexts by an enormous variety of commentators – and as with all such words, it runs the risk of meaning very little.

Taken at its most general level, globalization can be defined as the growing interconnectedness and interrelatedness of all aspects of society. Many theorists such as Anthony Giddens or Ulrich Beck argue that it can be understood as a process, that it can be identified in almost every dimension of contemporary life and that whilst in no sense a novel development in human history, it has become considerably more pronounced since the mid-twentieth century. However, its profile as a keyword stems largely from a more specific association with changes in the world economy in recent decades (and since the end of the Cold War in particular). For most non-academic commentators, globalization is first and foremost about the development of a global-scale, capitalist free market economy that is entwining economic activity across national borders in new and unprecedented ways. From an academic perspective, however, it has a plethora of further usages. It is applied to various different dimensions of social life in the contemporary world, spanning cultural, technological, informational, environmental and political transformations – to name but a few of the more significant spheres of globalization's conceptual reach.

Yet no matter what point of entry you take into the globalization debate, like all such generalized keywords, globalization is arguably becoming more of a problem than a solution for understanding the world. It is used now in so many contexts with such reckless abandon by all kinds of people that it is very easy to become both overwhelmed and confused by the sheer diversity of issues this phenomenon is being applied to. For those who seek to study globalization from an academic perspective, the situation is little better. Academic journals and bookstore shelves are brimming with titles that include this word. There are literally thousands of books that claim to cover some aspect of the globalization debate, and it would take years to read even half of the articles produced from a search of databases of academic publications. Such a volume of information, discussion and argument is bewildering, certainly from the perspective of the students I teach about globalization. I am often asked which article 'is most important' or which book is 'the one I need to read'. What is more, the continued development of the Internet offers seductive and dangerous resources for those interested in understanding globalization. A search on Google returns hits of staggering proportions: hundreds of thousands of documents, reports, news articles and dedicated sites referring to globalization. The temptation for many of my students is to rely heavily on such sources of information and analysis. The problem, however, is the lack of editorial control over such resources and the absence of guidance as to both the quality and veracity of information and analysis on offer. The rise of Internet-based free-access encyclopaedia resources is in one sense a marvellous development, but since many rely on voluntary non-specialist and only loosely moderated postings, the editing of many entries leaves much to be desired. The situation is reminiscent of Douglas Adams' description of his fictional forerunner to the Internet, *The Hitchhiker's Guide to the Galaxy* (1979), which is described as being 'very unevenly edited' – although at least where entries are 'wildly inaccurate', they are 'definitively inaccurate'.

Which brings me to the key purpose of this book. In writing a 'dictionary' of globalization, I have sought to offer a different kind of text on the debate itself. In no real sense can this book be exhaustive. It is not a dictionary in a conventional sense; it does not adopt the approach of the *Oxford English Dictionary* to the English language, nor is it simply a glossary of key concepts in the approach adopted by other social science 'dictionaries'. Rather, the aim is to provide a critical commentary on the contemporary globalization debate that enables the reader to navigate a path for themselves through the vast and burgeoning literature on globalization. By navigate, I mean that the 'definitions' in this 'dictionary' are more than simple statements of facts. The globalization debate is far too embroiled in unresolved philosophical, conceptual and political issues for anyone to claim to be able to offer a purely factual and incontestable set of 'definitions'. Rather, the entries in this book seek to offer a concise assessment of the position and significance of a concept, thinker or organization in relation to the wider globalization debate. The goal is to help readers understand how different parts of the debate around globalization are linked to each other and to offer a variety of ways in which they can develop these linkages in their own understanding. In other words, this book is a 'short-cut' tool that aims to facilitate a more rapid development of a critical understanding of the major thinkers, concepts and different arguments that dominate contemporary academic understanding of globalization. It is not a substitute for reading widely across the globalization literature but rather should enable those who wish to study globalization to derive greater value out of their forays into the debate.

However, in order to achieve that goal there is the need to provide an overview and context to the entries that follow. The remainder of this introduction takes up this task by offering a critical perspective on the major aspects of the globalization debate. The next section considers the historical development of ideas about globalization and explores the antecedents to contemporary globalization theories in classical social and political economy schools of thought. This should allow those trying to come to grips with the startling immediacy of this debate to understand how its philosophical and conceptual development has a longer history than much contemporary commentary leads one to believe. It also then offers an overview of the evolution of the current debate over the last couple of decades. The third section then moves to consider the contemporary debate in depth, outlining five major strands in the literature and pointing to the key issues and topics that characterize each one. Whilst by no means comprehensive, this should provide the reader with a broad understanding of the main dimensions to the globalization debate as it currently stands. Section 4 then moves on to the rather more difficult question of whether and how globalization as a (singular) concept can be theorized. A series of underlying concepts and abstractions that have been used to construct globalization theories are discussed, grouped together into four couplets: time and space, territory and scale, system and structure, and finally process and agency. The aim is to offer the reader an initial insight into how theorists have sought to develop a common theoretical basis for understanding the concept. Finally, this chapter ends with some guidance on the entries that follow through this dictionary, and also how these entries need to be used in relation to wider reading.

2   *The emergence of the globalization debate*

Although now widely circulated in popular discussions, the concept of globalization has emerged over the last two decades from a number of distinct intellectual traditions and academic disciplines. Even in the early 1990s the word was not familiar to anyone outside a limited group of academics, and even within this sphere there were relatively few journal articles which mentioned this term.

Three distinct academic origins to the current usage can be identified. The first is in business and management theory dating back to the 1960s. Amongst a number of management gurus and within US business schools a number of commentators published what were initially business manuals concerned with how to run and improve the competitiveness of large US multinational firms. This represented a new, 'cutting-edge' area of management science at the time when US firms sought to expand their operations into more countries around the world. By the 1970s, the debate around the development of the multinational business organization had produced a sizeable literature and a number of theorists began to argue that firms needed to become global in the scope of their operations rather than replicating multiple national-scale operations. Key management thinkers began to refer to this process as 'globalization' and by the 1980s this was already becoming one of the key vogue concepts pushed in both the academic literature on management and in the popular business literature. Commentators like Kenichi Ohmae, many of whom were themselves business practitioners working for large corporations or management consultancies, argue that the issue of globalization at firm level was the key challenge for businesses in the latter part of the twentieth century.

Second is a diverse set of academic contributions across social and cultural theory, which again stem from the 1960s. Most notable amongst these is Marshall McLuhan's idea of the 'global village', which sought to capture the way in which modernity was increasingly integrating global society through new forms of communication. Also important are concepts that emerged from the burgeoning environmental movement, which began to propagate a conceptual understanding of the Earth and its natural resources as a finite entity. The first pictures of the Earth from space, along with subsequent pictures taken from Moon orbit of a distant and small Earth, provided substantial impetus behind the idea that all human society existed together in close and inevitably entwined proximity. Likewise, James Lovelock's ecologically based 'Gaia' thesis presented a set of arguments about the nature of the global environment and the potentially negative impacts of human society and development on that environment. The idea of 'Spaceship Earth' undoubtedly continues to resonate in debates around the global environment today.

Third, but no less important than the others, are a series of academic literatures across political economy and the social sciences that were more specifically concerned with post-Second World War international economic development and politics. During the 1960s, a number of different strands of academic theory were engaging with the 'development-as-modernization' paradigm which had characterized the new Bretton Woods institutions' approach to the developing world. Many drew on classical social, political and philosophical theories including Marx, Weber and Durkheim. Notable predecessors to globalization theories include those of Andre Gunder Frank and others on 'dependent development', contending that the Third World was held in a state of underdevelopment by the capitalist First World. Similarly, Immanuel Wallerstein's 'world systems analysis' developed this theoretical line in arguing from a Marxian perspective that the capitalist world economy was characterized by core–periphery relations and that a capitalist world system had become 'global in scope' during the twentieth century.

However, it was not until the late 1980s that globalization as a term began to become common currency between these various discrete literatures and spheres of discussion. Crossover between academic disciplines began to occur, and the occasional journalist or policy commentator started to use the word. This was certainly catalysed by the end of the Cold War and the 'triumph of free-market capitalism'. This process accelerated through the 1990s as globalization usage 'took off', first measurably in the number of academic articles, then quickly in book titles and newspapers. By the mid-1990s the word had ceased to be obscure jargon and could be found across the Internet and popular media. Its entrance into all major global languages and everyday usage probably became assured when mass protests at G8 summits began to be attributed to the 'anti-globalization' movement in the later 1990s.

In terms of understanding the nature of this increasingly vast debate, the political scientist David Held and his co-authors offered what has become an increasingly definitive (although not unproblematic) academic account of the development of the debate spanning the social sciences and humanities. They proposed three emerging schools of thought across the globalization debate through the 1990s. The first school is the *hyperglobalists* who regard globalization as the key concept that defines a new epoch in human history. From this approach, one of the most important shifts has been the significance of nation-states. Many hyperglobalists regard the nation-state as an anachronism: they have become unnatural, even impossible, units of business in the contemporary world. The hyperglobalists, as characterized by Held and his co-authors, are largely contributors emerging from the business and management studies approach. Hyperglobalists argue for the emergence of a borderless world where economic activity becomes denationalized and there are new patterns of winners and losers.

The second school of thought proposed by Held and his co-authors is the *sceptics*. This approach is also focused on the economic realm but derives more from a political economy analysis of macroeconomic data on flows of trade, foreign direct investment (FDI) and other forms of finance. The key argument made by sceptics like Paul Hirst and Grahame Thompson is that recent levels of economic interdependence are not historically unprecedented. In fact, according to their interpretations of trade data the world economy was considerably less integrated at the end of the twentieth century when compared with the end of the nineteenth. The view that nation-states have become defunct or less prevalent is also strongly contested. They suggest that globalization, at least as described by the *hyperglobalists*, is a myth and that the hyperglobalist approach is flawed and politically naive. A number of commentators who fall within this broad school also make arguments, grounded in broad macroeconomic analysis, that there is greater regionalization, rather than globalization, occurring. They point to the development and intensified economic interconnectedness within regional trading blocs such as the EU, NAFTA and ASEAN. More recently, others have also sought to debunk the hyperglobalist conception of transnational firms as truly global corporations, again pointing to the regional focus of many of the world's largest firms.

The third, *transformationalist*, school of thought represents the approach developed by Held and his co-authors at the end of the 1990s as the globalization debate matured. They seek both to widen the scope of the concept and also to move beyond the relatively polarized terms of the hyperglobalist and sceptical schools. At the heart of what they term the *tranformationalist* thesis is the argument that, in the twenty-first century, globalization is a central driving force behind the rapid social, political and economic changes that are reshaping modern societies and the world order. Whilst acknowledging elements of the sceptical contributions, they suggest that overall globalization processes are historically unprecedented and that globalization is a powerful transformative force. It amounts to a massive shake-out of societies, economies and governance. Writing at the end of the 1990s, Held and his co-authors thus argue that the future direction of globalization is unclear. In arguing that the phenomenon is 'a contingent historical process replete with contradictions', they feel unable to make claims about its future trajectory.

In the last few years, this typology of the globalization debate has become widely cited in the academic and policy literatures. It has become an accepted framework for mapping the emergence of the debate and has been used by subsequent contributors as a starting point. However, it is important to realize that Held and his co-authors' account is not unproblematic, and a number of developments have called into question aspects of their approach. First, and probably foremost, both the coherence and the comprehensiveness of these distinct schools of thought on globalization are questionable. It is not difficult to take issue with the 'pigeon-holing' of contributors into one school or the other since many adopt a very different approach to fellow 'sceptics' or 'hyperglobalists'. It can thus be argued that there were and are more schools of thought on globalization than Held et al. identify and that, in characterizing the debate in this manner, they have inadvertently undermined the ability to recognize the nuances in various contributors' positions.

Second, there is the issue of what we might term the politics of knowledge. Held et al.'s review of the 'state of the art' of the globalization debate in the late 1990s attempts to present an academic and objective analysis of the concept and its validity for the contemporary world. Such a perspective is grounded in a social scientific tradition with philosophical roots in classical sociology and political economy. It aspires to offer a value-free explanation of what globalization can be understood to be. However, recent critical traditions within the social sciences – ones drawing upon postmodern and poststructural philosophical traditions – cast doubt on the ability of the theorist to adopt an objective and value-free position. Critics such as Douglas Kellner would suggest that all knowledge and our theories of the world are heavily subjective and politicized. And social-scientific analyses of globalization are perhaps increasingly vulnerable to such criticism because the concept itself has become so heavily politicized and contested in all spheres of life. Radical anti-globalization theorists have suggested that academic theorization of globalization incorporates a range of implicit subjective assumptions about the nature of globalization that can be contested. For those who view globalization as a political project, it is becoming increasingly difficult to accept an academic objective account.

Third and finally, there is the conception of globalization in the singular which is the outcome of Held and his co-authors' analysis of the debate. As transformationalists, their argument re-theorizes globalization as 'a powerful transformative force'. The concept itself, however, is an abstraction. Whilst Held et al.'s analysis of the multiple global transformations under way at the end of the twentieth century is well supported through lengthy reviews of an interdisciplinary academic literature, the concept itself is taken as a pre-given. The implicit assumption is that globalization is 'something' (a process, a force) which explains what is going on. Yet the concept itself remains abstract in this kind of wide-ranging analysis. Whilst Held et al. discuss a wide range of both causes and effects of greater interconnectedness, the common foundations of these changes to contemporary society are debatable. I will return to this issue in the fourth section.

3 Navigating the contemporary debate

In recent years the literature on globalization has split into a wide variety of directions. Given the sheer volume of contributions, there is an increasing need to differentiate between sub-categories of the debate – not least because individual commentators often fail to identify and/or demarcate where they are coming from. Book covers of all kinds excel at trumpeting an important and provocative contribution to the globalization debate but it is only upon looking inside that a tight focus on, for example, transnational firms or development economics becomes apparent. It is therefore an important first step in navigating the oceanic globalization literature to realize what more specific issues a contributor is seeking to engage with. In that context, I offer in this section a series of sub-groupings around which major tranches of the literature can be brought together. Of course, this in no way implies rigid boundaries between these sub-debates. Many contributors develop arguments that transcend these divisions, or in fact seek to tackle all of them in one enormous brushstroke as often happens with popular, journalistic globalization bestsellers. However, that does not diminish the argument for developing an understanding of the more detailed features of these sub-debates because a large volume of literature (and often that which gains most theoretical and analytical traction on an aspect of globalization) is highly focused. I provide here a brief overview of the key elements of at least five of the sub-debates of which I think no student of globalization should be ignorant.

The first is the most common by far: economic and technological globalization. A wide variety of academic and policy thinkers have contributed to arguments about the nature of economic integration and the trajectory of the global economy. In broad terms, the global economy is now larger, more geographically extensive and produces more goods and service than at any previous point in history. Trade has also increased in volume at the global scale, although it has increased much more substantially still at the level of regions such as Europe (facilitated by trading bloc agreements). Furthermore, the organization of this production has been transformed radically in recent decades. Where most developed economies had nation-based firms in the 1950s and 1960s, the rise of multinational and transnational firms has been central in shifting the production of manufactured goods into a 'global factory'. Semi-skilled manufacturing jobs have moved to developing countries and transnational corporations (TNCs) have emerged from nation-states across the globe in all industries, so that economic activity has become very much globalized. With new forms of information and communications technologies, and mirrored by global financial integration, the global productive economy has moved beyond the scale of nation-states and even regional trading blocs. Such a shift has also had profound impacts on the physical built environment of human society, with cities increasingly becoming nodes in globalized networks of relations, and key global cities such as New York, London or Tokyo taking up new functions in acting as centres of power and control in the global economy.

Second, and related, this economic globalization feeds into a strand of the globalization debate concerned with the political and governmental dimensions of contemporary globalization. At the centre of this is the ideological basis to contemporary global capitalism and the relationship with national governments and institutions of supranational governance. Many point to the fact that since the end of the Cold War and the so-called triumph of capitalism (Francis Fukuyama's 'end of history'), free-market neo-liberal economic development has become the accepted approach to economic activity across the globe. The post-Second World War supranational institutions (the International Monetary Fund (IMF), the World Bank, the World Trade Organization (WTO)) have actively sought to encourage and propagate policies in this respect across the globe. Yet globalization in general has presented serious challenges to the very basis of governance in the world today: the nation-state. The rise of transnational corporations (TNCs), global financial integration and supranational institutions has removed certain power held by nation-states and has led many to argue that national sovereignty has been eroded. A considerable proportion of the globalization literature is concerned with how global governance is developing, and what kinds of transnational governance structures should be developed in the twenty-first century.

Third, the nature of sociocultural globalization forms another identifiable segment in the debate. Also related to debates about the future of nation-states in a world where cultural identities are becoming increasingly hybridized and cultural flows permeate borders through the global media, a key discussion has focused on whether or not cultural globalization is producing a homogenous global culture (often further reduced to Americanization). Whilst undoubtedly globalization is producing new global cultural linkages and commonalities, some positive and some negative, increasingly the idea of a singular 'global culture' is contested, with thinkers such as John Tomlinson and Arjun Appadurai suggesting that cultural globalization produces greater diversity as well as commonalities. Also important in this sphere of the debate is the impact of increasing transnational migration and flows of people around the globe. At one level theorists like Leslie Sklair point to the development of an increasingly mobile global economic and political elite – the transnational capitalist class – who exist in an increasingly transnational community. At another, the underbelly of globalization is also being highlighted as low-skill and low-paid workers are increasingly moving in mass migrations. There is also a growing interest in how globalization processes affect a variety of related world societal changes. For example, the emergence and development of diasporic transnational communities where identities and communities are developing in a manner above and beyond the scale of territorial nation-states.

Fourth, a growing segment of the globalization literature is highly focused on environmental issues. The feasibility of and need for sustainable development in the twenty-first century is central, with many commentators arguing that contemporary transnational institutions are inadequate to tackle current levels of environmental degradation across the globe, let alone develop policies that will redress this in the future. Key areas of discussion in the literature concerned with global environmental politics are issues that clearly have implications for the entire population of Earth and their future well-being: global warming, sea-level change, natural resource depletion and the destruction and commercialization of biodiversity.

Fifth, and finally, an already large proportion of the existing globalization literature can be loosely described as being part of a critical/radical or anti-globalization strand. Whilst a range of different areas of criticism are covered by this part of the literature, the central focus is mainly the failings and inadequacies of contemporary neo-liberal economic globalization rather than a broad engagement with all aspects of the academic globalization debate. The critical literature argues that the path of global economic development is producing greater inequality in the world and not delivering social justice. Commentators like Samir Amin, Martin Khor and Vandana Shiva point to the growing wealth and power of a small capitalist elite at the global scale and argue that TNCs are driven primarily by greed and profit, at the expense of society and the environment. A key target is also the concentration of power and control in unaccountable and undemocratic supranational bodies – notably the Bretton Woods institutions and the WTO. Whilst earlier contributions tended to focus on developing a critique of neo-liberal globalization, more recently there have been a series of arguments made by thinkers like Walden Bello about alternative forms of globalization. However, the majority of the theoretical alternative perspectives developed have been grounded in neo-Marxian analyses that continue to struggle to develop what many regard as a feasible and mainstream alternative to global capitalist development.

In reality, of course, I would reiterate that there can be no clear demarcation between different strands of the globalization debate and, by the very nature of the topic, many contributors straddle several of these different segments. Readers of this dictionary should therefore be careful not to pigeon-hole commentators within a given set of sub-debates whilst also appreciating the often quite distinct positions from which articles or books with 'globalization' in their titles are approaching the issue.

4   Theorizing globalization – one phenomenon or many?

The central philosophical and conceptual question at the heart of the globalization debate is whether or not this concept captures a singular, identifiable phenomenon which is relevant and applicable to the multitude of transformations with which it is associated. This is a difficult question and one to which I will not seek to offer a final answer. However, this section considers the various underlying features of globalization in general which are argued by leading theorists to provide a justification for the claims made about its almost universal significance to contemporary social life in the twenty-first century. I suggest that four major underlying philosophical couplets underpin contemporary globalization theories. These represent the main underlying philosophical 'building blocks' around which are being constructed the theories of what globalization as a phenomenon in the world can be understood to 'be'.

The first, and perhaps most important, concerns space and time. Many of the leading theoretical contributors to the globalization debate have argued that the phenomenon can be demarcated as a transformation in the nature of our own and other people's experience of space and time. Sociologist Anthony Giddens has made one of the most important contributions in this respect. He argues that modern life is characterized by the stretching of our experience of space and time – a process he calls time-space distanciation. Social relations are becoming 'stretched' in all their forms, facilitated by information and communications technology, the global media and transport. This is a feature of contemporary modernity in Giddens' view and it represents a fundamental shift in the nature of social systems. In effect, globalization is a process involving the radical reorganizing and reconfiguration of relationships between individuals, groups and organizations, so that regardless of whether or not individuals become more globally mobile, multiple distant influences affect their lives. The geographer David Harvey develops a similar theoretical line of argument in seeing globalization as characterized at root by time–space compression. Other theorists also have in various ways considered how globalization can be conceived of as a common phenomenon through its impact on our experience of time and space.

Second, the concern with globalization as a spatio-temporal phenomenon also relates to two spatial concepts that globalization theorists use as theoretical building blocks: territory and scale. In the case of the former, theorists such as Giddens have argued that the experience of globalization processes is characterized by what he terms 'deterritorialization'. This is where social relations become 'detached' from their places of origin and transferred to new locales (reterritorialized). According to John Tomlinson, deterritorialization thus expresses the 'novelty of the contemporary transformation of place'. Territory is also important to those like Saskia Sassen who see globalization as being generically characterized by 'transborderness'. Furthermore, this transformation of the relationship between social practices and territory is often conceptualized as now being constituted at different scales. This represents another key concept in globalization theories. Considerable debate about globalization in the abstract has sought to use a multi-scalar (local, national, regional, global) framework to try to understand the transformation of social relations in a globalized world. For example, both Giddens and Harvey cited above draw on classical social theory that globalization can be understood as being articulated in the dialectical relationship between the global and local scales. Concepts such as glocalization have been developed by some in order to capture better the scalar nature of globalization processes.

A third conceptual couplet in globalization theories is that of system and structure. In developing a unified theorization of globalization, a number of theorists have argued that globalization is a world systemic phenomenon and is occurring at a structural level in the contemporary world. Growing interconnectedness in this sense is a feature of global society that is occurring beyond the scale of individuals or small groups and is related to meso-scale interactions in the world – by which theorists often mean nation-states in the international state system or market forces in the global trading system. Whilst individual people in their multitude make up this system, organizations and wider collective interactions are (more) important in explaining contemporary globalization. In this sense, theorists such as Leslie Sklair have argued for the utility of 'global system theory'. Similarly, in international relations theory, contributors such as Robert Cox seek to understand the global-scale structures of governance that are emerging as products of the international state system along with the structural relations that exist between these entities.

Fourth, and finally, are the concepts of process and agency. Globalization is widely argued to be processual in nature – although not one process but many in the view of Anthony Giddens. David Held and his co-authors offer a framework for understanding the key processes of globalization in the abstract. They argue that it can be understood around four major spatio-temporal processes: the stretching of social relations (extensification), the increasing intensity of exchanges (intensification), the speeding up of global flows (velocity) and the impact propensity of global interconnectedness (impact). These are the key processes that, they argue, characterize both the contemporary phase of globalization and earlier historical phases. Not all theorists agree, however, that globalization is one (or many) processes. The underlying disagreement to a large extent depends on how power and agency are understood. For those who draw upon poststructuralist philosophical traditions, a processual conceptualization of globalization implies a coherence and rigidity in agency in the contemporary world that does not exist in reality. The power relations and social agency driving global interconnectedness in this viewpoint are inconsistent, contradictory and sometimes work to produce disconnection. This opens up the critical space to contest whether the phenomena captured in the concept of globalization are the consequence of transformations that can be demarcated as one or more processes.

Overall, each of these four conceptual couplets I think identifies a key thread of discussion common across many theoretical attempts to understand globalization. The 'million-dollar' question behind much globalization theory, however, remains whether there is one phenomenon out there worth theorizing in general. It could be argued that globalization is such a diverse concept that seeking ever more specific sub-concepts, sub-forms and sub-categories of increasingly differentiated elements to globalization is a misguided undertaking. Social theorists might be better to abandon the project of 'grand globalization theory' in favour of more targeted theory that really gets to grips with key aspects of contemporary societal transformation. A critical researcher into globalization should always be asking themselves what 'big theory' is adding to our understanding. Smaller theories may be more appropriate. Which direction the theoretical debate about globalization takes remains to be seen.

5   Using the entries in this book

The entries in this book are loosely divided into three categories: institutions and organizations; concepts, phenomena and processes; and 'thinkers'. All have been compiled in order to offer a wide-ranging set of reference sources that can provide the reader with a resource to draw upon as they research a particular aspect or issue within the debate. They cannot be a substitute for wider reading around topics but provide a first point of entry and subsequent guidance in identifying key issues that are relevant. However, in that respect, I have avoided Harvard referencing within the text body in favour of a more targeting approach with respect to further reading. For each entry, a small number of recommended further readings are suggested that are intended to be directly relevant to that entry. At the end of the dictionary, there is also a section of 'additional readings' which offers a list of major 'overview' texts and readers, as well as more focused shorter readings around major sub-dimensions to the globalization debate. Words in **bold type** in the dictionary text are cross-references to other entries.

The first group of entries – organizations and institutions – is the most factual, and tends to be shorter. The entries aim to provide key information about institutions and organizations that regularly are cited in the globalization debate. Much of this information might be sensibly expanded by further research and reading on the Web. This is not the case for the next two groups, however, where there is a clear need to engage with the academic literature. The entries pertaining to concepts and phenomena seek to offer a snapshot insight into the key features that have been identified across the globalization literature. Often there is disagreement and debate, and this is flagged up wherever possible. I try to point the reader to a range of sources, including websites, that may be useful in building a more detailed understanding of the issues.

The final category of 'thinkers' is perhaps the most important but also the one where most caution should be exercised. The entries offer what is a necessarily and unavoidably subjective assessment on my part as to the most important aspect of a given individual's contribution to the globalization debate. I have tried to identify, therefore, what a given thinker is 'best known for' and the key elements of his or her contribution. Quite clearly, to summarize what in some cases is a life's work in academic thought which has produced numerous lengthy contributions to the globalization debate, it is impossible to cover the range or depth of a given thinker's views in the space available. Rather, the entries should be seen both as an initial briefing on that thinker and also an attempt to offer some guidance on their place in the debate – where they are coming from, how their work has been received, including both criticism and praise. I have for the longer entries tried to offer a pithy assessment of each thinker and possible avenues of critical engagement with their work. These assessments should not, therefore, be treated as final judgements and I would anticipate that plenty of readers who use this book may disagree with an aspect or the entirety of the perspective given by some entries in light of further reading. Such is the nature and vigour of the globalization debate.

Overall, an important final point is that those using this book remember there is no overarching ideological narrative to the entries. As an author, I have sought to offer a balanced and impartial view of the particular strengths and weaknesses of given perspectives rather than construct any kind of argument through the entries. I leave it up to readers to use this book as the beginning of the process for developing their own views, not the end point to be taken unquestioningly. Globalization, whatever you think about it, has become one of the most important ideas of our time. It is a concept that is shaping the world we all live in and I would encourage everyone to engage with the debate in as much detail as possible.

A–Z of Globalization

9/11

The US form of the date of the world's largest terrorist attack. On the morning of 11 September 2001, a group of Islamic terrorists, part of the al-Qaeda network, hijacked in mid-air four commercial airliners operated by American Airlines and United Airlines. The hijackers took over the planes' controls and deliberately crashed one into the Pentagon in Washington and another two into the twin towers of the World Trade Center in New York. Fire caused by the crashes led to the collapse of the two Trade Center towers. A large number of people were evacuated but when the towers collapsed hundreds more were killed, many of whom had been trapped on the upper floors. Several hundred New York City fire-fighters and police who had entered the towers to rescue victims were also killed. Counting fire-fighters, police, tower workers and passengers on the airliners, the death toll at the World Trade Center exceeded three thousand people. A total of 189 people who worked at the Pentagon were killed, and another sixty-four died on the airliner that was crashed into it. Another forty-four people died on the fourth hijacked airliner, which crashed in a field near Pittsburgh after the passengers overpowered the hijackers. It is thought the intention may have been to crash this airliner into the White House. The attacks provoked outrage in the US and were important not just because of the number of people killed, but because this was the first attack on the territorial US itself since Pearl Harbor in 1941. In response, President Bush declared his global 'war on terrorism'.

The significance of 9/11 to debates about **globalization** is considerable in relation to the emergence of **global terrorism** and the reconfiguration of warfare. Al-Qaeda arguably represents a new kind of terrorist organization that is global in the scope of its goals, objectives, targets and form of organization. It is in a sense fighting a global guerrilla war with the wealthy countries of the West as its target. It has also led to new supranational attempts at improving global security as the international community has sought to combat al-Qaeda and other terrorist groups more effectively. The impact of 9/11 has also been to undermine further the idea of **nation-state**s as actors in the geopolitical world, with the distinction between state and non-state actors becoming blurred in the consequent military response. 9/11 led directly to the 2001/2 war in Afghanistan as the US and **United Nations** Security Council focused attention on state regimes that supported the terrorists. Yet the 'war on terrorism' represents a shift in meaning of war from its modern sense of inter-state conflict to a more ambiguous conflict with terrorist organizations that have a much more complex relationship with territory and existing nation-states.

Further reading

The National Commission on Terrorist Attacks *The 9/11 Commission Report: The Full Final Report of the National Commission on Terrorist Attacks Upon the United States* (New York: W. W. Norton, 2004) [especially chs. 1, 2, 5 and 7]

Der Spiegel Magazine, transl. Paul De Angelis and Elisabeth Kaestner *Inside 9–11: What Really Happened* (London: St Martin's Press, 2002)

AGRICULTURE

The science and practice of producing crops and livestock from the natural resources of the earth. The primary aim of agriculture is to cause the land to produce more abundantly and at the same time to protect it from deterioration and misuse. The diverse branches of modern agriculture include agronomy, horticulture, economic entomology, animal husbandry, dairying, agricultural engineering, soil chemistry and agricultural economics. Agriculture has become a key area of debate in the context of **globalization** at the regional and global scale. Two areas are perhaps most important. First, agricultural subsidy has become a major point of contention in world trade negotiations and the relationship between the **global North** and **global South**. The US and **European Union** continue to subsidize agricultural production heavily and to refuse to open up markets to developing countries. The **Doha Development Round** remains stalled over agricultural tariffs and it represents a key area where the global North continues to enjoy favourable trading conditions. Second, as with other industries, the sector is becoming increasingly dominated by large **transnational corporation**s based in the wealthier countries of the global North. In recent decades these firms have spread their operations across regional and global markets for many commodities and foodstuffs.

A major strand of critique of (economic) globalization has thus arisen around agriculture. Despite increased levels of production through the **development** of industrial agriculture across the globe, poor farmers in developing countries remain excluded from lucrative markets in the global North, and agricultural markets and resources are becoming increasingly dominated by large TNCs. The outcome in many developing countries is unsustainable cash-crop production, the increased use of pesticides and increased debt amongst small farmers. Critics also point to capital-intensive, corporate-controlled agriculture being spread into regions where peasants are poor but, until now, have been self-sufficient in food. In much of the developing world where industrial agriculture has been introduced through globalization, higher costs are making it virtually impossible for small farmers to survive. The globalization of (non-sustainable) industrial agriculture is argued to be evaporating the incomes of **Third World** farmers through a combination of devaluation of currencies, increase in costs of production and a collapse in commodity prices related to excessive First World agricultural subsidy. Other points of contention include the development of intellectual property claims on plant species by agricultural TNCs and the genetic modification of key foodstuff crops.

Further reading
Bove, J. and Dufour, F. *The World is Not for Sale: Farmers Against Junk Food* (London: Verso, 2001)
Lang, T. and Heasman, M. *Food Wars: The Battle for Mouths, Minds and Markets* (London: Earthscan, 2004)

AID

'Aid', in the context of the **globalization** debate, tends to refer to foreign aid: economic, military, technical and financial assistance given on an international, and usually intergovernmental, level. Usually commentators make no clear distinction between aid given as a grant, with no repayment obligation, or as a loan. Aid has been a longstanding and contentious aspect of international **development** and has thus also become a subject of debate in its relationship to economic and **political globalization**.

When measured in all its forms, the largest long-term donor of aid since the end of the **Second World War** has been the US. At the end of that war, the US donated aid to meet a number of different objectives: to facilitate the reconstruction of the shattered First World economies, to strengthen the military defences of its allies and friends and to promote **economic growth** in underdeveloped areas. During the **Cold War** US aid was very much targeted on supporting states (and conflicts) that would inhibit the spread of communism. However, by the 1980s, aid as administered under presidents Reagan and Bush, was increasingly used to promote American investment, national interests and free market economies. Thus many commentators argue that the way the US used aid has been an important political tool in promoting **free trade** and an integrated neo-liberal global economy. Many nations in Europe and some in the Middle East and East Asia also have significant aid programmes. For a period during the mid- and late 1990s, Japan was the world's largest foreign aid donor, with significant flows of aid also coming from France, Germany and Great Britain. Since 2001, as a result of Japanese cutbacks in foreign aid, the US has overtaken Japan to become once more the world's largest donor nation.

Furthermore, in recent decades, an increasing proportion of aid has been largely channelled through the **World Bank** and **International Monetary Fund**. About 15 per cent of foreign aid is currently provided by international bodies. These include the World Bank and its affiliates, the International Development Association and the International Finance Corporation; regional **development** banks; the European Development Fund; the UN Development Program; and specialized agencies of the **United Nations**, such as the UN Food Agriculture Program. In 2000 US foreign aid amounted to $10 billion (less than 0.6 per cent of the federal budget) with the share of the gross domestic product (GDP) for foreign aid dropping from 2.75 per cent in 1949 to 0.1 per cent in 2000. In 2004 the US began the **Millennium Challenge Account** aid programme, which targets aid towards poorer nations with good governance and open economies. The programme places fewer restrictions than previous US aid schemes on how participating nations use the aid. In 2005 there were moves by a number of **G8** countries, led by the UK, to increase the percentage of GDP the wealthier countries give as aid.

Further reading
Burnell, P. *Foreign Aid in a Changing World* (Milton Keynes: Open University Press, 1997) [esp chs 1, 6, 10 and 12]

ALBROW, MARTIN

Albrow's key contribution to the **globalization** debate comes from a sociological perspective and considers the question of whether the contemporary era justifies 'the sense of rupture' with the past that appears to 'pervade the public consciousness of our time'. Albrow argues that it does and that a history of the present needs an explicit epochal theory to understand the transition to what he terms the *global age*. He suggests globality is displacing modernity and that there is a general decentring of state, government, economy, culture and community. This necessitates a recasting of the theory of such institutions and the relations between them. This is not a negative analysis, however, as he suggests that contemporary globalization also creates the potential for society to recover its 'abiding significance' in the face of the declining **nation-state** through a new kind of citizenship.

Further reading
Albrow, M. *The Global Age* (Cambridge: Polity Press, 1996) [esp. ch. 1]

AL-JAZEERA

The term for the (Arabian) peninsula in Arabic, used as the name of an Arabic television channel based in Qatar. The station was launched in 1996 with financial assistance from the emir but has subsequently aimed to become self-financing through advertising and subscription revenues. Many of the original employees came from the BBC World Service's Arabic Language Service which had closed after two years of operation. The channel's viewing audience has grown steadily in recent years and now rivals the BBC's world-wide audiences.

Al-Jazeera first gained widespread and controversial exposure outside the Middle East in 2001 when it broadcast videos in which Osama Bin Laden and Sulaiman Abu Ghaith defended and justified the **9/11** attacks. The US government argued that al-Jazeera was engaging in propaganda on behalf of terrorists. Al-Jazeera countered that it was merely making information available. **CNN** cut its ties with al-Jazeera for several months as a consequence. Since then, the station has continued to court controversy in its coverage of events, including the wars in Afghanistan and Iraq. In 2003 it was temporarily banned in the US by a number of organizations during the invasion of Iraq. However, a documentary based on its coverage of the war won a string of awards in 2004 and the station continues to maintain its commitment to independence and impartiality in news coverage.

Further reading
Miles, H. *Al Jazeera* (London: Abacus, 2005)

ALTER-GLOBALIZATION

A term deriving primarily from a recent, mainly French, critique of the **anti-globalization movement**. Groups such as the Association for the Taxation of Financial Transactions for the Aid of Citizens (ATTAC), based in France, prefer alter-globalization to **anti-globalization** because they wish to differentiate themselves from the simplistic negative opposition implied in anti-globalization. Alter-globalization is more positive in its conception as it supports certain forms of greater interconnectedness (globalization in general) but demands that values of democracy, economic justice, environmental protection and **human rights** be put ahead of purely economic concerns. In that sense, advocates of alter-globalization share many aspects of the wider anti-globalization movement's critique of neo-liberal **economic globalization**. It argues that most supranational institutions (such as the **World Trade Organization**, the **International Monetary Fund** and the **World Bank**) have to date worked in favour of First World economic interests. In France, a more radical form of alter-globalization has been confused to some extent with communist-derived internationalism since both oppose a globalization that would prioritize the transnational capitalist class over ordinary people. Although recently ascendant in terms of usage, several commentators argue that alter-globalization should be more widely used to distinguish much of the critical resistance to aspects of neo-liberal economic globalization from true 'anti-globalization' groups who are against *any* kind of globalization (for example, nationalists and protectionists).

Further reading
Mittelman, J. 'Alterglobalization', ch. 8 in *Whither Globalization? The Vortex of Knowledge and Ideology* (London: Routledge, 2004) pp. 89–97

AMIN, ASH

A professor of human geography, Amin has made a sustained contribution to the debate around theoretical conceptions of **globalization** as a phenomenon. His arguments have emerged from an academic perspective on regional economic **development**, manufacturing production systems and how these relate to territoriality and space.

Writing with fellow geographer Nigel Thrift, Amin argued that early theorization of globalization in the 1990s was insufficient to understand and theorize the impacts of this phenomenon on local economies. He emphasized, with Thrift, the significance and usefulness of theorizing the interaction of global–local relations through the concept of place as 'a setting for social and economic existence' and for 'forging identities, struggles and strategies of both a local and global nature'. Echoing other geographical contributors such as David **Harvey** and Doreen **Massey**, Amin has thus argued that regions such as Silicon Valley or the City of London have been successful in the global economy because of a complex set of historical factors and the sociocultural embeddedness of economic activity in those places. More recently, Amin has made a number of contributions concerning the nature of the embeddedness of firms in and between regions in the **global economy** and proposed that globalization needs to be understood in what he terms 'relational and topological' ways – that is by a theoretical emphasis on understanding how linkages and relationships between different actors (individuals, firms, regulatory organizations, governments) affect **economic growth** and development. Such an approach represents a theoretical attempt to push theorizations of globalization beyond the strongly territorial terms of much of the debate.

Further reading
Amin, A. and Thrift, N. 'Living in the Global', ch. 1 in *Globalization, Institutions and Regional Development in Europe* (Oxford: Oxford University Press, 1994)

AMIN, SAMIR

An Egyptian economist whose work focuses on global **development**. In *Capitalism in the Age of Globalization* (1997) he argues that **globalization** is polarizing, avoidable and not desirable. He deconstructs the **Bretton Woods institutions** – notably the **International Monetary Fund** and the **World Bank** – and argues that they are largely managerial mechanisms which protect the profitability of capital. He rejects the equation of development with market expansion, and instead asserts the need for each society to negotiate the terms of its interdependence with the rest of the global economy. More recently, he has focused on the role of the US, suggesting that what he sees as the ongoing American project to dominate the world through military force has its roots in European liberalism, but has developed certain features of liberal ideology in a new and uniquely dangerous way. Notably, he continues to emphasize the proposition that the American state has developed to serve the interests of capital alone, and is now exporting this model throughout the world.

Further reading
Amin, S. *Capitalism in the Age of Globalization* (London: Zed Books, 1997)

AMNESTY INTERNATIONAL

A **human rights** campaigning non-governmental organization (NGO), founded in 1961, that now operates at the global scale. Amnesty promotes a vision of the world in which 'every person enjoys all of the human rights enshrined in the [**United Nations'**] Universal Declaration of Human Rights and other international human rights standards.' It works to achieve this goal by undertaking research and action that is 'focused on preventing and ending grave abuses of the rights to physical and mental integrity, freedom of conscience and expression, and freedom from discrimination', within the context of promoting all human rights. Amnesty cites three major methods by which it works to achieve this. First, it addresses governments, intergovernmental organizations, armed political groups, companies and other non-state actors. Second, Amnesty is perhaps best known for trying, through accurate, impartial and persistent publicity, to 'make visible' the often invisible human rights abuses occurring around the world. Staff, members and supporters of the organization mobilize public pressure on governments and others to stop the abuses. Third, in addition to its work on specific abuses of human rights, it also has a broadly educational approach, urging all governments to observe the rule of law and to ratify and implement human rights standards. The organization therefore runs a wide range of human rights educational activities and it seeks to encourage intergovernmental organizations, individuals and all organs of society to support and respect human rights.

Amnesty is important in relation to the **globalization** debate as one of the key globalizing NGOs that has developed in recent decades.

Its goals have always been global in scope and it has thus been an important agent in promoting both a global-scale political consciousness and movement behind the UN's declaration on human rights, and also as an international civil society actor promoting the development of international standards, laws and societal norms.

Further reading
Clark, A. 'Amnesty International in International Politics', ch. 1 in *Diplomacy of Conscience: Amnesty International and Changing Human Rights Norms* (Princeton, N.J.: Princeton University Press, 2001)

ANTI-GLOBALIZATION
A conceptual position which is both ambiguous and contested in its meaning but most commonly used to refer to the political position of the **anti-globalization movement**, and in particular the opposition of component groups to contemporary neo-liberal **economic globalization**. However, the conception of anti-globalization is as broad as the concept of **globalization** itself and therefore subject to the same vast scope in meaning. To adopt an anti-globalization position can in its broadest sense also mean any opposition to societal integration. In that sense, extreme forms of territorially based regionalism or nationalism could also be described as anti-globalizationist in their rejection of new forms of interconnectedness. A small number of isolationist nation-states (Iran, North Korea) also characterize elements of this position.

With regard to its most common usage around the anti-globalization movement, there is considerable disagreement. Elements within the 'movement' contest the applicability of the concept and argue that this is a term created by the empowered global elite who support the project of neo-liberal economic globalization. Commentators point out that opposition to the latter does not amount to an anti-globalization position, as the movement itself is about forging transnational political linkages and the development of a global-scale opposition to certain sets of policies and doctrines. This leaves anti-globalization as a paradoxical concept, since whilst it is regularly used to describe resistance to policies and practices seen as engendering new forms of interconnectedness, it also is associated with a wide range of social practices that can be understood as globalizing. In this context, recent contributors have proposed the concept of **alter-globalization** to overcome the entirely oppositional implication of anti-globalization and replace it with an alternative, more desirable form of global societal interconnectedness.

Further reading
Held, D. and McGrew, A. 'Making Sense of Globalization', ch. 1 in *Globalization/Anti-globalization* (Cambridge: Polity, 2002)

ANTI-GLOBALIZATION MOVEMENT

A loose confederation of organizations and groups seeking to resist the processes of (**economic**) **globalization** which have emerged since the early 1990s. Many see the origins of the anti-globalization movement at the global scale in the Zapatista uprising in the southern Mexican state of Chiapas in early 1994. The **Zapatistas** were protesting about state-led land reforms in the context of the impact of Mexico entering the **North American Free Trade Agreement**. Although they were a regionally based resistance movement, the Zapatistas' ideological approach, in combination with their tactics of resistance (using the **Internet** and the global media), provided the conceptual platform for a range of other anti-globalization groups around the globe. During the 1990s, use of the Internet enabled disparate resistance organizations to develop linkages and threads of common argument against economic globalization and the impacts it was having on local communities. Importantly, and contrary to the perception of many in the West, the impetus behind the anti-globalization movement thus stemmed from organizations in developing countries.

The anti-globalization movement itself became solidified into a larger global movement primarily through a series of mass protests at meetings of the **G8** and **World Trade Organization**. The first of these was the **Seattle** protest in 1999 which set the precedent for subsequent influxes of protestors into meetings of world leaders or supranational bodies that were perceived to be driving forward neoliberal economic globalization at the expense of the world's poor and the **environment**. This led to sometimes violent clashes between protestors and police at subsequent meetings in Genoa, Quebec, Barcelona and at **Gleneagles**. In Western countries such as Britain, the anti-globalization movement has also made other pivotal protests, notably on May Day in London and other UK cities where a variety of anti-capitalist groups engaged in direct-action protests.

However, there is doubt about the coherence of this movement. Critics pointed to the diverse and sometimes contradictory goals of the large number of organizations involved. The anti-globalization movement has also been argued to be weak on offering alternatives to neo-liberal globalization with the initial energy of the movement directed towards criticism. Early alternatives tended to centre around anarchist ideologies or revisions to unreconstructed Marxist theories which many saw to be unrealistic projects in mainstream politics. However, since 2001 and the events of **9/11**, it has been suggested that the nature of the anti-globalization movement has changed. Whilst some right-wing commentators have argued its time has passed, others have suggested that it has become more mature and trenchant in its criticism of neo-liberal global capitalism and has begun to develop more moderate, detailed and politically feasible recommendations about how the ravages of global capitalism might be tamed. Organizations such as the **World Social Forum** have started to organize increasingly large conferences aimed at proposing positive and feasible alternatives to neo-liberal economic globalization. Whilst some lament the move away from radical and confrontational protest tactics, the anti-globalization movement is arguably now developing a more realistic and pragmatic series of proposals for moderating the negative effects of globalization.

Further reading
Held, D. and McGrew, A. *Globalization/Anti-globalization* (Cambridge: Polity, 2002)
Kingsworth, P. *One No, Many Yeses* (London: Faber & Faber, 2003)

APEC *see* Asia Pacific Economic Cooperation.

APPADURAI, ARJUN

A social theorist at the University of Chicago, Appadurai positions cultural analysis at the centre of his discussion of the global present in his book *Modernity at Large* (1996). In seeking to theorize what he terms the 'new global cultural economy' that has emerged in the context of late twentieth-century **globalization**, he proposes an elementary framework for exploring 'the disjunctures and differences' identifiable. Five forms of global cultural flow are outlined, which he suggests enable an understanding of these disjunctures.

These he terms '-scapes' because they refer to a fluid, irregular cultural landscape and 'characterize international capital as much as they characterize international clothing styles'. They are not 'objectively given relations that look the same from every angle of vision' but are rather deeply perspectival constructs which are specific to actors and circumstances. First are *ethnoscapes* which are described as 'landscapes of persons who constitute the shifting world in which we live: tourists, immigrants, **refugees**, exiles, guest workers and other moving groups'. These moving groups 'can never let their imaginations rest too long, even if they wish to'. Second, *technoscapes* refer to the also ever-fluid fact that technology, both high and low in form as well as mechanical and informational, moves at high speeds across various kinds of previously impervious boundaries. Third, *financescapes* have become a 'more mysterious, rapid and difficult landscape to follow' as currency markets, national stock exchanges and commodity speculations move through national turnstiles at blinding speed. To these three, Appadurai adds *mediascapes* and *ideascapes*, which are closely related to the flow of images. The former refer to the distribution of electronic capabilities to both produce and disseminate information that spans television, newspapers, magazines and film, whilst the latter are concentrations of images that are often directly political in nature such as state ideologies (e.g. democracy) and counter-ideologies.

Appadurai's five '-scapes' have been widely influential in developing theoretical debates about the nature of globalization as a phenomenon and his arguments remain at the centre of analysis on the nature of the global cultural economy.

Further reading
Appadurai, A. 'Disjuncture and Difference in the Global Cultural Economy', ch. 13 in Lechner, F. and Boli, J. (eds) *The Globalization Reader* (2nd edn; Oxford: Blackwell, 2004)

ARMS CONTROL

A broad term alluding to a range of political concepts and aims which generally refer to disarmament and can apply from the individual scale concerning small arms to the international and global scale concerning nuclear weapons. In the context of contemporary **globalization** debates, the concept is largely applied to the latter, with a particular emphasis on weapons of mass destruction (WMD).

Historically, attempts at controlling arms have long existed and have been a major element of emerging attempts at global political governance since the late nineteenth century. It is only since the Hague Peace Conferences of 1899 and 1907 that these attempts have been multilateral and have been accompanied by growing political demands for international legislation to prohibit inhumane weapons and to regulate the growing global arms trade. The Hague conferences involved twenty-six mainly European states but in the aftermath of the **First World War**, the then sixty-four recognized **nation-state**s met from 1932 to 1934 at the Geneva World Disarmament Conferences.

During the **Cold War**, arms control took on a new impetus with the development of nuclear weapons (and more effective chemical ones). Aside from a few global-scale constraints (the Treaty on the Non-proliferation of Nuclear Weapons), the majority of postwar initiatives have been regional rather than global in nature such as the Intermediate Nuclear Forces Treaty (Europe) and the Pacific Nuclear Weapons Free Zone. Some agreements have acquired almost universal ratification such as the 1925 Geneva Protocol; others have had very limited international support – for example, the Inhumane Weapons Convention. The most significant Cold War agreements concerned the limitation of US and Soviet stocks of nuclear weapons through the Strategic Arms Limitation Talks (SALT) and Strategic Arms Reduction Talks (START). In the post-Cold War period, however, significant shifts are occurring as the nature of military threats evolves in the contemporary world. President Bush announced his intention to withdraw from SALT to develop new space-based defences to ballistic missiles. However, the contemporary situation is complicated as the threat from WMD shifts to new non-state actors with the rise of **global terrorism**.

Further reading
Held, D., McGrew, A., Goldblatt, D. and Perraton, J. 'The Expanding Reach of Organized Violence', ch. 2 in *Global Transformations* (Cambridge: Polity, 1999)

ASEAN *see* Association of South-East Asian Nations.

ASIA PACIFIC ECONOMIC COOPERATION (APEC)

An organization consisting of a group of Pacific Rim countries that meet with the purpose of improving economic and political ties. The first meeting took place in Canberra, Australia, in 1989, and APEC now holds annual meetings as well as having standing committees on a wide range of issue such as communications and fishing rights. Since 1993, the heads of government of each member state have hosted a summit in rotation (apart from Taiwan). In 1994, APEC stated the 'Bogor goals', called after the summit in Bogor, which aimed to free up trade and investment between members by cutting tariffs to between zero and five per cent in the Asia-Pacific area for industrialized economies by 2010 and developing economies by 2020. The 2001 summit in Shanghai was important in initiating the **World Trade Organization**'s **Doha Development Round**.

Further reading
Miranti, R. and Wei-Yen, D. (eds) *APEC in the Twenty-First Century.* (Singapore: Institute of South Asian Studies, 2005)

ASSOCIATION OF SOUTH-EAST ASIAN NATIONS (ASEAN)

An organization established on 8 August 1967 with the signing of the Bangkok Declaration by the foreign ministers of Indonesia, Malaysia, the Philippines, Singapore and Thailand. ASEAN was conceived as having three main objectives: to promote the economic, social and cultural **development** of the region through cooperative programmes; to safeguard the political and economic stability of the region, particularly in relation to the influence of 'big powers'; and to serve as a forum for the resolution of intra-regional differences. In that sense, ASEAN (like the **European Union**) is more than just the regional economic trading bloc that it is sometimes represented as being in the **globalization** literature. It is certainly a supranational organization that has also always had political and sociocultural goals as part of its *raison d'être*.

ASEAN remained an alliance of five nations until January 1984 when Brunei Darussalam became a sixth member. Vietnam then joined eleven years later, in 1995, and Laos and Myanmar joined two years after that, in 1997. Cambodia was also due to join in 1997 but because of internal political struggles at the time this was deferred until 1999. There are now ten ASEAN members but Papua New

Guinea has also been an 'observer' since 1995. It also conducts dialogue meetings with other countries and organizations, collectively known as the ASEAN dialogue partners; these are Australia, Canada, China, North Korea, South Korea, the US, India, Japan, Mongolia, New Zealand, Russia and the EU. Overall, ASEAN now represents 8 per cent of the global population and has a combined GDP of around $700 million.

ASEAN is seen to have been broadly successful on a number of fronts in achieving various forms of regional integration in the southeast Asian region. On the political front, since the mid 1970s, ASEAN has had a stated goal of achieving political and security dialogue between its members with an aim of promoting peace and stability. No tension between member states has escalated to a state of armed confrontation in the three decades of the organization's existence. In economic and trade terms there is also plenty of evidence of success at fostering trade and cross-investment between the southeast Asian economies. Since 1997, the member states have tried to accelerate the pace of economic integration in order to generate a competitive ASEAN economic region within the global economy.

However, in the aftermath of the Asian Financial Crisis of 1997, ASEAN member states have also expressed reservations about allowing unchecked and unregulated processes of globalization. In that sense, the role of ASEAN as a mediator rather than an unquestioning facilitator of globalization has been propagated to some extent. Various key figures in ASEAN have expressed the view that whilst economic integration and the opening up of markets is an important economic developmental goal for the southeast Asian region, ASEAN can also act to protect member states and their societies from the worst ravages of unregulated globalization. There remain arguments about the need to maintain social cohesion and promote **development** within ASEAN which at times do not sit comfortably with the neo-liberal agendas of organizations such as the **World Trade Organization**. Consequently, as with the EU, ASEAN occupies a complex position as a supranational political-economic organization in the wider context of globalization.

Further reading
Tan, G. *ASEAN: Economic Development and Co-operation* (2nd edn; Singapore: Times Academic Press, 2003) [esp. Introduction]

ATLANTIC FREE TRADE AREA

An idea that has been mooted from time to time in both North America and Europe. Since the formation of the **North American Free Trade Agreement** (NAFTA) in 1993, the US has continued to look for new ways to form more effective trading partnerships. The US Senate discussed a proposal to form a closer trading alliance with Europe in 1996, and several policy commentators on both sides of the Atlantic have subsequently argued the case for closer trading agreements. However, trade relations between the US and the **European Union** continue to be tense, with disputes on a wide range of sectors including agricultural products and arms. There remain those in Britain and the US who suggest the 'special relationship' should be extended to a trans-Atlantic trade alliance between the two countries, but this seems unlikely, considering Britain's existing position within the EU.

Further reading
Treverton, G. 'An Economic Case for the New Era', ch. 3 in *America and Europe: A Partnership for a New Era* (Cambridge: Cambridge University Press, 1998)

AXIS OF EVIL

A phrase that has become common in the context of (political) **globalization** since its use by US President George W. Bush in his State of the Union address in January 2002. He used it to describe state 'regimes that sponsor terror', originally labelling Iraq, Iran and North Korea as specific examples. Later in 2002, John Bolton, then US Under Secretary of State, added Libya, Syria and Cuba to the list. The criterion for membership of this group was that they were 'state sponsors of terrorism that are pursuing or who have the potential to pursue weapons of mass destruction (WMD) or have the capability to do so in violation of their treaty obligations'. The term is often used interchangeably with 'rogue state' and is reminiscent of the Axis powers (Germany–Italy–Japan) in the **Second World War** as well as President Reagan's description of the Soviet Union as an 'evil empire'. The expression is important as it is taken by many globalization commentators as a key concept in the dominant US-led view of global political relations: this is that these states are anti-, or at least only imperfectly, democratic, that they repress their populations and that they are not engaged in the peaceful development of a global economy and society. The 'axis of evil' concept certainly provoked strong criticism from many left-wing commentators around the globe, including from within the US. It is argued that the use of 'axis' constructed a representation of strength and coherence between the three original states that did not exist. The phrase has also been attacked for crudely equating a broad non-compliance with the US vision of global development with 'evil'. Many Muslim states are strongly hostile to the term, notably because it is seen to be often closely linked to Islamic regimes.

Further reading
Levine, M. *Why They Don't Hate Us: Lifting the Veil on the 'Axis of Evil'* (London: OneWorld Publications, 2004)

BANK FOR INTERNATIONAL SETTLEMENTS (BIS)
A financial international organization established under the Hague agreements of 1930. It was later joined by the other **Bretton Woods institutions** in 1944. The bank's main purpose is to seek to influence reserve policy among the central banks of its members with the principal goal being to ensure stability in the global financial system through an effective regime of regulation. Thus it aims to provide a 'well-designed financial safety net, supported by strong prudential regulation and supervision, effective laws that are enforced, and sound accounting and regulation regimes'. Most commentators agree that historically it has had less power to do so than is necessary. More recently, the bank has also aimed to address specific concerns with the growth of Offshore Financial Centres (OFCs), Highly Leveraged Institutions (HLIs), Large and Complex Financial Institutions (LCFIs), deposit insurance and the spread of money laundering and accounting scandals.

In recent years a range of academic and policy commentators have expressed doubts about the bank's mandate, its programme, its effectiveness and the desirability of any existing institution taking the lead role in accounting reform. These criticisms have been particularly trenchant in the aftermath of serious failures around money-laundering law enforcement and major breaches of prudence and supervision in the US (e.g. Enron and WorldCom). Its critics also include leading practitioners such as the financier George **Soros** who has argued that there is no will to enforce effective financial regulation in the present competitive global financial industry, where nations effectively compete to offer less regulation. As with the **International Monetary Fund** and **World Bank**, the bank has also been criticized for having a culture of secretiveness. However, overall, it has not received as much critical attention from **anti-globalization** critics as the other Bretton Woods institutions, the main line of critique generally echoing concerns about its effective ability to achieve a sufficient degree of regulation in the context of **global financial integration**.

Further reading
Baker, C. *The Bank for International Settlements: Evolution and Evaluation* (Westport, Conn.: Greenwood Press, 2002)

BAUMAN, ZYGMUNT

Spanning sociology and philosophy, Bauman addresses the conceptual issue of time–space compression as an underpinning process that defines **globalization**. He sees the problem of what globalization 'is' as being centred around a new speed and flux which divides human experience between the haves and have-nots of cyberspace. Bauman thus sees technological time–space compression as a polarizing process in society with new 'elites' choosing cybernetic isolation and the rest of the population being cut off. His argument is that new global media are not truly interactive, but in fact privilege a small global elite. Politically, Bauman argues that globalization refers primarily to global effects that are unintended and unanticipated rather than to global initiatives. It is therefore about the growing experience of the weakness of individuals, organizations and most particularly states. Overall, Bauman's contribution has thus focused on the human meaning of globalization as opposed to technical aspects of the processes it encompasses.

Further reading
Bauman, Z. *Globalization: The Human Consequences* (Cambridge: Polity Press, 1998) [esp. ch. 3]

BECK, ULRICH

Beck is probably best known for his writings on the **environment** and the contemporary 'risk society' in which we live. More recently, however, he has turned his attention to **globalization** and made a series of arguments both about the nature of the phenomenon and its impacts. For Beck, globalization represents primarily a scare-word corresponding to the escape of politics from the **nation-state**. He suggests that contemporary **economic globalization** amounts to a politicization because it permits employers to disentangle and recapture the power to act that was restrained by the political and welfare institutions of democratically organized capitalism. In this view **transnational corporations** can play an important role in shaping not just the economy but wider society too. Beck sees this as a fundamental attack on modern national societies for a number of reasons. First, TNCs can export jobs to lower-cost and less-regulated places. Second, informational technologies break down the national label of labour by dispersing goods and services. Third, TNCs can therefore play countries off against each other in processes of 'global horse-trading'. Fourth, the sites of investment, production, tax and residence are all in the hands of the TNCs and their leading employees.

Overall, therefore, Beck reads economic globalization as a negative process which for him 'completes what has been driven forward by intellectual postmodernism and politically by individualisation – the collapse of **modernity**'. Neo-liberal economic globalization, he argues, will ultimately produce unemployment on a huge scale as global capitalism becomes a form of accumulation without work. In order to counter this conceptually, he differentiates between **globalism** (the view that the world market eliminates or supplants political action), *globality* (the fact that we have for a long time been living in a world society) and globalization (the processes through which sovereign states are criss-crossed and undermined by transnational actors). The processes of globalization in this view are dialectical and create transnational social links and spaces, revalue local cultures and promote third cultures. Beck posits that the extent and limits of successful globalization can thus be assessed through three parameters: extension in space, stability over time and the social density of the transnational networks and image flows. He sees the emerging world society being produced by these processes as not a mega-national society containing and dissolving national societies within itself, but a world horizon characterized by multiplicity and non-integration. Globalization, then, does not lead to the emergence of a world state but rather to a society without world state/government encompassed by a globally disorganized capitalism. The response that is needed, he argues, is that globalist ideology must be countered if social values and the values of social democratic welfare societies are to be maintained in the context of globalization processes.

Beck's contribution is impassioned but open to a number of critical lines which call into question both his theorization of what globalization is and the problems it poses. First, his conceptualization of globalization can be argued to be economistic and narrowly focused on the nation-state. Conceptually, many commentators have argued for a much broader definition of what globalization is as an abstract process. Second, Beck's arguments are very generalized and focused on the negative aspects of TNCs and their impacts on nation-states. His analysis asserts this and does not expand these arguments with any significant empirical support. It is, in short, a very one-sided perspective. Third, he occupies a very Euro-centric perspective in his arguments and in that sense there are many questionable assertions that can be contested: for example, the idea that shifting employment to the developing world does not create jobs. His view of IT and the workless global capitalist economy is in that sense contradicted by a considerable amount of evidence.

Further reading
Beck, U. *What is Globalization?* (Cambridge: Polity, 2000) [esp. Introduction and part II)

BELLO, WALDEN

Policy commentator Bello has made a sustained series of radical contributions critiquing contemporary **economic globalization** and the nature of contemporary global economy. He founded and heads Focus on the Global South, a policy research institute based in Bangkok, Thailand. Broadly aligned with other 'anti-globalization' commentators, Bello has been particularly critical of **development** as a concept deployed through the **Bretton Woods institutions** in the postwar period. He argues these institutions are now trying to manage the unmanageable, especially in the uncontrolled development of global financial markets and the integration of a singular global form of capitalism. In his key contribution *Deglobalization* (2002), he argues that neo-liberal economic globalization and the supranational institutions that have propagated it are facing a crisis of legitimacy, especially across the **global South**. Bello points to the manifest failings of economic globalization: recurrent financial crises, the ever-widening gulf between developing and industrialized countries, the persistence of gross inequalities and mass poverty. This amounts in his view to a crisis of global capitalism and necessitates a radical shift in the nature and form of world economic management. He thus argues for an alternative he calls *deglobalization*. This does not amount to a withdrawal from the international economy but is rather about 'reorienting economies from an emphasis on production for export to production for local market'. To do this, countries need to draw on their financial resources for development from within rather than becoming dependent on foreign investment. They need to carry out income and land redistribution as well as deprioritizing growth in favour of maximizing equity. Deglobalization is also about not leaving strategic economic decisions to the market and about scrutiny of the private sector and state by civil society. Perhaps most importantly, he argues that **transnational corporation**s need to be excluded in favour of communities and more local productive organizations. Bello certainly occupies a radical position within the debates and provides a more detailed and academically grounded 'alternative' proposition than many anti-globalization commentators. However, it is difficult to envisage how the political capacity to implement many of his recommendations could be generated in the current international political climate.

Further reading
Bello, W. *Deglobalization: Ideas for a New World Economy* (London: Zed Books, 2002) [esp. chs 1, 2 and 7]

BIODIVERSITY
The concept coined by the conservationist Thomas Lovejoy in 1980 that refers in simple terms to the number of species in a given habitat. It is estimated there are in the range of three to thirty million species on earth, of which 2.5 million have been classified, including 900,000 insects, 41,000 vertebrates and 250,000 plants. The remainder are invertebrates, fungi, algae and micro-organisms. Biodiversity is affected by resources, productivity and climate. The more pristine a diverse habitat, the better chance it has of surviving a change or threat – either natural or human – because that change can be balanced by an adjustment elsewhere in the community. A damaged habitat may be destroyed by breaking the food chain

with removal of a single species. Biological diversity is thus known to help prevent extinction of species and is argued to be important for the continued sustainability of many ecosystems upon which human societies depend. Further arguments for the preservation of biodiversity include the varied potential of as yet unknown uses of biological products that may be lost through species extinction: medical treatments developed from plants, for instance.

The key relevance to **globalization** of debates around biodiversity is the fact that, although other species remain to be discovered, many are becoming extinct through deforestation, pollution and human settlement. This is seen to be a consequence of both the scale and nature of global economic **development** and is also a source of international political contention. Notably, much of the existing (or remaining) diversity is found in the world's tropical areas, particularly in the forest regions and marine environments where natural resources have historically been less damaged by human activity. These are also often in countries with the lowest incomes.

The preservation of global biodiversity has thus become a key issue and one that requires political action and agreement at the global scale. At the 1992 United Nations Conference on Environment and Development (the 'Earth' Summit) more than 150 nations signed the Convention on Biological Diversity which is intended to protect the planet's biological diversity. The convention has three main goals: the conservation of biological diversity; the sustainable use of its components; and the fair and equitable sharing of benefits arising from genetic resources. However, in reality the current trajectory of global economic development continues to have negative (and perhaps accelerating) impacts on biodiversity, and it is likely this will remain an urgent issue in the coming decades.

Further reading
Gaston, K. and Spicer, J. *Biodiversity: An Introduction* (Oxford: Blackwell, 2003) [esp. chs 1 and 5]

BIS *see* Bank for International Settlements.

BLACKBURN, ROBIN

Blackburn is a US-based historian whose main contribution has concerned **financial globalization** and its implications for the global economy. In particular, he argues, in *Banking on Death* (1999), that pension funds, increasingly important in the global economy as a source of finance, have been depleted by wasteful promotion and used as gambling chips by ruthless and overpaid top executives. He labels this 'grey capitalism', where employees' savings are sequestrated from them and pressed into the service of corporate aggrandizement. Even the best companies find it hard to run a business and a pension fund at the same time – especially when the latter is larger than the former. The fund managers' notorious short-termism and herd instinct, and their failure to curb the greed and irresponsibility of the corporate elite, lead to obscene inequalities and a blighted social landscape. Across Western economies, Blackburn argues, ageing societies will generate increased costs but, so long as the new life course is properly financed, all age groups can gain. He thus proposes a public regime of asset-based welfare, drawing on Keynes, that could ensure secondary pensions for all and foster a more responsible, egalitarian and humane pattern of economic development at the global scale. Blackburn has also written regularly on global financial regulation, notably being critical of the emerging 'post-Enron' policies aimed at addressing the risk of future financial crises and scandal.

Further reading
Blackburn, R. *Banking on Death or Investing in Life: The History and Future of Pensions* (London: Verso, 1999) [ch. 1]

BLAIR, TONY

Prime Minister of the UK since 1997, Blair has regularly spoken and written on the issue of **globalization** and has sought to create a new form of international politics in the post-**Cold War** and post-**9/11** world. His Government's support for the US-led wars in Afghanistan and Iraq and his political attempts to influence a range of global issues, including climate change, debt, **development** and the future of the **European Union**, mean that Blair's contribution to both the shape of and the debate about globalization is significant. In a number of speeches during his first term in government Blair laid out the argument that **nation-state**s can no longer behave independently or be treated in isolation in an increasingly interconnected world. He argues that international politics, through institutions such as the EU and the **United Nations**, need actively to engender a sense of global community and that individuals and the states in which they live should behave as global citizens. However, Blair's political leadership has been controversial as this perspective on global society has also been invoked by him in support of the war on terror and recent wars in the Middle East. Critics argue that his arguments are used as selective justifications to defend First World self-interest and that his post-Westphalian interpretation of twenty-first century globalization reinforces (whether intentionally or not) a new form of imperialism.

Further reading
A wide range of commentary articles on Tony Blair's policies and approach to globalization can be found on <www.opendemocracy.net/globalization>.

BRETTON WOODS INSTITUTIONS
The organizations set up as the result of the UN Monetary and Financial Conference held during the first three weeks of July 1944, while the **Second World War** was still raging. Representatives of forty-four Allied nations met at the Mount Washington Hotel in Bretton Woods, New Hampshire, which led to the signing over the following year of the Bretton Woods Agreements. The conference established the International Bank for Reconstruction and Development (later divided into the **World Bank** and the **Bank for International Settlements**) and the **International Monetary Fund**. These organizations became operational in 1946 after a sufficient number of countries had ratified the agreement. They have subsequently become known as the Bretton Woods institutions.

In the immediate postwar period the stated aim behind the formation of these institutions was to provide a stable international economic environment in order to promote growth and **development** after the chaos and destruction of the war. A further key pillar of this strategy was the Bretton Woods system of fixed exchange rates which was presided over by the IMF. The system's purpose was to provide exchange-rate stability and thus facilitate **economic growth** in the (capitalist) world economy. It was largely conceived by the then Assistant Secretary of the US Treasury, Harry D. White, and the British economist John Maynard Keynes. In effect, it pegged all currencies to the US dollar which was itself pegged to the US's gold reserve at $34 per ounce. Exchange rates were therefore unable to change in relation to the dollar unless the IMF took the view that a given currency was over- or undervalued and agreed to a revaluation.

The Bretton Woods exchange-rate system lasted until the early 1970s when the US withdrew its guaranteed dollars-for-gold rate. Thereafter the system moved to the current one of floating exchange rates. However, the Bretton Woods institutions themselves remained and have played an increasingly central (and contentious) role in the development of the global economy. Those critical of neo-liberal **globalization** see the Bretton Woods institutions and their descendants (such as the **World Trade Organization**) as having an increasingly outdated ideological perspective and argue that their policies have not sufficiently fulfilled the key promise of raising global living standards and prosperity in the way conceived sixty years ago. For much of the **anti-globalization movement**, the Bretton Woods institutions are a key target for reform.

Further reading
Stiglitz, J. 'The Promise of Global Institutions', ch. 1 in *Globalization and its Discontents* (London: Penguin, 2001)

CALLINICOS, ALEX

A British political scientist, Callinicos sees no alternative to capitalism but the classical socialist economy and society. His major contribution to the **globalization** debate concerns the **anti-globalization/** capitalist movement and what possible alternatives exist. In his *Anti-Capitalist Manifesto* (2003), he defines socialism as a society that 'gives priority to human needs and subjects allocation of resources to democratic control'. He relies heavily on **Marx** for his conception of capitalism and argues that **globalization** has not in effect altered its intrinsic qualities as a system of eocnomic organization. He therefore sees contemporary resistance to neo-liberal globalization as an extension of class conflict to the global scale. For Callinicos, this is still about revolution, albeit a global one, and the overthrow of market-led corporate global capitalism. He is concerned therefore with how the **anti-globalization movement** can develop as a political force that can offer an alternative to global capitalism.

Further reading
Callinicos, A. *An Anti-Capitalist Manifesto* (Cambridge: Polity, 2003) [Introduction and part I)

CANCÚN

The purpose-built holiday resort of Cancún at the tip of the Yucatán peninsula in southern Mexico that was the venue for the Fifth Ministerial Conference of the **World Trade Organization** in September 2003, part of the **Doha Development Round** of trade negotiations. At Cancún, the developing tensions of the Doha Round of negotiations came to a head with members adopting inflexible negotiating positions and the polarization between the developed and developing countries being highlighted. This led to the collapse of the talks. Importantly, however, a number of developing countries mobilized against what they perceived as the US and EU's disproportionate level of control over the proceedings, and organized themselves as the Group of 20 (G20) to create a stronger voice in negotiations.

At the 1999 **Seattle** Ministerial Conference, several groups of developing countries released statements criticizing their exclusion from key decision-making processes at the WTO, such as informal, closed-door 'green-room' meetings. In Cancún, a number of NGOs, including the World Development Movement, Oxfam and Third World Network, issued similar complaints. A memo was drafted to the WTO which called for more transparent and democratic decision-making in the Doha Round. Specifically, they asked that the WTO stop holding unrecorded informal meetings or 'mini-ministerial' meetings in which developing countries are rarely invited to participate. They also asked that meetings and their location be announced in good time and that all agenda additions or omissions be made as a whole group. A request was also made that underfinanced developing country delegations receive special assistance to ensure that they can participate fully. However, during Cancún, none of the suggestions made by civil society groups was implemented. At the end of the meeting, a number of commentators trumpeted the outcome as a significant success for developing countries but others have pointed out that the US and other powerful countries in effect 'bought off' many of the G20 with subsequent bilateral agreements. Overall, therefore, Cancún is important in representing another incremental step towards redressing the power imbalance between developed and developing states but it cannot truly be said to have led to a radical reconfiguration of the global trading system.

Further reading
Jawara, F., Kwa, A. and Sharma, S. *Behind the Scenes at the WTO: The Real World of International Trade Negotiations* (London: Zed Books, 2004)

CASTELLS, MANUEL

Professor of Sociology at UCLA Berkeley, Manuel Castells has made key contributions to the **globalization** debate stemming from a career-length academic interest in social interconnectedness, particularly in relation to economies, cities and technological **development**. However, in his major tri-volume contribution, *The Information Age*, Castells has extended his analysis of globalization across the realms of society, politics and culture. In that sense, his contribution to the globalization debates spans a far greater breadth than that of many theorists.

Castells' work tackles globalization through a number of inter-linked conceptual themes which arguably represent his most significant contributions. The first of these is informational capitalism. His key argument is that information technologies have transformed the nature of economic activity in recent decades, and that this is a central factor behind contemporary globalization. He argues that 'the new economy' is both informational and global in nature, and that these are its two essential defining features. The informational aspect derives from the fact that the productivity or competitiveness of units or agents in the economy (firms, regions or nations) fundamentally depends on their capacity to generate, process and apply efficiently knowledge-based information. The global characteristic rests on the fact that the core activities of production, consumption and circulation, along with their components (capital, labour, raw materials, management, information, technology, markets), are all organized on a global scale – either directly or through a network of linkages between economic agents. The economy has thus become both informational and global because under the new historical conditions of the contemporary era, productivity is generated through and competition is played out in **global networks** of interaction.

In this sense, Castells places the shift towards informational capitalism at the heart of his understanding of globalization as a process. He argues that in the contemporary period, a global economy has developed which is distinct from the earlier world economy described by theorists such as **Wallerstein** or Braudel. The key distinction for Castells is that the contemporary global economy has the capacity to work as a unit in real time on a planetary scale.

Second, and related, is the concept of the network society. The network metaphor enables Castells to think through new forms of interconnectedness which escape simplistic territorial approaches to understanding social interrelatedness. He argues that increasingly extensive network forms can be identified in a range of institutions and organizations from economic enterprises to political bodies. He also deploys this concept, for instance, in theorizing how national identities are being reconfigured or new social movements such as the **Zapatistas** have developed in the era of contemporary globalization.

The third concept is the space of flows. From his early work on the developing interconnectedness of global cities in the 1980s, Castells has argued that contemporary globalization is characterized by society becoming increasingly constructed around flows: flows of capital, information, technology, organizational interaction, images, sounds and symbols. For Castells, flows are thus not an element of social organization under current globalizing conditions but they are 'an expression of the processes dominating economic, political and symbolic life'. Spatial practices have thus taken on a new spatial form as a consequence of globalization (the space of flows), which can be summed up as 'the material organization of time-sharing social practices that work through flows'.

Overall, Castells has made an extremely wide-ranging contribution to thinking about how contemporary society is changing in the context of technological change and globalization. Much of this has drawn diverse literature together. From a critical perspective, the main potential problem with this approach is the extent to which his generalized vision of the network society, informationalism and the space of flows offers explanatory power in all the many contexts he seeks to apply it. Given the overarching nature of his theoretical vision, this view of the nature of globalization is inevitably more convincing in some areas than others.

Further reading
Castells, M. 'Global Informational Capitalism', ch. 27 in Held, D. and McGrew, A. (eds) *The Global Transformations Reader* (2nd edn; Cambridge: Polity, 2003)
Castells, M. 'The Other Face of the Earth: Social Movements against the New Global Order', ch. 2 in *The Power of Identity* (2nd edn; Oxford: Blackwell, 2004)

CHOMSKY, NOAM

American professor of linguistics, Noam Chomsky, has long been an important and extremely prolific contributor to radical debates on politics, international conflict and international **development**. He has taught at the Massachusetts Institute of Technology since 1955 and first gained recognition as a (broadly) left-wing political commentator for his objections to US involvement in the Vietnam war. Although not opposed to electoral democracy, he defines himself as being in the tradition of anarchism, a political philosophy he summarizes as challenging all forms of hierarchy and attempting to eliminate them if they are unjustified. His contributions to the **globalization** debate span a range of areas, although Chomsky himself has only more recently made use of the term to any great extent in his writing. At least four major areas of the contemporary globalization debate can be identified where Chomsky has made detailed and consistent contributions across his work. First, Chomsky has long been critical of the concentration of power and control in multi- and now **transnational corporations**. Chomsky in particular has sought to highlight how big business has endeavoured to shift societal perceptions to further profit and has highlighted how this is a threat to democracy. This is a similar position to **anti-globalization** commentators such as Naomi **Klein**. Second, Chomsky has long been opposed to the politics of **neo-liberalism** and their extension to the global scale. He sees many aspects of contemporary **economic globalization** as characterizing 'predatory capitalism' which is benefiting a privileged elite at the expense of the poor majority. In particular, he has offered detailed intellectual critiques of the philosophical basis of neo-liberalism, pointing to the mismatch between the visionary and progressive ideas in the philosophical works of Adam Smith and the implemented doctrine of neo-liberalism in the contemporary world. Third, Chomsky has also been a major critical commentator analysing the development of US power in the international sphere. In a similar vein to Michael Hardt and Antonio **Negri**, he sees the **Bretton Woods institutions** as constituting the core of a 'new imperial age'. Fourth, Chomsky has also made important contributions to the debate around the development of **global terrorism** in the aftermath of **9/11**. Whilst denouncing the atrocity of 9/11, Chomsky traces its origins in US foreign policy and actions on the international stage. A long-time critic of the relationship of the militaristic-technological mode in which the US has promoted its interests and the development of the global economy, he sees the evolution of al-Qaeda as a global-scale organization as being in response to the 'new imperial age' of US-led neo-liberal economic globalization and an unchecked global capitalism.

Further reading
Chomsky, N. *Profits over People: Neoliberalism and the Global Order* (New York: Seven Stories Press, 1998)
Chomsky, N. 'Dilemmas of Dominance', ch. 4 in *Hegemony or Survival: America's Quest for Global Dominance* (London: Penguin, 2004)
Fox, J. *Chomsky and Globalisation* (London: Icon Books, 2001)

CLUB OF ROME

A German-based global think-tank which was founded in 1953. It deals with a wide variety of international political issues and is probably most famous for its 1972 report *The Limits to Growth*. The report, which sold over thirty million copies in over thirty languages raised the question of the impact of human **development** on the earth's finite natural resources. It predicted that **economic growth** would not continue indefinitely because of natural resource limitations, especially oil. The oil crisis in 1973 brought this to particular public attention. The Club fell into a period of lower profile during the 1980s and question marks were raised about its future. However, the 1990s saw a period of renewal and a refocused wider agenda with the Club currently seeking to address the core issues of **development**, the **environment**, governance and education.

Further reading
The Club of Rome's current declaration is available at <http://www.clubofrome.org/archive/declaration.php>.

CNN

The US-based Cable News Network, launched on 1 June 1980. CNN has since expanded to include a number of cable and satellite networks, twelve websites, two private place-based networks and two radio networks. Its coverage is now truly global and the network has bureaux in over forty-two countries, fed by a further nine hundred news agency affiliates worldwide. CNN has launched many regional and foreign-language networks in the last decade or so and was responsible for the first major news website on the **Internet** in 1995. The global reputation of CNN was perhaps most firmly established during the 1991 Gulf War where saturation coverage was carried around the world. CNN has developed a series of regional editions in recent years to meet foreign demand for less US-centric news coverage and makes increasing use of local reporters. The channel has been criticized by both right- and left-wing commentators for political bias.

Further reading
Volkmer, I. *News in the Global Sphere: A Study of CNN and its Impact on Global Communication* (Luton: University of Luton Press, 1999)

COLD WAR

The shifting struggle for power and prestige between the Western powers and the communist bloc from the end of the **Second World War** in 1945 until 1989, although its origins pre-date the war in the mutual suspicion that had existed between the West and the Soviet Union since the Russian Revolution. With respect to global interrelatedness, the Cold War is important in that it extended the ideological differences (communism versus capitalist democracy) to worldwide proportions. In a famous speech in 1946, Winston Churchill warned of an implacable threat that lay behind a communist 'iron curtain'. The US took the lead against the expansion of Soviet influence, rallying the West with the Truman Doctrine, under which immediate aid was given to Turkey and Greece. Also fearing the rise of communism in war-torn Western Europe, the US inaugurated the European Recovery Program (the Marshall Plan); this encompassed the strategic aim of restoring prosperity to Western Europe and containing the spread of communism, which also fostered the foundation of what is now the **European Union**. Beyond Europe, the Cold War saw a series of military conflicts in developing countries at the margins of both blocs. The Korean and Vietnam wars (the latter including Laos and Cambodia), along with the support of nationalist China (Taiwan), represented one major area of Cold War conflict. However, both the US and Soviet Union supported various state regimes or groups in Africa (for example, Congo and Angola) and Latin America (Nicaragua, Cuba, Chile and Colombia), which in effect extended the conflict to these regions.

During the later 1960s and 1970s there was a period of lesser tension between the blocs until President Reagan revived Cold War policies and rhetoric in the 1980s, referring to the Soviet Union as

the 'evil empire' and escalating the nuclear arms race. Some historians argue this stance was responsible for the eventual collapse of
Soviet communism while others attribute the collapse to the inherent
weakness of the Soviet state. From 1989 to 1991 the Cold War came
to an end with the opening of the Berlin Wall, the collapse of communist party dictatorship in Eastern Europe, the reunification of
Germany and the disintegration of the Soviet Union.

Further reading
Sewell, M. *The Cold War* (Cambridge: Cambridge University Press, 2002)
  [esp. chs 2, 3 and 7]

COMPARATIVE ADVANTAGE

The theory that explains why it can be beneficial for two countries to
trade, even though one of them may be able to produce every kind of
item more cheaply than the other. What matters is not the absolute
cost of production, but rather the ratio between how easily the two
countries can produce different kinds of things. It was first described
by Robert Torrens in an essay on the corn trade (1815). Contemporary
understandings of comparative advantage are, however, generally
attributed to another nineteenth-century political economist, David
Ricardo. In *The Principles of Political Economy and Taxation* (1817) he
explains the theory through an example involving England and Portugal. In Portugal it is possible to produce both wine and cloth with
less work than it takes in England. However, the *relative costs* of producing those two goods are different in the two countries. In England
it is very hard to produce wine, and only moderately difficult to
produce cloth. In Portugal both are easy to produce. Therefore, while
it is cheaper to produce cloth in Portugal than England, it is cheaper
still for Portugal to produce excess wine, and trade that for English
cloth. And conversely England benefits from this trade because its
cost for producing cloth has not changed but it can now get wine at
closer to the cost of cloth. In comparative advantage theory, if one
entity (for example, a firm or a country) is able to produce more efficiently than another entity it has what is termed an absolute advantage. This means that, assuming equal inputs, the entity with an
absolute advantage will have a greater output.

The theory is famously counter-intuitive and often misunderstood.
However, it is crucial to understanding contemporary **globalization**
because it is the basic underlying theoretical argument for **free trade**

and regional trading blocs such as the **European Union**. It is, of course, problematic in this respect as an abstraction that rarely, if ever, captures the complexity of the real world and actual existing trading relationships.

Further reading
Review article by Douglas Irwin on international trade available at <http://www.econlib.org/library/Columns/Irwintrade.html>.

COSMOPOLITAN DEMOCRACY
An ideal model for a desirable future political system, for which a number of political theorists have argued. At its heart, the concept of cosmopolitan democracy is based around the idea of the need for a transnationally applicable set of basic rights. David **Held** has outlined a vision for this future, centred on six main pillars. First, in an era when the global order is being made concrete in multiple, overlapping power networks which encompass human bodies, welfare, culture, voluntary organizations, the economy, international ties of dependence and organized violence, then the scope for cosmopolitan democracy arises out of these varied networks and out of a multidimensional balance of power among nations, organizations and people.

A second element is that all groups and organizations claim a relative autonomy, which is expressed in certain rights and duties. This pattern of what is permitted and forbidden, Held argues, must be tied together in fundamental principles of cosmopolitan democratic law, which then need to be spelt out individually for the fields of action of the social, the economic and the political.

Third, these legal principles need to be legitimated and guaranteed by transnationally and locally articulated parliaments and courts – the model for this is the European Parliament and the European Court of Justice – which would have to be established in transnational spaces of South America, Asia and Africa.

Fourth, **nation-state**s will need to cede parts of their power and sovereignty to transnational institutions and organizations, and develop a new understanding of themselves as nodal points and co-ordinators of transnational dependence.

Fifth, individuals in this model may come to belong to different national and transnational power areas, and thus exercise rights to participation and self-determination from the local up to the global level.

Sixth, public money will be needed for everyone – regardless of whether they are involved in the private sector, domestic labour or public civil employment. This will guarantee the exercise of political freedom.

Ulrich **Beck** has argued that this idealized sociological model is all very well but that this is a picture-book vision which is more a hope than a feasible future. He sees the ideal of cosmopolitan democracy as only achievable in the era of globalization through the emergence of a transnational state or at least similar structures that can mitigate the effects of the undemocratic and increasingly powerful **transnational corporation**s. Furthermore, many of Held's basic tenets for cosmopolitan democracy appear to have had a difficult time in recent years. In particular, attempts at the construction of new transnational legal institutions such as the **International Criminal Court** have been hampered by key state players such as the US refusing to participate. Likewise, in the current configuration of politics in an expanded EU, the future role and strength of institutions such as the European Parliament are unclear, with some questioning whether these institutions can ever be effective mechanisms of democracy on the regional scale. The issue that remains in doubt therefore is whether Held's contention, that a coherent form of transnational cosmopolitan democracy can be developed from an array of cooperative procedures and relations of dependence, can in fact ever be achieved in the complex world of international politics.

Further reading
Beck, U. *What is Globalization?* (Cambridge: Polity, 2000) [ch. 2]
Held, D. 'Cosmopolitanism: Ideas, Realities, Deficits', ch. 15 in Held, D. and McGrew, A. (eds) *Governing Globalization* (Cambridge: Polity, 2002)

COX, ROBERT

Writing from a political science perspective, Cox has argued that it is important to adopt a historical perspective on **globalization**. During the 1990s, he represented a key critical voice pointing to the rhetorical and ideological underpinnings of much commentary on globalization – its construction, for example, as an inevitable phenomenon and as the logical culmination of market forces. He argues that globalization has become a hegemonic ideology that is presented as a solution to polarizing social forces. As ideology it shields the perpetuations of spatial and temporal inequality and leads to the fragmentation and 'break down' of opposition. This is what those opposing (neo-liberal) globalization should seek to resist.

Further reading
Cox, K. 'Introduction – Globalization and its Politics in Question', in Cox, K. (ed.) *Spaces of Globalization: Reasserting the Power of the Local* (London: Guilford Press, 1997)

CULTURAL GLOBALIZATION

In general, the integration and intertwining of cultural practices, ideas and tropes at the planetary scale (usually in the contemporary period), although it is a widely contested and unclear sub-concept in the **globalization** literature that has been used to describe and explain a wide variety of different phenomena. It is commonly conceived as one dimension of globalization's many forms and, as with other dimensions, commentators are quick to point out that there is nothing especially novel about this phenomenon that warrants its distinction from earlier forms of cultural interrelatedness and that, even more than with **economic** or **political globalization**, culture and cultural phenomena are intangible and amorphous.

Notwithstanding this perspective, a number of important contributions to the globalization debate have argued that cultural issues are at the heart of globalization as a wider phenomenon. John **Tomlinson** argues that the modern world displays complex connectivity which he sees as the rapidly developing and ever-densening network of interconnections and interdependencies that characterize modern social life. Culture is central to the development of complex connectivity because it is the order of life in which human beings construct meanings through practices of symbolic representation. He makes the argument that the degree of globalization is greatest in the cultural arena because cultural symbols 'can be produced anywhere and at any time and there are relatively few resource constraints on their production and reproduction'. In that sense, culture is intrinsically more globalizing on account of the ease of the 'stretching' of relations involved and the inherent mobility of cultural forms and products. Culture cannot be meaningfully extracted from the economic, political or social realms and it is also 'ordinary' (after the sociologist Raymond Williams) in so far as it describes a whole way of life. It is not the exclusive property of the privileged but includes all manner of everyday social practices.

For many globalization theorists such as Martin **Albrow**, the key debate around cultural globalization rests around the longstanding association of culture with fixed localities. Globalization is argued to weaken the ties of culture to places, and the impact of globalization is in the transformation of localities through the process of **deterritorialization**. Whilst many have taken this process to be a negative, as is most widely evident in the ongoing debate about the erosion of national cultures by globalization processes, Tomlinson suggests that in fact deterritorialization also has positive benefits. In particular he argues that it furnishes people with a cultural resource which they lacked previously. This does not mean that everyone is experiencing the world as cultural cosmopolitans, and much less that a single **global culture** is developing (as Arjun **Appadurai** argues), but that 'the global' increasingly exists as a cultural horizon within which more and more people (to varying degrees) frame their existence.

These more recent responses to earlier negative views of cultural globalization (often seen as **cultural imperialism**) as a potential destructive and disempowering process in relation to identity, locality and **nation-states** have produced an important shift in the terms of the debate. However, such abstract theoretical arguments have limitations when held up against the 'messy reality' of the globalizing world. Most of these limitations revolve around the problematic and ambiguous status of culture itself as a concept. First, for example, because the concept itself remains hard to define, ascertaining the degree of cultural integration in contemporary globalization is a problematic undertaking since cultural entities in practice cannot be isolated in the first place. Second, and relatedly, the same point applies to the notion of 'pure' cultural forms in localities or nations. Dialectical theories of deterritorialization posit that cultural attributes can be meaningfully thought to exist out of places and localities. In reality, isolating a cultural attribute is a largely arbitrary theoretical practice which conceals the fact that most cultural attributes or tropes have a complex form of connectivity in time and space. Culture was never simplistically tied to locality, and cultural ideas have always easily been transmitted to distant places. Deterritorialization is in that sense a misconstrued concept, as culture never in fact exists out of space and place. Third, if the cultural dimension is the key central dimension to globalization, the question could be raised as to what extent it is helpful and meaningful to try to theorize cultural globalization as a distinct process from other forms of societal interconnectedness. Whilst the same is true for all aspects of the wider phenomenon, economic globalization or political globalization do at least manifest themselves more directly through organizational and institutional forms. The tangible impacts of cultural globalization are less clear, which thus provides weaker justification for the concept itself.

Further reading
Albrow, M. 'Travelling Beyond Local Culture', ch. 16 in Lechner, F. and Boli, F. (eds) *The Globalization Reader* (2nd edn, Oxford: Blackwell, 2004)

Appiah, K. and Gates, H. *A Dictionary of Global Culture* (London: Penguin, 1998)

Tomlinson, J. *Globalization and Culture* (Cambridge: Polity, 1999) [esp. ch. 1]

CULTURAL IMPERIALISM

In broad terms, the practice of promoting the culture or language of one nation in another. It is usually the case that the former is a large, economically or militarily powerful nation and the latter is a smaller, less affluent one. Cultural imperialism can take the form of an active, formal policy or a general attitude. Historically, this has therefore had a long relevance in human history from the ancient empires to the influence of China or of European colonial powers in recent centuries. However, in the contemporary period, cultural imperialism is widely associated with **cultural globalization** and arguments in particular relating to the transmission and dominance of American culture (Americanization). Most countries outside the US feel that the high degree of cultural export through business and popular culture (popular and academic books, films, music, and television) threatens their unique ways of life or moral values where such cultural exports are popular. Some countries such as France have experimented with policies that try actively to oppose Americanization and Western consumer culture. Arguments about cultural imperialism also continue to dominate discussions of **development** in the postcolonial context.

However, the concept itself is problematic. It covers a range of interpretations spanning a continuum from 'forced acculturation' of a subject population to the voluntary embracing of a foreign culture by individuals who do so of their own free will. Since this presents a number of very different interpretations, the validity of the term can be called into question. It has, moreover, been pointed out that the term is also understood differently in particular discourses – for example, as 'media imperialism' or as 'discourse of nationality'. Furthermore, since culture itself is dynamic and fluid, delimiting one distinct culture from another is difficult (and becoming ever more so in the age of global media). A number of theorists of cultural globalization such as John **Tomlinson** argue that the power relations associated with cultural interactions in the contemporary world are complex and are leading to new hybrid cultural forms. These are not necessarily easily fitted into simplistic accounts of cultural imperialism understood in terms of one coherent national culture dominating another.

Further reading
Said, E. *Culture and Imperialism* (London: Penguin, 1994) [esp. Introduction]
Tomlinson, J. *Cultural Imperialism: An Introduction* (London: Lightning Source, 2003)

DALY, HERMAN

Former senior economist in the environmental department at the **World Bank**, Herman Daly published a strong critique of the principles and ideologies underpinning global economic **development** in *Beyond Growth: The Economics of Sustainable Development* (1996). Daly argues that the purpose of the (global) economy should be to create 'greatest good for an optimum number of people over the long run' and that the postwar global economy has not been very successful in this respect. He points to the limitations that others critical of neo-liberal **economic globalization** identify: the growing wealth imbalance, the cruel 'efficiencies' of capital flowing in and out of communities and questions about the Earth's capacity to sustain human life. The significance of his contribution is that he questions emerging notions of (environmental) sustainability in relation to **economic growth**. He argues that sustainability needs to be defined as 'development without growth beyond environmental carrying capacity, where development means qualitative improvement and growth means quantitative increase'. He further argues that continuous growth is not only impossible in the long run, but undesirable, and that what is needed is a 'steady-state' economy that improves living standards through qualitative improvement with no increase in what he terms 'throughput' – the materials and energy that the economy turns from raw inputs into waste. His work is thus important for its continuing critique of neo-liberal economic globalization's basic assumption that global economic growth can be both achieved and sustained. More recently he has joined other environmental and ecological economists in advocating the **localization** of economic activity as a means of achieving greater sustainability.

Further reading
Daly, H. *Beyond Growth: The Economics of Sustainable Development* (Boston, Mass.: Beacon Press, 1996)

debt *see* international debt.

DEMOCRATIZATION
In the broadest sense, a system of government which embodies or is based on the belief in freedom and equality between people, and in which power is either held directly by the people themselves or by elected representatives. In reality, it is the latter which forms the model for modern democratic states. Democratization, in a simple sense, is therefore the process by which systems of government become democratic. The implicit assumption held by most commentators on democratization is that democratic governance (of some form) is the most desirable form of governance in the contemporary world.

Historically, some **nation-state**s have developed democratic forms of government whilst others have not, but during the last century there was a continued promotion of and trend towards nation-states adopting democratic systems of governance. The demise of the Soviet Union and other communist states as a system of governance has been proclaimed as representing the triumph of democracy in the late twentieth century that has led to the democratization of many former communist nations. Institutions such as the **United Nations**, **International Monetary Fund** and **World Bank** have also (in principle at least) embodied the desirability of democratization and the creation of democratic governance structures in the countries of the less developed world.

However, contemporary **globalization** complicates the democratization issue. Critics such as Edward Goldsmith and Susan **George** have argued that various globalization processes undermine the democratic accountability of states and other institutions. They point to the increasing concentration of power in a variety of non-democratic organizations and groups, including **transnational corporation**s, the **transnational capitalist class**, elite political groups and unaccountable supranational institutions such as the IMF or World Bank. These new governance actors do not replicate the structures of democratic accountability that existed in traditional democratic political institutions. In this way, democratic accountability is being eroded by globalization. However, other theorists point out that at the same time the integration of political structures and globalization of values and forms of political practice simultaneously continues to promote democratization.

The political science literature has thus been concerned with the best way of achieving democratic accountability in the contemporary era of globalization. This requires the democratization of supranational institutions and other bodies as well as the development of better democratic structures in many existing nation-states where democracy has only ever been weakly developed. However, there are a variety of models which different theorists see as the best way of promoting democratization. Anthony **McGrew**, for example, identifies a number of different normative concepts of democracy that can exist beyond borders: **cosmopolitan democracy**, radical democracy and transnational deliberative democracy.

In sum, the democratization debate is largely focused on the problematic issue of which form of supranational democracy best delivers 'good **global governance**' and what policies are desirable as a consequence. In the 1980s, the perceived weakness of governments in delivering democracy led to a policy shift towards new local organizations – NGOs, charities and other agencies were seen as offering democratization where weak nation-states had failed. Yet in the 1990s there was a reaction to this, as researchers showed that these pressure groups and other civil society organizations were unrepresentative and had poor democratic credentials. Current thinking therefore argues that to achieve democratization of contemporary global governance requires the simultaneous incorporation of a wide range of governance actors; these include supranational institutions, governments, NGOs, advocacy groups, TNCs and other agents of civil society. However, this 'ideal' is far more difficult to achieve in reality than some of the political science literature appears to acknowledge.

Further reading

Dahl, R. *Democracy and Its Critics* (New Haven, Conn.: Yale University Press, 1989)

Grugel, K. 'Democratization and Globalization', ch. 7 in *Democratization: A Critical Introduction* (Basingstoke: Palgrave Macmillan, 2001)

Keohane, R. 'Governance in a Partially Globalized World', ch. 16 in Held, D. and McGrew, A. (eds) *Governing Globalization* (Cambridge: Polity, 2002)

DENATIONALIZATION

In a straightforward sense, the process of uncoupling processes, entities or forms of practice from **nation-state**s. In the context of the **globalization** debate, it is most commonly used to refer to the process by which **economic globalization** is severing the linkage between economic activity and national territorial spaces (national **sovereignty**) and nation-based organizations. Most often, these organizations are those of political governance but commentators on economic globalization have also used the term with respect to **transnational corporation**s.

However, commentators such as Saskia **Sassen** have argued that this denationalization of national territory should not be understood in any simplistic form as a wholesale displacement from the national scale to the global. She argues that specific and highly specialized forms of denationalization are occurring within nation-states as entities, and that these are manifested differently in different countries. Thus a considerable segment of the globalization literature has been concerned with how the national scale is only one of several traditional conceptions of scale that have been destabilized by contemporary global interconnectedness. Thus, as Sassen points out, denationalization needs to be treated with caution as globalization is producing 're-scaling dynamics' that cut across institutional size and across institutional encasements of territory produced by the formation of nation-states.

Further reading

Sassen, S. 'Globalization or Denationalization?' *Review of International Political Economy*, 10 (2003), 1–22

DETERRITORIALIZATION

The concept most commonly used to refer to the process by which there is a loss of the 'natural' relation of culture to geographical and social territories. John **Tomlinson** argues that the complex connectivity that is emerging in contemporary global society is weakening the ties of culture to place and that this 'troubling phenomenon' involves a simultaneous penetration of 'local worlds by distant forces' and the dislodging of everyday meanings from their anchors in the local environment. However, Tomlinson also argues that deterritorialization is 'not all bad news' in so far as it also furnishes people with a cultural resource that they lacked previously – a cultural awareness that is in many senses 'global'. He thus echoes the arguments of Roland Robertson and Anthony **Giddens** who also characterize deterritorialization as a process whereby people's 'phenomenonal worlds', though locally situated, are becoming for the most part truly global.

Beyond debates around **cultural globalization**, the term is also used in a vaguer and often more confused manner in discussions of economic activity and other dimensions of globalization. There is, for example, a debate about the extent to which both financial capital and transnational firms' activities have become deterritorialized. Certainly in the case of the latter, however, the specific meaning of the word is problematic since most economic activity at least in part occupies some physical territorial space or place.

Further reading
Tomlinson, J. 'Deterritorialization: The Cultural Condition of Globalization', ch. 4 in *Globalization and Culture* (Cambridge: Polity, 1999)

DEVELOPMENT

A descriptive term for the process or transformation through which the poorer countries of the world achieve the standards of living experienced in the so-called developed countries of the West. The meaning and theories of what development 'is' have been profoundly affected by the **globalization** debate. Theories of development have changed substantially over the last fifty years. At the start of the postwar period, development was largely seen as the need for the poor countries of the '**Third World**', as they became known, to 'catch up' with the more advanced and wealthier economies of the capitalist Western First World (and to a lesser extent the communist Second

World). A strong element in this was the argument that the more developed world needed to intervene and direct the development of poorer countries in order to modernize their institutions to permit **economic growth.**

However, from the late 1960s, this *modernization theory* was challenged from within the developing world by the Latin American *dependencia* school and neo-Marxian **world systems analysis.** World systems analysis in particular can be seen as a forerunner of one kind of globalization theory in so far as it argues that the less developed world's weak structural position in a global political and economic system was to a large extent responsible for the poorer countries' continued lack of economic growth. The policy response prescribed was that poorer countries should 'de-link their economies from the world market'.

In the 1980s this view of development encountered a number of crises. In particular, the rise of neo-liberalism as an ideological basis for emerging theories of **economic globalization** offered a different explanation of the development 'problem' from that of the Marxian critiques. It also offered very different policy prescriptions as a consequence. The interventionist paradigm of postwar development theory was challenged as neo-liberal theorists argued development was an inherently universal and increasingly global economic process. A lack of development was primarily seen as a domestic problem which was caused by 'rent-seeking' bureaucrats and corrupt politicians in less developed countries. If the world capitalist economy were left to work unfettered, argued the neo-liberals, then development would be achieved in the low-income economies of the world. In that sense, development theory has been caught in an 'impasse' since the late 1980s as proponents of neo-liberal economic globalization argued that the best development policy was one of non-intervention. From an economic perspective, many commentators have argued that globalization *itself* has now become the new word for mainstream development. They suggest that **globalism** is a development ideology which implies the growth of a world market, increasingly penetrating and dominating 'national' economies.

Overall, many aspects of the development debate are therefore now entwined with questions of globalization. It is impossible to discuss theories of development without engaging with different theoretical perspectives on globalization. In the last decade, from a number of different angles, different academic disciplines have questioned whether neo-liberal globalization really can achieve development. A growing body of research suggests that in many parts of the world income inequalities are widening rather than narrowing as a consequence of global economic integration. This has provoked calls for the return of a revitalized interventionist approach to development, albeit at the level of supranational institutions of **global governance** rather than at the scale of **nation-state**s.

Further reading
Desai, V. and Potter, R. (eds) *The Companion to Development Studies* (London: Edward Arnold, 2002) [esp. Introduction]
Schuurman, F. (ed.) *Globalization and Development Studies: Challenges for the 21st Century* (London: Sage, 2003) [part I in particular]

DIASPORIC COMMUNITIES

Communities of people who share common cultural, ethnic, linguistic and other attributes but who are scattered across various **nation-state**s and territories around the globe. The term is often used interchangeably with the notion of the transnational community. Literally, a diaspora is a spatial distribution one might achieve by dipping a paintbrush into a tin of paint and flicking it across a large canvas. In this sense the concept refers to any spatially and territorially scattered community. However, Stephen Vertovec identifies three broad meanings of the term 'diaspora' as it has been increasingly used in contemporary debates, which push the term beyond the physical scattering of communities: 'diaspora as social forms', 'diaspora as types of consciousness' and 'diaspora as modes of cultural production'. Diasporic communities thus have both a real and imagined dimension, with community members' sense of identity and cultural belonging being an important aspect of their definition.

The development of global-scale diasporic communities has been a historical process running back many centuries and related to various population migrations for a variety of reasons. Important migrations that have led to significant contemporary diasporic communities include the Jewish and Black diasporas. However, in the context of contemporary **globalization**, various commentators argue that the size, number and extent of diasporic communities have increased. In the twenty-first century people are in a position to extend their connections to their home country with ever greater intensity and to establish networks globally. Improved transport and communications have allowed a greater degree of coherence to newer diasporas of (often) recent economic migrants, for example, the Indian and Chinese diasporic communities. Importantly, in a socio-cultural and political sense, diasporic communities demand a recon-figuration of the concept of the nation-state and its relationship to cultural identity. They are a key issue in debates about the emergence of new postnational societal forms in the contemporary world.

Further reading
Braziel, J. and Mannur, A. 'Nation, Migration and Globalization', ch. 1 in *Theorizing Diaspora* (Oxford: Blackwell, 2003)
Gilroy, P. 'The Black Atlantic as a CounterCulture to Modernity', ch. 1 in *The Black Atlantic* (London: Verso, 1996)

DICKEN, PETER

Dicken's work represents a very important contribution to theoretical and empirical understandings of the evolving global economy. Coming from a geographical perspective, his major research has concentrated on the nature of the restructuring of economic activity across the global economy since the 1970s. Some time ahead of the emergence of the conceptual language of the **globaliza-tion** debate, Dicken pointed to the dramatic geographical 'shifts' in the organization of production as **multinational corporations** reorganized their activities across **nation-state**s and regions in response to the falling profitability of production in advanced industrial economies in the 1970s. His work provides a key, empiri-cally founded basis for understanding what he argues is the pivotal role of **transnational corporation**s in the contemporary global economy.

As theorists in the later 1980s began to address how production was becoming increasingly concentrated amongst a small number of growing TNCs, Dicken's work has been important in providing a theoretical understanding of the forces underlying the development and behaviour of the world's largest firms. His earlier arguments concerning MNCs' shift of production activity developed into a wider-ranging theoretical approach for understanding the globalization of manufacturing production. In particular, his research has concen-trated on exploring how firms are embedded in local and regional institutional and national contexts, as well as how technology has shaped and affected these interrelationships. This has led him recently to make a series of arguments about the nature of globalization as a phenomenon in general.

First, he argues, in line with a number of theorists, that globalization is a set of tendencies and not some kind of final condition. However, he emphasizes that these tendencies are both geographically and organizationally uneven, with neither a single predetermined trajectory nor a fixed end point. Second, he suggests that (economic) globalization cannot be understood as a single transformative force. Whilst his work has concentrated on the nature of TNCs, he is careful to argue that other institutions and entities are important in shaping global economic activity – most notably the state.

Third, the implication of this is that what Dicken sees as the processes of globalization are not simply unidirectional in a way that might be construed, for example, as being from global to local. Instead he argues that globalization processes have to be understood as being deeply embedded, produced and reproduced in particular contexts. This is a broadly dialectical conception (although he does not state that explicitly) in so far as specific 'assemblages of characteristics of individual nations and of local communities' will in Dicken's view not only influence how globalization processes are experienced but will also influence the nature of those experiences themselves.

Dicken's work has been well received and forms an important contribution to understanding the complexity of the processes captured in the concept of **economic globalization**. His book *Global Shift* (2004) is one of the most comprehensive and detailed empirical overviews of global economic activity in the social sciences. However, a number of more specific areas of potential critical engagement with his theoretical approach are worth mentioning. First, in seeing TNCs as primarily articulated between the global–local scales, it could be argued that this oversimplifies the complexity of relationships that are not easily fitted into a given scale. His later research seems to acknowledge this as it has focused ever more closely on the organizational complexity of TNCs at different scales. Second, his analysis relies heavily on the concept of territoriality and this can be seen as a poor surrogate for the mass of factors influencing firms' activities in the global economy. Again, Dicken's recent work has addressed this issue in seeking, for example, to think through how the spatiality of TNCs might be conceived. However, there is no strong sense of the role of cultural and institutional context in Dicken's usage of the term 'embeddedness'. Third, his approach to understanding the activities of TNCs and other global economic actors pays relatively little attention to power relationships, which other commentators on the global economy argue is essential to an effective understanding of the activities of TNCs.

Further reading
Dicken, P. '"Placing" Firms: Grounding the Debate on the Global Corporation', ch. 2 in Peck, J. & Yeung, H. (eds) *Remaking the Global Economy* (London: Sage, 2003)
Dicken, P. *Global Shift: Reshaping the Global Economic Map in the 21st Century* (4th edn; London: Sage, 2004) [esp. Introduction]

DIVISION OF LABOUR

The specialization of the functions and roles involved in production. Among the different categories of division of labour are territorial, in which certain geographical regions specialize in producing certain products, exchanging their surplus for goods produced elsewhere; temporal, in which separate processes are performed by different industrial groups in manufacturing one product, as the making of bread by farmers, millers and bakers; and occupational, in which goods produced in the same industrial group are worked by a number of persons, each applying one or more processes and skills. Historically, this is argued to have occurred in the modern period (since around 1600) with the development of capitalism and industrialization. This emergence of a different, modern division of labour activity occupied thinkers from Adam Smith to Karl **Marx** and Emile Durkheim in the nineteenth century. In its classical conception, the division of labour is thus about the specialization and concentration of the workers in their individual sub-tasks. This leads to greater skill and greater productivity in their particular sub-tasks than would be achieved by the same number of workers each carrying out the original broad task. Marx and Durkheim developed this to point to the alienating effect that this has on the individual.

However, during the twentieth century, the concept became closely tied to the standardization of production (often associated with Fordism), the introduction and perfection of machinery and the development of large-scale industrialization. Importantly, a number of theorists have argued that it has a territorial and geographical dimension. In the post-**Second World War** decades, a range of social scientific theorists argued that a new international division of labour (NIDL) has occurred as lower-skill manufacturing employment shifted from the advanced Western economies to newly industrializing countries (NICs) in Asia. More recently, this global shift in labour division has become further complicated as the global economy has developed with an ongoing dramatic switch of manufacturing employment to formerly less developed countries such as China and the rise of service-sector employment in more developed economies.

Further reading
Mittelman, J. 'Rethinking the International Division of Labour', ch. 2 in *The Globalization Syndrome* (Princeton, N.J.: Princeton University Press, 2000)

DOHA DEVELOPMENT ROUND
The round of trade negotiations initiated by the **World Trade Organization** at the Fourth Ministerial Conference in Doha, Qatar, in November 2001. Importantly, the Doha Round represented a response by the WTO to increasing criticism that trade negotiations are not sensitive enough to the concerns of developing countries. Hence, the Doha Round gained the title of the '**development**' round. It focuses specifically on the role of trade in development and on the areas most important to developing countries, such as **agriculture** and implementation issues (how developing countries could implement trade rules). It was heralded by the WTO as a bold step forward in redressing trade negotiations' favouritism towards the advanced economies of the more developed world.

However, the Doha Round quickly ran into difficulties. When the Ministerial Conference in **Cancún** ended abruptly in 2003, no progress had been made on agriculture, and developed and developing countries disagreed vociferously on whether to add the four Singapore issues to the agenda (trade and investment, competition policy, transparency in government procurement and trade facilitation). This antagonism between developing and developed countries and the lack of progress has many commentators sceptical about Doha as to whether the WTO's attention to development is just rhetoric. Little of the development agenda has actually been accomplished to date. In agriculture, for example, the US and Japan have resisted making any commitments, and the EU has made only very limited moves towards dismantling agriculture supports and reforming its subsidy programme. At Cancún, developed and developing countries were unable to come to a consensus on a proposal, and were even more polarized on the issue of subsidies and domestic supports. In that sense, since Cancún, the Doha Development Round has been effectively locked in stalemate.

Further reading
Las Das, B. *WTO: The Doha Agenda. The New Negotiations on World Trade* (London: Zed Books, 2003)

DRUG TRAFFICKING
The trade in illegal narcotic drugs which is increasingly occurring at the global scale. Although hard to measure, it is estimated that this trade is worth in excess of US $400 million per annum. It is one of the major components of the developing global black economy and as such shadows the **globalization** of production, distribution and consumption evident in the rest of the global economy. As with legal commerce, the illegal drug trade is multilayered and often multinational, with layers of manufacturers, processors, distributors, wholesalers and retailers. Financing is also important, generally involving money laundering to hide the source of the illegal profits and revenue streams. All of these are made more complex by their illegality, but tend to follow the same economic logics as conventional legal business activity.

As a global industry, the drug trade is a very fragmented industry with the most popular product, cannabis, being grown locally by many individuals with little collaboration. Similarly, drugs like LSD have very low profit margins and are often produced and sold on a small-scale, localized basis. The main organized drug cartels deal with cocaine, heroin and ecstasy (MDMA). Largely manufactured drugs also induce the foundation of satellite organizations that supply some of the needed chemical precursors. In places where alcohol is illegal, such as Saudi Arabia or Iran, it may also be the subject of illegal trading. The drug trade also reflects a global pattern of production and consumption, with a large proportion of the manufacturing occurring in less developed countries (Latin America, southeast Asia, central Asia) and considerable demand and consumption occurring in wealthier countries (North America, Europe, Australia and Japan).

Further reading

Buruma, Y. 'Drugs and Transnational Organized Crime: Conceptualization and Solutions', ch. 16 in Vellinga, M. (ed.) *The Political Economy of the Drug Industry: Latin America and the International System* (Miami: University of Florida Press, 2004)

See also The Drug Policy Alliance website: <http://www.dpf.org/homepage.cfm>.

ECONOMIC GLOBALIZATION

A sub-concept in the **globalization** debate that can be broadly divided into five relatively distinct realms of discussion. First, at the macroscale, economic globalization has been taken to refer to the long-term historical integration of economic activity through trade across continents, regions and, more recently, national borders. In that sense, David **Held** and his co-authors point out that the integration of economic activity stretches back into antiquity, and that human history over the last three millennia has seen a variety of different local, regional and globally extensive trading systems. They suggest, however, that during the nineteenth century in particular, empire-building set the context for the rise of international capitalism. Yet it was only in the mid-twentieth century, after the conflicts of two world wars, that an international political environment was created that has permitted the current phase of economic globalization. From the 1950s, international trade grew more rapidly than output under the conducive supranational climate created by the General Agreement on Tariffs and Trade (GATT), now the **World Trade Organization**. This argument concerning the nature of economic globalization has been contested by some, notably Paul **Hirst** and Grahame **Thompson** who argued that current levels of trade are not as historically unprecedented as globalization theorists have suggested.

The second dimension is the emergence of global markets. The emergence of global **free trade** in the last fifty years has provided the basis for markets in both commodities and services to become more extensive than ever before as a network of trading relations between regions and countries has developed.

Third, many theorists have highlighted the key role of **global financial integration** in economic globalization. This debate has focused on the liberalization of international restrictions on the movement of capital, currencies and other financial transactions which has been concomitant with trade liberalization. Whilst commentators such as David Held point out that there is a long historical evolution to this transnational 'enmeshment' of finance through nineteenth-century imperialism and the operation of the classical gold standard, it is again argued that the post-**Second World War** period, in particular after the demise of the Bretton Woods system, has witnessed a dramatic globalization of financial activity. This can be distinguished in terms of both the increased intensity and extensity of financial flows.

A fourth dimension to economic globalization is the role of economic actors and in particular the development of multinational and **transnational corporations**. Again, whilst there is a long history to the internationalization of business enterprises, it is primarily the growth in numbers and the extensiveness of corporate operations in the last fifty years that is emphasized as distinctive in contemporary economic globalization.

Fifth, and finally, theorists of economic globalization have also argued that this process has also transformed labour both in terms of the nature of labour markets and, more recently, the nature of working practices. Labour markets have themselves become globalized, although to a far lesser extent than other markets, but more important is the impact on regional and national labour markets of globalized production. With regard to working practices, a number of globalization theorists have pointed to the development of new patterns of working related to the needs of TNCs with rising levels of expatriation, international business travel and the increasing importance of information and communications technology.

Further reading

Greider, W. *One World Ready or Not* (New York: Penguin, 1997) [esp. Introduction]

Held, D., McGrew, A., Goldblatt, D. and Perraton, J. 'Global Trade, Global Markets', ch. 3 in *Global Transformations* (Cambridge: Polity, 1999)

Hirst, P. and Thompson, P. 'The Limits to Economic Globalization', ch. 28 in Held, D. and McGrew, A. (eds) *The Global Transformations Reader* (2nd edn; Cambridge: Polity, 2003)

ECONOMIC GROWTH

An issue at the centre of debates about whether **globalization** in general is a positive phenomenon. Given that the most common meanings attributed to globalization relate to economic integration and the development of the global economy, the degree to which economic growth is being achieved as a consequence is axiomatic.

There are many different definitional cuts at economic growth itself, and also many arguments about how it might best be measured. In simple terms, the most common understanding of economic growth, usually of a region or nation, is a positive change in the level of production of goods and services over a certain period of time. Nominal growth is defined as economic growth including inflation while real growth is nominal growth minus inflation. This tends to be measured using changes in gross domestic product (GDP) over time, although there are a number of technical arguments amongst economists as to whether the changes to the GDP overall or expressed per capita is a better indicator.

However, using changes in real GDP as a surrogate for economic growth is not without its problems. For example, real GDP in a country may increase at the same time as population. At the national level, the total output of goods and services is therefore increasing and there is real economic growth whilst at the same time individuals will see their personal wealth decline. Some have sought further to broaden definitions of economic growth to cover an increase in the potential or scope for increased wealth generation. Economic growth can therefore be taken in this way to refer to an increased capacity to produce and/or better use economic resources. From this perspective, economic growth can still occur in a situation of decreasing GDP.

In the globalization literature, these differences in definition, measurement and interpretation have fuelled debates about whether or not the current phase of **economic globalization** is leading to an increase in production and wealth at the global scale. Organizations such as the **International Monetary Fund** and **World Bank** point to the consistent trend of year-on-year rises in total global GDP since the **Second World War** and in particular since the beginning of the 1990s. (Economic) globalization is argued to be the key factor in this growth as greater efficiencies through international trade, competition, integrated markets and the economies of scope and scale gained by **transnational corporations** have increased global output. From the IMF perspective, globalization has been central to the fact that more people have become wealthier and at a faster rate than ever before.

Yet the critics of this perspective from the **anti-globalization movement** and elsewhere argue that this big story of economic growth is debatable. Aside from highlighting the unquestionable fact that economic growth has been highly uneven both socially and geographically, some critics have drawn starkly different conclusions from the same data as the IMF: that economic growth rates have in fact slowed dramatically in the last decade. They point to the falling annual economic growth rates in many countries in recent years, arguing that the relationship between economic growth and global economic integration is not necessarily a strong one.

Overall, economic growth remains a highly contentious phenomenon in the globalization debate. Given that many of the supranational policies aimed at promoting globalization rest on the argument that they promote higher levels of economic growth, it is inevitable that this has become the focus of so much attention by globalization's proponents and critics. In many ways, it is the key battleground between different ideological views of globalization.

Further reading

Dollar, D. and Kraay, A. 'Growth is Good for the Poor', ch. 21 in Lechner, F. and Boli, J. *The Globalization Reader* (2nd edn; Oxford: Blackwell, 2004)

Wade, R. and Wolf, M. 'Are Global Poverty and Inequality Getting Worse?', ch. 37 in Held, D. and McGrew, A. (eds) *The Global Transformations Reader* (2nd edn; Cambridge: Polity, 2003)

EHRENREICH, BARBARA

Writing from a journalist's viewpoint, Ehrenreich addressed the nature of **globalization**'s 'underside', as she describes it, by examining low-paid work in developed and developing countries. Most recently in *Global Woman* (with Arlie Hochshild, 2002), she has examined how, as a consequence of globalization, women are on the move in the contemporary world as never before historically. Popular images focus on the global business class and affluent travellers, but Ehrenreich's work highlights the increasing **migration** of millions of women from poor countries to rich ones. These include maids, nannies, waitresses, sex workers and other low-level service jobs. She argues that these migrant female workers are easing a 'care deficit' in rich countries by creating a 'care deficit' in their own (poor) countries.

Further reading
Ehrenreich, B. and Hochshild, A. 'Introduction', in *Global Woman: Nannies, Maids and Sex Workers in the New Economy* (Cambridge: Granta Books, 2002)

EMPIRE

In the context of the **globalization** debate, a concept associated most widely with the work of Michael Hardt and Antonio **Negri**. In a book of this name (2000), they defined empire as 'the political subject that effectively regulates' the 'irresistible and irreversible globalization of economic and cultural exchanges'. The term is in effect therefore their replacement concept for national-based political **sovereignty**. Sovereignty has taken a new global form which they call 'empire', and is distinct from 'imperialism' in so far as they argue that imperialism was really an extension of the sovereignty of the European **nation-state**s beyond their boundaries. In contrast, 'empire' as the state of sovereignty under contemporary globalization establishes 'no territorial centre of power and does not rely on fixed boundaries or barriers'. It is thus 'a decentred and deterritorializing apparatus of rule that progressively incorporates the entire global realm within its open, expanding frontiers'. In their view, this new form of sovereignty merges hybrid identities, flexible hierarchies and plural exchanges through 'modulating networks of command'. The rise of empire has therefore 'merged the national colours of the imperialist map of the world into an imperial global rainbow'. The concept is therefore used to refute the simplistic arguments put forward by some in the globalization literature that the nineteenth century was a period dominated by the British Empire and the twentieth was dominated by the US. One-nation imperialism is over: globalization has produced a regime that encompasses 'the whole of the civilized world'.

Further reading
Hardt, M. and Negri, A. 'The Political Constitutions of the Present', part I in *Empire* (Cambridge, Mass.: Harvard University Press, 2000)

ENVIRONMENT

A wide-ranging concept that in a literal sense means the surrounding conditions that influence humans and the societies in which they live.

However, in the context of the contemporary **globalization** debate, environment is largely taken to refer to the natural and physical environment on planet Earth. The environment, in this sense, is therefore deeply embedded in many aspects of the globalization debate. Three major dimensions can be identified.

First, conceptualizations of globalization have heavily influenced environmental theory. If Marshall McLuhan's 'global village' encapsulated the social and cultural dynamics of globalization, then notions of 'spaceship Earth' and James Lovelock's Gaia theory have equally promoted the consciousness of the interconnectedness of the Earth's physical and biological system along with humans' relationship to them. The environment is argued by many globalization theorists to be an example of how various globalization processes have bound the fate of human societies together. Ulrich **Beck** in particular argues that modernity has created, through technological development, a situation where we live in a global risk society. Many environmental problems can no longer be regarded as existing within local areas, regions or nation-states. In the contemporary world, the environment has become a global issue and environmental problems need to be addressed at that scale.

Second, contemporary environmental politics is therefore argued to be at the forefront of debate about the wider implications of globalization. **Global warming**, sea-level change and the degradation of the stratospheric ozone layer are key global environmental problems that have forced nation-states and regional blocs to come together to seek a solution. The summits on **sustainable development** over the last thirty years (Stockholm, Rio and Johannesburg), as well as agreements such as the **Kyoto Protocol** on greenhouse gas emissions, thus represent key aspects of developing **political globalization**. They also serve as major examples of the difficulties **nation-states** and other organizations in **global civil society** face in addressing cross-border environmental problems. At the grassroots level, environmental concerns have also been important factors in the objections raised by the **anti-globalization movement**. The actions of unaccountable **transnational corporation**s across the developing world have spawned a range of resistance movements that have become prominent at the global scale.

Third, environmental thought has become more intertwined with debates about **economic growth** and development. This has inevitably pushed environmental concerns into the mainstream discussion about globalization. Theories of sustainable development, for example, have increasingly identified the interrelatedness of environmental degradation in developing countries with processes across the wider global economy. Contemporary commentators such as Jerry **Mander** and Walden **Bello** argue that poverty and environmental problems go hand in hand in the developing world, and that they cannot be addressed without global-scale change.

Environmental concerns are thus very much at the centre of the debate about the wider implications of globalization as a general phenomenon, and tackling these problems is also argued to be one of the key challenges presented by globalization. In that sense, the development of supranational agreements, protocols and institutions that have the capacity to arrest environmental degradation and manage the global environment is becoming a top priority. In many ways this means that the environment is likely to become an ever more central feature of the globalization debate.

Further reading

Connelly, J. and Smith, G. *Politics and the Environment: From Theory to Practice* (London: Routledge, 1999) [esp. Introduction and chs. 7, 8 and 10]

Held, D., McGrew, A., Goldblatt, D. and Perraton, J. 'Catastrophe in the Making: Globalization and the Environment', ch. 8 in *Global Transformations* (Cambridge: Polity, 1999)

World Commission on Environment and Development (WCED) 'From One Earth to One World', ch. 47 in Lechner, F. and Boli, J. (eds) *The Globalization Reader* (2nd edn; Oxford: Blackwell, 2004)

EURO

The currency of twelve of the twenty-five nations that in 2005 formed the **European Union**, along with four outside it. At present the member states using the Euro are Austria, Belgium, Finland, France, Germany, Greece, Ireland, Italy, Luxembourg, Netherlands, Portugal and Spain. Overseas territories of some of these 'Eurozone' countries also use the currency. The Euro was established by provision in the Maastricht Treaty (1992) with the core aims of enhancing the EU's single market and facilitating **free trade** between member states. The currency was introduced in a non-physical form at midnight on 1 January 1999 (in banking, electronic transfers etc.) but new notes and coins were not introduced until 1 January 2002. There was a short changeover period of two month for most countries adopting the new currency. The establishment of the Euro represents an important process in supranational financial integration and is thus argued to be both a response to and a propagator of contemporary global economic integration.

Further reading
Martin, A. and Ross, G. (eds) 'Introduction: EMU and the European Social Model', in *Euros and Europeans: Monetary Integration and the European Model of Society* (Cambridge: Cambridge University Press, 2004)

EUROPEAN UNION (EU)

An economic and political supranational body comprised, in 2005, of twenty-five member **nation-states**. It was formed in March 1957 with the signing of the Treaty of Rome by six founding European states: France, West Germany, the Netherlands, Luxembourg, Belgium and Italy. The Treaty formed two institutions – the European Economic Community (EEC) and the European Atomic Energy Community (Euratom) – which were merged in 1965 to form the European Commission. After a lengthy period of slow development the community enlarged from six to twelve members with the accession of the UK, Denmark and the Irish Republic in 1973, of Greece in 1981 and of Portugal and Spain in 1986. In 1990 these states aligned themselves more closely in political terms with the signing of the Maastricht Treaty and the shift in name from Community (EEC) to Union (EU). During the 1990s, followed by referenda, the twelve were joined by Austria, Finland and Sweden. With the collapse of communism in Eastern Europe, many East European countries stated their desire to join the EU from the outset, and a further ten states (including also Malta and Cyprus) enlarged the EU to twenty-five member states in 2004. A political debate is now continuing around the increasingly contentious issue of whether further states should join, most notably Turkey.

In the context of this historical development trajectory, the EU is bound into a number of dimensions of the **globalization** debate, of which four are highlighted here. First, as an economic regional trading bloc and a political unit the EU is the archetypal supranational political institution that many argue is central to the ongoing wider processes of globalization. In this line of argument, the EU is an emerging form of governance above the scale of **nation-state**s that is superseding their role and power. Likewise, for those who bemoan the negative effects of globalization on democratic accountability, the EU with its weak parliament and bureaucratic Commission is seen as an example of the problems associated with **political globalization**. Second, and relatedly, the EU shares the same underlying economic rationale as has prevailed in the global institutions of **economic globalization**. Broadly, the economic logic of the EU is that regional economic integration will promote efficiency, investment and greater **economic growth**. Third, however, a contrasting strand of the globalization debate has argued that the development of the EU and other similar trading blocs undermines the concept of globalization in favour of increased regionalization. A number of commentators argue on the back of empirical analysis that the world economy is becoming more regionalized, not globalized, in terms of trade, markets and labour. Fourth, the fractious political debate around how the EU as an idea and an institution should develop in the twenty-first century embodies many of the key issues raised by wider globalization. Aside from the debates about economic issues such as growth and employment, the growing power of the supranational EU embodies debates about the erosion of national culture as well as the ability of national governments to remain sovereign over their own territorial spaces.

Overall therefore, the position that the EU occupies as an institution in relation to globalization is varied. For some it embodies globalization processes whilst for others it represents a reaction to and check on those same processes. As arguably the world's most sophisticated and certainly largest supranational trading bloc it is likely that the EU will become an ever more pivotal institution in debates over globalization in the coming decades.

Further reading
McDonald, F. and Dearden, S. *European Economic Integration* (London: Prentice Hall, 2005)
Pinder, J. *The European Union: A Very Short Introduction* (Oxford: Oxford University Press, 2001)
See also the EU's main website: <http://europa.eu.int/index_en.htm>.

FALK, RICHARD

The most widely cited contribution by Richard Falk to the **globalization** debate is his book *Predatory Globalization* (1999), although he has written widely in relation to globalization on **international law, human rights, global terrorism** and **global governance**. In *Predatory Globalization*, he argues globalization corresponds at its core to the expansion of capitalism and the creation of one single global market, without oversight or regulation, and backed by 'neo-liberal' free market ideology. Falk argues that in general most aspects of this process are having adverse effects on human well-being and in that sense the process is inherently 'predatory'. The key symptom of globalization in this view is that the **nation-state** has been changed 'from above'. Falk sees states as no longer able to act freely, even if they utterly reject globalization. This is also an ironic process, in so far as the most fervent defenders of globalization such as the US are themselves also limited in their range of freedoms. All states have to conform to the neo-liberal view of globalization in which free markets are sacrosanct. If they do not sign up to this project, they are cast out. In that sense, the attempts by the social democratic states of Europe to maintain a significant degree of welfare intervention are doomed to failure. Falk argues that these states will sooner or later have to succumb to neo-liberal globalization and become 'quasi-states' – simply agents of **economic globalization**.

In this context, Falk argues that there is a need for resistance and that this is possible. He suggests that **global civil society** needs to develop in order to combat the worst effects of globalization. This amounts to 'globalization-from-below'. This in effect will lead to a 'scaling-up' of the kinds of political struggles which occurred at the sub-national scale in many states during the nineteenth and early twentieth centuries: worker rights, social justice, protection of public goods and so on. In that sense, he takes an optimistic line, arguing that disagreement amongst those who control the levers of global capitalism can be exploited to further a progressive political agenda. He proposes a series of normative initiatives, such as 'renouncing the use of force' and 'protecting the common heritage of mankind' (*sic*) that should form a plan of action for global civil society. More recently, he has suggested that the state 'may make a come-back' and that global governance could be reconfigured progressively with a new collaborative endeavour between nation-states and civil society organizations.

Overall, Falk's contribution to the debate is significant and wide ranging, and it is impossible to cover the breadth of it here. However, a number of critical points emerge from his perspective. First, his analysis of the negative effects of globalization tends to be at the generalized level and there is not the sensitivity to the complexity of outcomes that various globalization processes generate for states, organizations and individuals in the contemporary world. Second, and in common with others writing on global governance, the prescriptions for tackling the negative effects of neo-liberal globalization are developed only to a limited extent. There is little detailed elaboration of how civic society, for example, should tackle the power of major actors in the global economy. Third, the 'foe' in Falk's analysis may not be as coherent as he implies. Elsewhere in the globalization literature, there are commentators who would question the coherence of the neo-liberal project Falk squares up to, and whether the 'bad' neo-liberal capitalists and the 'good' civil society organizations form distinct sides. Finally, of course, Falk's analysis does define globalization in rather narrow terms as the neo-liberal economic project, and a wider interpretation of the concept may allow a better understanding of the nuances of the way in which economic integration has developed. Overall, his approach can be seen as unjustifiably one-sided in casting globalization as primarily a negative transformation.

Further reading
Falk, R. *Predatory Globalization: A Critique* (Cambridge: Polity Press, 1999) [esp. Introduction and chs. 1, 8 and 9)
Falk, R. *The Great Terror War* (New York: Arris Books, 2003)

FDI *see* foreign direct investment.

FINANCIAL GLOBALIZATION
The integration of financial markets and systems beyond the national and regional scale. Whilst both popular and academic commentators have often highlighted the financial aspects of **globalization** as creating dramatic and potentially highly destabilizing effects in the contemporary world, financial globalization as a process can be identified as an impact aspect of global economic **development** for at least a couple of centuries. Whilst financial integration, most notably in the classical gold standard period from 1870–1914, is identifiable in the imperial age during the eighteenth and nineteenth centuries, it is twentieth-century financial globalization which has been important in shaping the contemporary global economy.

In the post-**Second World War** period, the integration of global finance was a key activity of the **Bretton Woods institutions** in the capitalist First World. The turbulence of the interwar decades led to recognition of the need for a stable international financial system of exchange rates. The Bretton Woods system fixed all major currencies to the US dollar which itself was fixed to gold at thirty-four dollars per ounce. The **International Monetary Fund** oversaw the system, bailing out countries which encountered balance-of-payments difficulties. However three main changes have produced the basis for a phenomenal expansion of financial flows in the 1980s and 1990s: the demise of the Bretton Woods system in the early 1970s, the formation of the Organization of Petroleum Exporting Countries (OPEC) cartel and the rise of 'Eurocurrency markets'. During the 1970s, the key consequence of OPEC was an unprecedented transfer of funds from the oil-importing to the oil-exporting countries. Leading oil exporters had a large surplus which they invested in international money markets, greatly increasing the liquidity of international banks. Much of this money was lent to developing countries. Concurrently, emerging 'Eurocurrency markets' allowed currencies to become increasingly detached from national economic controls. By the 1980s, these new global markets for currencies, facilitated by new information and communications technologies, were joined by an enormous number of new financial products such as swaps, options and other derivatives. From the 1980s onwards, the process has also been fuelled by the progressive deregulation of cross-border financial flows as states have removed capital controls and other constraints on financial movements under the broad paradigm of the neo-liberal **Washington Consensus**.

Within the wider globalization debate, financial globalization has been important in a number of contentious areas. First, the development of global money markets has been seen as instrumental in eroding the **sovereignty** of **nation-state**s. Globally integrated financial markets now often possess far greater leverage in financial terms than nation-states with their currency reserves. As the speculations against overvalued currencies in the European Exchange Rate Mechanism (ERM) in the 1990s showed, states have increasingly lost the capacity to intervene to defend currency values or effect devaluation. Second, the development of integrated financial markets and new forms of financial products has led many from an **anti-globalization** perspective to argue that there is a lack of accountability and anti-democratic effect as a consequence of financial globalization. Third, **global financial integration** has regularly been questioned with respect to the stability of the global economy. Processes of financial globalization are seen as key factors in creating crises in the financial system in recent decades which potentially threaten the stability and security of the global capitalist economy. From the 1980s debt crisis to the Asian financial crisis of the 1990s, it has been argued that financial integration could catalyse through crisis global economic collapse, or at least severe recession.

Further reading
Garrett, G. 'Global Markets and National Politics,' ch. 33 in Held, D. and McGrew, A. (eds) *The Global Transformations Reader* (2nd edn; Cambridge: Polity, 2003)
Held, D., McGrew, A., Goldblatt, D. and Perraton, J. 'Shifting Patterns of Global Finance', ch. 4 in *Global Transformations* (Cambridge: Polity, 1999)
Noble, G. and Ravenhill, J. (eds) *The Asian Financial Crisis and the Architecture of Global Finance* (Cambridge: Cambridge University Press, 2000)

FIRST WORLD WAR
The war (1914–18) precipitated by the assassination of Archduke Francis Ferdinand of Austria-Hungary by a Serbian nationalist in Sarajevo in 1914. However, the war was the outcome of a series of factors leading up to this point: important were economic rivalry between the imperial powers (Germany, France, Great Britain, Russia and Austria-Hungary), strong militarism and nationalism in many of these nations and territorial conflicts in continental Europe. With regard to previous conflict, the unification of Germany and France's loss of Alsace and Lorraine at the end of the Franco-Prussian war (1870–1) provided an important context.

The war itself is important with respect to **globalization** because it represented the most globally extensive conflict that had ever occurred in human history to that date. It also led to an enormous lost of life, with conservative estimates suggesting at least ten million people died as a consequence of it. The First World War saw nations across the globe drawn into the conflict through imperial ties with the European powers, and people from all the major continents were involved in fighting (although this mostly occurred in Europe, western Asia, the Mediterranean basin and the north Atlantic). The war was also important in its impact on military technologies, strategies and forms of combat. The First World War was the first fought between industrialized nations and, beyond the Western and Eastern Fronts, much of the strategy of the war was concerned with starving combatant nations of foreign imports of fuel, food and raw materials. Thus the 'arena of conflict' extended to a global scale, whilst the war also penetrated domestic societies within nations to unprecedented levels.

Finally, at least two aspects of the settlement at the end of the war are worth highlighting. First, the peace treaties (and in particular the Treaty of Versailles) imposed such stringent conditions and reparations on Germany that many historians have argued a second global-scale conflict was inevitable. In that sense, the First and **Second World War** are inextricably linked. Second, the aftermath of the war saw the foundation of the first major attempt to develop supranational political governance – the **League of Nations**. Whilst the League achieved only limited success, it represented the predecessor of the contemporary **United Nations** and is thus important as the first major supranational political institution of the modern international system.

Further reading
Howerd, M. *The First World War* (Oxford: Oxford University Press, 2002)

FOREIGN DIRECT INVESTMENT (FDI)
The movement of capital across national frontiers in a manner that grants the investor control over the acquired asset. It commonly entails investment in or purchase of production facilities in the recipient state. Thus it is distinct from a portfolio investment (equity investment) which may cross borders, but does not offer such control.

In a historical sense, FDI dates back to the medieval period with, for example, the Peruzzi company in Florence, Italy, operating across Europe, and it was also an important aspect of the development of European colonialism. Whilst most nineteenth-century imperialism involved mostly portfolio investments, FDI represents a significant factor in the internationalization of production. However, in the context of contemporary debates about **globalization** it is the growth and emerging patterns of FDI in the last century or so that are important.

In the early decades of the twentieth century, most FDI originated from Britain. However, in the US new kinds of firms were sourcing

FDI that were distinct from earlier trading firms, particularly in that they began to invest in productive assets overseas as opposed to trade-based activities. The pace and intensity of FDI flows increased considerably after the **Second World War**, with US firms being the primary source. Between 1945 and 1960 the US accounted for three-quarters of all FDI. However, in the 1960s and 1970s FDI has been sourced increasingly from Europe and Japan. In recent decades, the Asian (and to a lesser extent) Latin American economies have also become sources, reflecting the rise of **multinational corporations** and **transnational corporations** from economies in these regions. FDI has thus grown hugely in importance in the global economy, with FDI stocks now constituting over 20 per cent of global GDP.

Further reading
Held, D., McGrew, A., Goldblatt, D. and Perraton, J. 'Shifting Patterns of Global Finance', ch. 4 in *Global Transformations* (Cambridge: Polity, 1999)

FREE TRADE

In its contemporary usage, trade or commerce carried on without such restrictions as import duties, export bounties, domestic production subsidies, trade quotas or import licences. The basic argument for free trade is grounded in the economic theory of **comparative advantage**: each firm, state or region should concentrate on what it can produce most cheaply and efficiently and should exchange its products for those it is less able to produce economically.

Historically, many states did not achieve free trade within their own borders until comparatively recently; for example, France still maintained internal trade barriers until the French Revolution (1789). On the international scale, Western Europe hosted a burgeoning free trade movement during the nineteenth century but the deteriorating trade and economic positions of the European powers led to growing levels of tariffs and trade barriers from the end of the nineteenth century. This trend continued through the early decades of the twentieth century and the high degrees of trade **protectionism** during the 1930s are often argued to have been contributory to the severity of the Great Depression. The experience of the 1930s certainly formed a major imperative behind the international regime of free trade that emerged post-**Second World War**. The **Bretton Woods institutions**, and especially the negotiations of successive GATT rounds aimed to free trade internationally and thus promote greater global economic prosperity. This stated rationale for free trade continues in the **World Trade Organization** and in the underlying logic behind regional trading blocs (for example, the **European Union**, the **Association of South-East Asian Nations** and the **North American Free Trade Agreement**).

However, critics of free trade argue that measures such as the creation of free trading blocs are detrimental to domestic economies. In the case of NAFTA, for example, opponents contended that the jobs of some American workers would be 'exported' to Mexico, where labour costs are lower. Many have continued to oppose the international impetus towards freer trade, arguing that the accords not only fail to protect jobs in more developed nations but also harm workers and the **environment** in less developed nations, where the laws are laxer or less strongly enforced. Furthermore, others argue that the contemporary global trading system is far from 'free' and intrinsically unfair. They argue that actual free trade has never existed and does not exist now. Current debates about the global trading system are thus shifting to questions of the 'terms of trade' between differently empowered states and regions in the global economy across different economic sectors.

Further reading
Irwin, D. 'The Case for Free Trade: Old Theories, New Evidence', in *Free Trade under Fire* (Princeton, N.J.: Princeton University Press, 2005)

FUKUYAMA, FRANCIS

A prolific political theorist and social commentator, Fukuyama gained a high profile in the early 1990s with his book *The End of History and the Last Man* (1993). Widely quoted but misinterpreted by many, Fukuyama argues from a political philosophical perspective that humankind has found its ultimate form of governance – liberal democracy – after a long historical period of experimentation. He points to the philosophies of Hegel and **Marx** who both believed that the evolution of human societies would end when mankind had achieved a form of society that satisfies its deepest and most fundamental longings. For Hegel this was the liberal state, while for Marx it was a communist society. Fukuyama argues that humanity will be led to liberal democracy which is what he means by 'the end of history'. The thesis in effect is an attempt to provide a global-scale theoretical account that contextualizes twentieth-century political history along with the rise and fall of different political philosophies (fascism, communism). Fukuyama's argument is that liberal democracy remains the only coherent political aspiration spanning the globe and this is his basis for optimism. This important contribution was the subject of enormous debate in the 1990s, notably in the aftermath of the collapse of the Soviet Union and the apparent spread of liberal democracy to more and more countries around the world. It is in this sense one of the most important perspectives on the nature of contemporary **political globalization**. However, it is also contested in so far as many critics have suggested Fukuyama's argument is too idealistic about both the universalism and coherence of liberal democracy as a form of governance.

More recently, amongst a large volume of subsequent publications on the nature of contemporary society, Fukuyama takes up the question of **global governance** in analysing the problem of 'weak' states. He argues again that in the twenty-first century there is a need to build strong liberal democracies across the globe and that this is the key to achieving global security. However, he also suggests this task is fraught with difficulties. In order for globalized liberal democracy to be successful, Fukuyama argues that what is essential is the formation of proper public institutions: an honest police force, uncorrupted courts, functioning schools and medical services and a strong civil service. Yet he suggests that whilst assistance with resources, people and technology across borders is relatively easy, state-building requires methods that are not easily transported.

Further reading

Fukuyama, F. *The End of History and the Last Man* (London: Penguin, 1993)

Fukuyama, F. *State-Building: Governance and World Order in the Twenty-First Century* (New York: Profile Books, 2004)

G8 (GROUP OF EIGHT)

The coalition of eight of the world's leading industrialized nations: France, Germany (West Germany to 1991), Italy, Japan, the UK, the US (who formed the G6 in 1975), Canada (who joined the G7 in 1976) and Russia (not participating in all events), as well as the **European Union**. The G8 holds an annual economic and political summit of the heads of government with international officials, though there are numerous subsidiary meetings and policy research. The purpose of these summits is to deal with the major economic and political issues facing the members' domestic societies and the international community as a whole. Starting with the 1994 Naples Summit, the G7 met with Russia at each summit (referred to as the P8 or Political 8). The Denver Summit of the Eight was a milestone, marking full Russian participation in all but financial and certain economic discussions. The 1998 Birmingham Summit saw full Russian participation, giving birth to the G8 (although the G7 continued to function alongside the formal summits). At the Kananaskis Summit in Canada in 2002, it was announced that Russia would host the G8 summit in 2006, thus completing its process of becoming a full member. The responsibility of playing host rotates throughout the summit cycle at the end of the calendar year, as follows: France, US, UK, Russia (as of 2006), Germany, Japan, Italy and Canada. Throughout the year, the leaders' personal representatives – known as sherpas – meet regularly to discuss the agenda and monitor progress.

The G7/8 summits have consistently dealt with macroeconomic management, international trade and relations with developing countries. Questions of East–West economic relations, energy and **terrorism** have also been of recurrent concern. From this initial foundation the summit agenda has broadened considerably to include microeconomic issues such as employment and the information highway, transnational issues such as the **environment**, crime and **drug trafficking** and a host of political-security issues ranging from **human rights** through regional security to **arms control**.

Because of the centrality in the process of **global governance**, the summit has always attracted significant attention both from the media and from a number of countries seeking admittance to this exclusive and powerful club. It has also become an increasingly important occasion for non-governmental and civil society organizations to lobby on behalf of their concerns. Since the Birmingham Summit in 1998, the annual meeting has become a focus for **anti-globalization** demonstrations. These protests have developed into large-scale affairs on a number of occasions with the most violent in 2001 at the Genoa Summit. The **anti-globalization movement** and other civil society organizations have also increasingly formalized their 'fringe' meetings around G8 summits.

Further reading
Hubbard, G. *Arguments Against G8* (London: Pluto Press, 2005)
See also the University of Toronto's information website on the G8: <http://
    www.g7.utoronto.ca/>.

GATED COMMUNITIES

In the first instance, physically 'fenced-off' housing developments
in cities or regions where there are considerable differences in
income. They are evident in urban development in Los Angeles and
other American cities, and neo-liberal **economic globalization** has
arguably led to the construction of a growing number of these communities in countries such as Mexico, Brazil, Venezuela and Chile,
where the affluent gate themselves off from the rest of society. Gated
communities take the form of physical enclaves with walls and
fences, and security guards as well as CCTV. Public access is
restricted and legal agreements tie residents to a common code of
conduct. A number of commentators have likened the **European
Union** to a gated community in its attempts to seal its external
borders against illegal immigrants.

Further reading
Blakely, E. and Synder M. *Fortress America: Gated Communities in the United
    States* (Washington, DC: Brookings Institute, 1997) [especially intro-
    ductory ch.]

GCC *see* global commodity chain; Gulf Cooperation Council.

GENERAL AGREEMENT ON TRADE IN SERVICES (GATS)

An agreement that came into force in January 1995 as a result of
the Uruguay Round GATT negotiations, with the aim of providing
for the extension of the multilateral trading system to services.
All members of the **World Trade Organization** are signatories to
the GATS and have to assume the resulting obligations. The
GATS agreement is intended to contribute to trade expansion
'under conditions of transparency and progressive liberalisation
and as a means of promoting the **economic growth** of all
trading partners and the **development** of developing countries'.
The WTO argues that trade expansion is not an end in itself,
but an instrument to promote growth and development. The link
with development is further reinforced by explicit references to

the objective of increasing participation of developing countries in trade in services and to the special economic situation and the development, trade and financial needs of the least developed countries.

GATS' contribution to world services trade rests on two main pillars: first, ensuring increased transparency and predictability of relevant rules and regulations; and second, promoting progressive liberalization through successive rounds of negotiations. Within the framework of the agreement, the latter concept is the key to improving market access and extending national treatment to foreign services and service suppliers across an increasing range of sectors. Whilst it has been argued that this involves deregulation, the Agreement in fact explicitly recognizes the right of governments to regulate and to introduce new regulations in order to meet national policy objectives, and the particular need of developing countries to exercise this right.

The agreement has, however, been criticized on a range of fronts in line with wider critiques of neo-liberal **economic globalization** and the **Bretton Woods institutions**. In particular, a major focus is the impact of GATS on services that are considered to be public goods or related to social welfare. Critics argue that GATS enables **transnational corporation**s to take control of basic social welfare services for profit: education and healthcare, for example. It is therefore seen from an **anti-globalization** perspective as further strengthening the vested commercial interests of large corporations and removing accountability and power from states for the provision of basic social services.

Further reading

World Trade Organization *A Handbook on the GATS Agreement* (Cambridge: Cambridge University Press, 2005) [esp. Introduction and chs. 1, 6 and 8]

See also, for a critical view, <http://www.gatswatch.org/>.

GEOPOLITICS

The concept coined by the Swedish political geographer Rudolf Kjellen at the end of the nineteenth century, referring to a form of social scientific analysis which combines politics, history and geography to explain the **development** of states and societies at the regional and global scale. Geopolitics traditionally indicates 'the links and causal relationships between political power and geographic space'. In concrete terms it is often seen as a body of thought assaying specific strategic prescriptions based on the relative importance of land power and sea power in world history. The geopolitical tradition had some consistent concerns, like the geopolitical correlates of power in world politics, the identification of international core areas and the relationships between naval and terrestrial capabilities. Geopolitics has been a central concept in debates around the nature of political and **military globalization**.

In the earlier part of the twentieth century, geopolitical analysis essentially arose as an attempt to theorize world politics and the relationships between the great imperial powers. Notably, the work of German geographer Friedrich Ratzel and British geographer Halford Mackinder was important in propelling this form of analysis to the centre of theories of emergent international relations. Mackinder's 'heartland thesis' (1904), in particular, posited that a large and successful **empire** could arise without a significant naval capability and that this empire would not be defeatable by the rest of the (Western) world forming a coalition against it. Mackinder's theory thus divided geography between the Old World (most of the Eastern Hemisphere) and the New World (the Western Hemisphere and what was called Oceania). Such ideas were important in the policies adopted by both sides in the **First** and **Second World War**s. In the latter part of the twentieth century, the term has been broadened to cover a range of debates about the nature of power in the international system: for example, US communist 'containment theory' in the 1950s and 1960s and Marxian theories such as **world systems analysis**.

Further reading
Dodds, K. *Global Geopolitics: A Critical Introduction* (London: Prentice Hall, 2004) [esp. chs. 1, 2 and 8]

GEORGE, SUSAN

A key voice of the **anti-globalization movement**, Susan George has written extensive critiques of neo-liberal **globalization** and the **Washington Consensus**. She is one of the key proponents of 'alter-globalization' and argues consistently that contemporary global **economic globalization** is deeply problematic and 'dangerous' for everyone on the planet apart from a very small elite minority. She is also one of the leading critics of the power of **transnational corporations**, arguing that there is an urgent need to 'save' democracy from the threat they present.

In *The Lugano Report*, George argues that global capitalism is in effect a timebomb waiting to go off. She sees economic globalization as a product of an emerging world government that is designed to protect capitalism and the vested interests of the wealthy few against the people. She satirically posits that if contemporary global capitalism is incapable of meeting the needs of the projected eight to twelve billion people on the planet in the twenty-first century, then the managers of globalization will take secret steps to reduce global population. The aim of this satire is to illustrate that there are viable alternatives to contemporary economic globalization and the neo-liberal Washington Consensus. The cornerstone of this alternative is the need to remove sovereignty from corporate hands and resolve to build a network of local organizations to create 'co-operative globalization' that will produce a global economy founded on healthier, more equitable societies.

In a subsequent book, she develops these themes in arguing that the real debate, 'which almost never takes place', should be how to limit the market and decide who pays the externalized environmental and social costs of (economic) globalization. This argument is illustrated by examining the behaviour of both supranational actors such as the **International Monetary Fund** and **Organization for Economic Cooperation and Development** and also specific transnational firms. She dismisses the corporate social responsibility movement as a 'fig leaf' designed to hide the continuing profit-driven motives of the corporations. George's alternative vision is primarily socialist in nature but not in the traditional state socialist sense. She argues the progressive ideal would be a hybrid form between socialism and democracy which would put key decisions about economics in the hands of small groups of individuals rather than those who seek purely to serve the interests of large corporations. She has also made substantial critical assessment of the effect of developing world debt on perpetuating poverty and social injustice in much of the world.

Susan George's sustained contribution to the globalization literature has made her an emblematic thinker amongst the anti-globalization and alter-globalization movements. Her arguments are well researched and supported by examples, although, as with other highly politicized commentators such as George **Monbiot**, she is selective as to which case studies and sets of evidence she uses. In that sense, George's argument is as much about making a political argument about what globalization should be as commentary on what it is. Her characterization of the effects of neo-liberal globalization tends to be largely negative and, from an academic perspective, less rigorous than is desirable given the force of the arguments being made. However, her impact on the wider globalization debate is undoubtedly significant.

Further reading
George, S. *A Fate Worse than Debt* (London: Penguin, 1994)
George, S. *The Lugano Report* (London: Pluto Press, 1999)
George, S. *A Better World is Possible if . . .* (London: Verso, 2004)

GIDDENS, ANTHONY

The work of the sociologist Anthony Giddens has been widely cited across both academic and policy literatures concerned with **globalization**. Giddens represented one of the first theorists to engage with globalization itself as a broad concept, and his arguments about how globalization may be conceived of in theoretical terms have been used by many commentators. He also has, as a consequence, been the target of considerable critical engagement.

Giddens argues that, on the general scale, globalization as a process is 'restructuring the ways in which we live, and in a very profound manner'. He sees it as being led from the West, with a strong imprint of American political and economic power but also as a wider process which affects all dimensions of life including the everyday. In that sense, Giddens' contribution to the globalization debate has been important for significantly criticizing the overprioritization of the economic realm over other aspects of social life. He extends his understanding and theoretical arguments to encompass, for example, the impact of globalization on sexuality, marriage and the family. Furthermore, he argues that globalization is not just a 'big phenomenon' out there in the world, but that it represents a series of processes cutting across all scales, including many at which the individual lives on a daily basis. Globalization, then, is an 'in here' phenomenon for Giddens which influences intimate and personal aspects of life. The transformation of family values or women's position in society across the globe is a prime example of this. In this way, Giddens sees contemporary globalization as a truly global revolution in everyday life, the consequences of which are being felt around the world in spheres from work to politics.

Giddens' work is also important for providing a theoretical framework for understanding what globalization 'is'. The axiomatic foundation to this is Giddens' arguments about **time–space distanciation** and how this relates to contemporary globalization processes. In *The Consequences of Modernity* (1991), Giddens provides a theoretical argument which amounts in effect to a theoretical basis for understanding what globalization is in abstract. Drawing on classical social theory (**Marx**, Durkheim, Weber), Giddens suggests that our contemporary condition of 'high modernity' is distinctive from earlier periods in that social systems have now become organized and stretched across space and time. Traditional social theory has studied society as comprised of social systems which are territorially bounded, whereas Giddens argues that high modernity has dissolved such territorially limited 'societies' and what we now need to theorize are social systems which are stretched in time and space. This process also rips social relations out of territorial contexts (disembedding) and re-embeds them in new territorial spaces in complex ways.

These arguments have been taken as the cornerstone of many subsequent contributions to the globalization debate by authors such as David **Held**, Martin **Albrow** and Robbie Robertson, and have come under close critical scrutiny (see Justin **Rosenberg**'s book *The Follies of Globalisation Theory*). The main areas of potential weakness in Giddens' approach derive mainly from the criticisms that have been levelled at the classical social theory from which he has developed his arguments and at the 'grand' claims his approach makes for globalization as a concept. First, a number of commentators have cast doubt on to what extent this overarching theoretical characterization of contemporary social systems is applicable as a generalization. Second, from a postmodern perspective, the coherence of these very social systems as meaningful entities in the world is questionable. Third, both his dialectical conception of time and space and the concepts of embedding/re-embedding have been criticized for being far too simplistic in their conceptualization of how social relations are constituted in space, time and territory. Overall, however, Giddens represents one of the most important and provocative thinkers on globalization and many of these critical lines of thought remain to be developed by the literature.

Further reading
Giddens, A. *Runaway World: How Globalization is Reshaping our Lives* (Cambridge: Polity, 1999)
Giddens, A. 'The Globalizing of Modernity', ch. 2 in Held, D. and McGrew, A. (eds) *The Global Transformations Reader* (Cambridge: Polity, 2003)

GLENEAGLES

The hotel in Perthshire, Scotland, that played host to the July 2005 **G8** summit. With climate change, debt cancellation and African **development** firmly on the agenda, the summit was also the focus of a long popular campaign on world poverty, which culminated in the **Live8** concerts across a number of developed countries just ahead of the meeting. In that sense, the Gleneagles summit has been argued to represent a significant move towards accommodating longstanding critiques of neo-liberal **economic globalization** by **anti-globalization** groups. Chaired by Tony **Blair**, the UK Prime Minister, the summit did conclude with a series of 'progressive' agreements. On climate change, the summit appeared to win a softening of the US position, with all G8 countries accepting the reality of **global warming** and signing up to a 'Plan of Action' aimed at reducing carbon emissions and developing a global-scale low-carbon economy. The key achievement was argued by **Blair** and others to be deals on debt cancellation for the poorest African states and a doubling of **aid** budgets by 2010. The summit also produced agreement on over fifty further measures aimed at accelerating African development, ranging across increases in peace-keeping forces and extra provision for **HIV/AIDS** drugs. Overall, the summit does represent a marked change in the rhetoric of G8 policy, although to what extent these stated policies will be effectively implemented and what impact they will have remain to be seen.

Further reading
See the UK Government website on the summit: <www.G8.gov.uk>.
And for a critical engagement the reports on: <www.corporatewatch.org.uk>.

GLOBAL APARTHEID

A number of **globalization** commentators argue that this concept has evolved to describe a new global paradigm: an international system of minority rule that promotes inequality, disparities and differential access to basic **human rights**, wealth and power. It is thus the opposite of global democracy and has been used to describe the emerging unjust outcomes of neo-liberal **economic globalization** by commentators such as Richard **Falk**. Current manifestations are argued to be the dominance of bilateralism and hegemonic behaviour of the US, the unbalanced and undemocratic process in the **World Trade Organization** and the disproportionate power of **transnational corporations** and the **Bretton Woods institutions**.

Further reading
See the resources on the Africa Action website: <http://www.africaaction. org/resources/globalapartheid.php>.

GLOBAL CITIES
A concept that originated primarily in the work of Saskia **Sassen**, who proposed her global city thesis in the early 1990s. Developing the arguments of theorists such as Peter Hall and Manuel **Castells** in the 1980s on 'world cities' and 'informational cities' respectively, Sassen argued that three cities had risen to the top of an emerging global urban hierarchy during the 1980s: London, New York and Tokyo. These cities warranted this new label primarily because Sassen argued they were fulfilling new and distinct functions in the spatial organization of a globally integrated economy. Principally, this involved being key command and control centres in an emerging global economy, as well as being the location of key financial and business services.

Subsequent commentators, including Sassen herself, have developed the concept of the global city to describe a much greater number of cities than the original three leading urban centres. Manuel Castells has argued that the functions incorporated in global cities exist through a network of cities spanning the globe and that 'global cityness' therefore represents a process. This could be construed as the urban manifestation of various phenomena captured in the concept of **globalization** and Sassen herself takes on board these arguments in the second edition of *The Global City* as she argues that global cities represent networked organizing hubs in the global economy of the twenty-first century. The list now extends far beyond the key centres at the top of the global urban system and the debate increasingly centres on the issue of to what extent key functions in the global economy exist across this urban system in a networked form as opposed to being concentrated in a few specific 'global cities'. The danger of course is that if all cities are now 'global cities', to what degree is the concept itself useful as an explanatory tool?

Further reading
Sassen, S. *The Global City* (2nd edn; Princeton N.J.: Princeton University Press, 2001) [esp. Introduction]

GLOBAL CIVIL SOCIETY

A phrase that has meant many different things over time and has been used, as with **globalization**, inconsistently in contemporary political analysis. Jan **Scholte** argues that for present purposes it can be taken to refer to the activities by voluntary associations to shape policies, norms and/or deeper social structures. Civil society is therefore something distinct from both official (governmental) and commercial circles, although the line can sometimes be blurred. An example would be a government-organized NGO or a business-lobbying organization concerned with social issues. In general, civil society is therefore taken to include a wide variety of non-governmental actors including academic institutes, community-based organizations, consumer protection bodies, criminal syndicates, **development** cooperation groups, environmental campaigns, ethnic lobbies, charitable foundations, farmers' groups, **human rights** groups and so on. Much of civil society is formally constituted in some organizational form but other civic activities, in particular at the grassroots, are *ad hoc* and informal.

Scholte suggests that the idea of global civil society began to become widespread during the 1990s as commentators began to discuss the role of 'international non-governmental organizations', 'transnational advocacy networks', 'global social movements' and a 'new **multilateralism**'. He argues that there are four features that can be identified in common across this literature. First, global civil society may address supraterritorial issues like transworld ecological change or transborder capitalism. Second, global civic networks may use supraterritorial communications like email and fax. Third, global civic activity may have a transborder organization with coordinated branches spread across the planet. Fourth, global civil society may operate on a premise of supraterritorial solidarity between, for example, women and workers. Scholte argues that these four attributes have often gone hand in hand, but not in all cases.

However, concepts of global civil society can be questioned on a number of fronts. First, there is a clear question as to what extent there exists any coherent global civil society. Despite the rhetorical assertion of linkages and collective intent and action, the numerous organizations and actors that constitute global civil society have very different interests, motivations and characteristics. The question has to be asked as to what extent all these social groups share any common characteristics. Second, their distinction from governmental, corporate or other power interests is often unclear and the relationship with other societal stakeholders complex. Commentators such as John **Keane**, Jan Scholte and Manuel **Castells** generally cast global civil society as an amalgam of organizations and groups resisting neoliberal **economic globalization** but this is not necessarily the case. There is no intrinsic reason why the various constituent groups of global civil society are a site of resistance to economic globalization, and in that sense the literature can be considered one-sided in its construction of this idea. Third, the common conception of global civil society as an alternative to the undemocratic consequence of **political globalization** is questionable. As several commentators acknowledge, many civic groups lack democratic structures, accountability consultation mechanisms and transparency. In that sense, this is a chaotic concept.

Further reading

Castells, M. 'The Other Face of the Earth: Social Movements against the New Global Order', ch. 2 in *The Power of Identity* (2nd edn; Oxford: Blackwell, 2004)

Keane, J. 'Unfamiliar Words', ch. 1 in *Global Civil Society* (Cambridge: Cambridge University Press, 2003)

Scholte, J. 'Globalization and (Un)Democracy', ch. 11 in *Globalization: A Critical Introduction* (2nd edn; Basingstoke: Palgrave Macmillan, 2005)

GLOBAL COMMODITY CHAIN (GCC)

In the words of Terrence Hopkins and Immanuel **Wallerstein**, 'a network of labour and production processes whose end result is a finished commodity'. In the **globalization** literature, there has been much work to try to analyse the increasingly complex form that global commodity chains take in the global economy. However, the simple definition has been criticized for being too limited and for not taking account of the structures and power relationships that exist within real GCCs. Contemporary usage of the concept tends to try to account for key agents within commodity chains and their differential power positions.

Further reading
Gereffi, G. and Korzeniewicz (eds) *Commodity Chains and Global Capitalism* (New York: Greenwood Press, 1994) [ch. 1]

GLOBAL COMMONS

The common pool of resources that exists on planet Earth over which no state or human organization can claim to have exclusive ownership. In the context of the **globalization** debate, the understanding of certain natural resources (and, increasingly, human-mediated resources) in these terms represents itself a shift in perception and is evidence that absolute **sovereignty** is an idea whose time has passed. Examples of the global commons that are widely discussed are Antarctica, the oceans, the atmosphere, outer space and telecommunications. These share a number of ownership and international management characteristics and are increasingly managed and regulated through **international law** and international treaties.

Further reading
Buck, S. *The Global Commons: An Introduction* (London: Earthscan, 1998) [esp. Introduction]

GLOBAL COMMUNICATIONS

A central facilitating factor in the historical development of **globalization**, and particularly in the phases of accelerated globalization experience over the last fifty years. Global communications have a long history stretching back to the age of European colonialism, possibly earlier. However, during the nineteenth century new forms of communications technology greatly increased the speed and capacity of communications systems. A key innovation was the invention of the telegraph which led to the foundation of the first international organization, the International Telegraph Union (ITU; now the **International Telecommunications Union**), in order to provide a set of standards for transcontinental communication. During the twentieth century, the development of telecommunications and radio, as well as transportation advances, further increased the scope of more effective communication between states and continents. However, in the post-**Second World War** period new communications technologies have vastly increased informational flows to the extent that commentators such as Manuel **Castells** argue we now live in a global informational society. Satellites have enabled global-scale coverage for telecommunications and televisual media, and the emergence of the **Internet** has linked an ever-growing proportion of the world population in ways that were previously unimaginable. More recently, mobile and wireless communications systems have further extended the penetration of forms of global-scale communications into people's lives where, for example, mobile phone handsets provide instantaneous telecommunications and email communication for users wherever they are.

With regard to how globalization is conceptualized, global communications were argued by some in the early 1990s as annihilating territorial and spatial differences. This technologically centred version of the hyperglobalist school contended in respect of economic **development** that activity could be located anywhere on the planet. Whilst the startling pace of innovation and capacity in communications technologies has and continues to be a key factor in major transformations occurring in the global space economy (for example, the shift of IT-based call-centres from Europe and North America to developing countries), the impact of increasing global communications capacity is more complex. A similar set of arguments can also be made in debates around **cultural globalization** and the relationship of cultural flows (or 'global culture-scapes', after Arjun **Appadurai**) to global communications. Again, early commentators argued that global communications were key in producing global cultural homogenization. This has been increasingly contested as research points to the ways in which new and more widely available global communications are creating new hybrid cultural forms. Overall, therefore, whilst the nature and extent of contemporary global communications are unprecedented and must be considered as a central facilitating factor in contemporary globalization, techno-centric and basic explanations of globalization and its sub-forms (economic, political, cultural etc.) as being driven by the emergence and evolution of global-scale communication have largely been dismissed as simplistic. The relationship between communication and globalization is being shown to be highly complex and varied by many current researchers in the field.

Further reading
Thompson, J. 'The Globalization of Communication', ch. 21 in Held, D. and McGrew, A. (eds) *The Global Transformations Reader* (2nd edn; Cambridge: Polity, 2003)

GLOBAL CORPORATION

A term that has only recently begun to permeate the academic and business literature and is generally used to refer to the world's largest firms. There is no clear distinction as yet between a global corporation as opposed to a **transnational corporation**, but theoretically the validity of distinguishing between the two concepts rests on to what extent the largest firms do not warrant a definition based around their relationship to the political container of the **nation-state**. The term 'global corporation' is generally used to suggest a firm that operates in many nation-states and that exhibits characteristics of being organized at the global scale in terms of core functions (management, marketing, organizational structure etc.).

Further reading
Dicken, P. 'Placing Firms: Grounding the Debate on the Global Corporation', ch. 2 in Peck, J. and Yeung, H. (eds) *Remaking the Global Economy* (London: Sage, 2003)

GLOBAL CULTURE

A problematic concept in academic debates about globalization. In the popular imagination, globalization has been widely associated with the idea that societies across the world are becoming similar in cultural terms. Early on in the 1990s academic commentators also proposed that integration was increasingly producing a common global culture centred in particular commonalities in consumption. Thus **transnational corporation**s, in marketing global brands, were at the centre of a process by which more and more people in the world shared a common cultural set of values and lifestyles. This idea was exemplified by the notion of people consuming **McDonald's** food and Coca Cola and purchasing clothing from companies such as Nike across the globe. During the later 1990s, this negative conception of the development of a global culture was developed by the popular **anti-globalization movement** and seen more widely as a downside of neo-liberal **economic globalization** and the power of TNCs.

However, within the academic discussion of globalization, the concept of a single global culture has become increasingly questioned. Several thinkers including Arjun **Appadurai** and John **Tomlinson** have argued that there is no identifiable global culture emerging. In contrast they suggest it is better to seek to understand the increasing volume and diversity of global cultural flows that are occurring; thus, whilst globalization is producing many new cultural forms in the contemporary world, they are multiple and unstable in nature (much as culture as a phenomenon is itself) and no clear process of cultural homogenization is identifiable. Furthermore, many other commentators have become concerned with the impact of global cultural interconnectedness with the rise of new forms of media (for example, the **Internet** and satellite television channels such as **CNN**) and global-scale communication in the contemporary period.

Further reading
Tomlinson, J. *Globalization and Culture* (Cambridge: Polity) [esp. ch. 1]

GLOBAL FINANCIAL INTEGRATION
A concept, often used interchangeably with **financial globalization**, referring to a range of transformations in organizations and the growing degree of interconnectedness of financial flows at the global scale. As David **Held** and his co-authors point out, global finance embraces three forms of money: credit such as loans and bonds, investment such as **foreign direct investment** and money (foreign exchange). Although cross-border financial flows have a long history, a European financial order first emerged in the sixteenth century. In the latter part of the nineteenth century, Held et al. argue, these flows became considerably more extensive and intensive as the domestic financial markets of states became increasingly enmeshed within international financial networks. Major currency values were regulated in this period (1870–1914) through the classical gold standard, and financial flows were intense, although primarily Eurocentric. However, after a period of turmoil between the world wars, it is in the latter part of the twentieth century that global financial integration has accelerated and deepened. Three major changes in the 1960s and 1970s provided the context for phenomenal expansion of financial flows: the development of Eurocurrency markets, the collapse of the Bretton Woods system and the oil price shocks. Since the 1980s, states have removed national capital controls, and technological

advances have facilitated financial market integration. The consequence is that national financial systems are increasingly embedded
in a global financial system where one of the key effects has been to
diminish the capacity of national governments to exert control on
their own fiscal circumstances. A number of theorists have also
argued that this integration is producing ever greater global systemic
risks, as evidenced by the financial crises in Russia and Asia during
the 1990s.

Further reading
Garett, G. 'Global Markets and National Politics', ch. 33 in Held, D. &
    McGrew, A. (eds) *The Global Transformations Reader* (2nd edn; Cam-
    bridge: Polity, 2003)
Held, D., McGrew, A., Goldblatt, D. and Perraton, J. 'Shifting Patterns of
    Global Finance', ch. 4 in *Global Transformations* (Cambridge: Polity,
    1999)

GLOBAL GOVERNANCE

An idea embodying a rejection of the conventional state-centric conception of world politics and world order. In that sense, instead of the
nation-state, the principal unit of analysis is taken to be the global,
regional or transnational system of authoritative rule-making and
implementation. From a theoretical perspective, theorists such as
James **Rosenau** argue this places 'rule systems' at the centre of the
theorizing process, with an emphasis on developing an analytical
understanding and explanation for the political significance of global,
regional and transnational authority structures.

David **Held** and Anthony **McGrew** suggest, from a review of the
literature, that the emerging institutional architecture of contemporary global governance has a number of characteristics. First, it is
multilayered in that it is constituted by and through the structural
enmeshment of several principal infrastructures of governance.
These are the superstates (for example, the **United Nations**), the
regional (the **European Union**, **MERCOSUR**, the Association of
South-East Asian Nations etc.), the transnational (**global civil society**,
business networks and so on) and the substate (community associations and city governments). National governments are sandwiched
between these layers. Second, global governance is often described
as polyarchic or *pluralistic* since there is no single locus of authority.
This does not imply any equality of power between participants but

simply that authority is fragmented. Third, global governance has a variable geometry in that the relative political significance and regulatory capacities of these infrastructures vary considerably around the globe and from issue to issue. Fourth, the system is structurally complex, being composed of diverse agencies and networks with both overlapping (functional and/or spatial) jurisdictions and also differential power resources and competencies. Fifth, and finally, national governments are not in fact sidelined in this system but are instead becoming increasingly crucial as strategic sites for bringing together these various infrastructures of governance and legitimizing regulation beyond the state.

One of the features of global governance that is emphasized is the reconfiguration of authority between various layers of infrastructures of government – evident in the expanding jurisdictions of both superstate and substate institutions. This is sometimes referred to as the New Medievalism since the large number of competing actors resembles the multiple levels of political authority that characterized medieval Europe. Furthermore, contemporary global governance is argued to involve a relocation of authority from public to quasi-public and to private agencies.

However, a number of critical commentators doubt the usefulness of focusing on global governance as distinct from **geopolitics** or that global institutions (or global civil society) are autonomous sites of power in global politics. International relations theorists offer three explanatory accounts of global governance from this perspective. First, the liberal institutionalist perspective argues that governance beyond the state is endemic since it arises from the functional benefits which states can realize through the strategic coordination of their policies and activities in an interdependent world. Second, the realists argue in contrast that geopolitics remains essential to understanding the conduct and dynamics of global governance. Governance beyond states is largely contingent on the policies and interests of the most powerful states. Third, and sharing the emphasis on geopolitics, the neo-Gramscian perspective sees this factor as having to be understood in the context of the structural imperatives of global capitalism. Overall, therefore, both the realist and Marxist (Gramscian) perspectives are highly critical of the unreflective nature of much of the existing literature on global governance which they see as perhaps descriptively accurate but unable to penetrate beyond the dynamics of global politics to the underlying structures of power.

Further reading
Held, D. and McGrew, A. 'Introduction', in *Governing Globalization* (Cambridge: Polity, 2002)
Scholte, J. *Globalization: A Critical Introduction* (Basingstoke: Palgrave Macmillan, 2000)

GLOBAL NETWORK

Broadly, the term referring to network linkages at the planetary scale, a number of identifiable forms of which have been discussed in the literature. The use of the term has become so widespread across several dimensions of the **globalization** debate that there is now an academic journal which bears this concept as its title. First, from an economic perspective, interest in network relationships has become a focus of discussion in analyses of the development of **transnational corporation**s and of how firms are interconnected at the global scale. The idea that they are embedded in global networks has been extended across both physical places or territories and in a sociological sense with respect to the role of social contact networks amongst key business people. Second, and related, Saskia **Sassen** and others have developed the global city debate with the idea that globalized cities exist as nodes in various global networks that are vital in running the global economy. Third, there is also considerable discussion of the role of global networks in debates about **political globalization** and the emergence of **global governance**. The term is however, increasingly used across all areas of the globalization debate.

Further reading
Sassen, S. 'Introduction', in *Global Networks, Linked Cities* (London: Routledge, 2002)
Zacher, M. and Sutton, B. 'International Regimes in Global Networks', ch. 1 in *Governing Global Networks: International Regimes for Transportation and Communications* (Cambridge: Cambridge University Press, 1995)

GLOBAL NORTH

The term increasingly used by academic and policy commentators in place of 'First World' (though less commonly used than '**global South**'). The countries covered by this term remain broadly the same in that they are the economically more developed ones (North America, Northern Europe, Japan, Australia and New Zealand). As with its opposite, the distribution of countries within the global North is not all within the northern hemisphere and in that sense it is a loose geographical metaphor similar to the notion of 'the West'.

GLOBAL PRODUCTION NETWORKS

This is the concept (GPNs) encapsulating the growing transnational organization of production and distribution within and among firms instead of through markets. Since international markets are not perfect, the costs of doing business for **transnational corporations** are significantly lower if they organize economic activity within the firm or through networks of firms. GPNs thus cover international production within firms and through external networks, be that through a variety of subcontractual or supplier arrangements. GPNs are now evident across most manufacturing sectors and, likewise, various service industries are becoming organized in a similar international form.

Further reading
Dicken, P. 'Webs of Enterprise': The Geography of Transnational Production Networks', ch. 8 in *Global Shift* (London: Sage, 2004)

GLOBAL SOCIAL DEMOCRACY

This is the concept encapsulating the extension of democratic forms of governance to a global scale, involving in particular a reconfiguration and strengthening of the supranational institutions of global governance. It is a much debated and highly contentious idea as to what it represents, what it is and what it should be. Within the wider **globalization** debate it represents the key concept in the academic Left's proposal for how **global governance** should develop and be developed over the coming decades.

According to David **Held** and Anthony **McGrew**, this is a form of global governance that extends the guiding principles of social democracy to the global scale. These principles are social justice, democracy, universal **human rights**, human security, rule of law and transnational solidarity. Their preferred form of global social democracy is a cosmopolitan democratic form that involves a series of both short- and long-term measures, as well as a requirement for certain institutional and political conditions. In the short term, a shift towards global social democracy requires reform of global governance via a representative Security Council, the establishment of a Human Security Council to coordinate global **development**, a **global civil society** forum, strengthened systems of global accountability and enhanced governance structures at all scales. It also requires economic reforms in the regulation of global markets, capital flows and **transnational corporation**s, as well as debt abolition and other measures to promote development.

In the long term, they envisage a shift of governance towards *double democratization* with effective national *and* suprastate governance as well as the enhanced provision of global public goods and global citizenship. In economic terms, global markets would also be tamed, with the formation of a World Financial Authority and Competition Authority. **TNC**s would be regulated through a mandatory code of conduct and there would be a need for a global tax mechanism. Held and McGrew also suggest market-correcting and market-promoting measures including mandatory global labour and environmental standards and privileged market access for developing countries.

Finally, the development of global social democracy along this model will require a whole raft of new institutional and political conditions, including activist states, a globally progressive coalition of developing states and civil society forces and strong multilateral institutions.

This perspective and proposed vision of the world is not however accepted as either feasible or desirable by many globalization commentators. First, as a critique of what is seen as a neo-liberal **Washington Consensus**, right-wing commentators clearly view global social democracy as a watered-down socialism that will inhibit the efficient development of global markets and the ability of the global economy to generate wealth. Second, and perhaps more importantly, there are also critics of this idea on the Left. The so-called 'globalization pessimists' such as John **Gray** conversely see the ideas for global social democracy as being little more than a weak payment of lip-service to progressive socialist and Marxian values by an agenda that really is little different from the one advocated by the neo-liberals. Third, other critics on the Left, such as Roger **Scruton**, have criticized the basis for theories of global social democracy as being obsessively focused on the problems of the Washington Consensus, arguing that the ideologues of the American Right are only one visible target (and not necessarily the most important) for a social democratic critique and political agenda. Fourth, and finally, even for those who share the ideological and political rationale for developing global social democracy, the feasibility and likelihood of global governance developing in this manner appears in many ways unrealistic and wishful thinking. The literature to date has had little to say on whether and how the global social democratic model is to be achieved.

Further reading
Held, D. and McGrew, A. 'Reconstructing World Order: Towards Cosmopolitan Social Democracy', ch. 9 in *Globalization/Anti-globalization* (Cambridge: Polity, 2002)
Held, D. *Global Covenant: The Social Democratic Alternative to the Washington Consensus* (Cambridge: Polity, 2004)

GLOBAL SYSTEM

With 'system' defined simply as 'an assemblage of inter-related elements comprising a unified whole', a concept that has a wide range of applications spanning the categories of economy, society and politics. Across the **globalization** literature as a whole, the key question in relation to this concept is whether and to what extent the various phenomena captured by the idea of globalization constitute a system at the global scale. Various thinkers and contributors in different areas of the debate argue that it does and that globalization represents a systemic phenomenon. For example, commentators regularly refer to the global financial system, systems of **global governance** and the global trading system. In more specific terms, the sociologist Leslie **Sklair** has argued that the global system 'is most fruitfully conceptualised as a system that operates at three levels, and knowledge about which can be organised in three spheres: the economic, the political and culture-ideology'. He argues that each sphere is characterized typically by a representative institution and cohesive structures of practice and is organized and patterned. He contends that the current period of globalization is dominated by capitalistic globalization where the primary agents and institutional focus are **transnational corporations**. This global systems theory contrasts, however, with a segment of the globalization literature that contests the coherence and systemic form of contemporary global interconnectedness. Thus the validity and utility of the concept remains the subject of debate relating to fundamental assumptions about how global society is constituted and how interconnectedness develops.

Further reading
Sklair, L. 'Sociology of the Global System', ch. 9 in Lechner, F. and Boli, J. (eds) *The Globalization Reader* (Oxford: Blackwell, 2000)

GLOBAL TERRORISM

A relatively recent phenomenon comprising primarily Islam-based terrorist acts in the last couple of decades. Notable incidents include the World Trade Center attacks on New York (1993 and 2001), the Madrid mass transit bombings (2003), the Bali resort bombing (2003) and the London Tube and Bus bombings (2005). Terrorism in general is regarded as dating back to the Reign of Terror (1793–4) during the French Revolution. The term refers to the unlawful use or threatened use of force or violence by a person or an organized group against people or property with the intention of intimidating or coercing societies or governments. It is most commonly grounded in ideological or political reasons and involves activities such as assassinations, bombings, random killings and hijackings. From a sociological perspective, it is the modern means of violent resistance for those alienated from the society in which they live. Over the last century, significant terrorist groups include the Italian Red Brigade in Italy, the Irish Republican Army (IRA) in Ireland, the Basque region separatists (ETA), the Tamil Tigers in Sri Lanka, the Palestinian Liberation Organization (PLO) in Israel and the Shining Path in Peru. More recently, new terrorist groups have emerged, including nationalist and religious groups in parts of the former Soviet Union such as Chechnya and the Islamic al-Qaeda.

However, it is the emergence of al-Qaeda in recent decades with the two attacks on the World Trade Center – **9/11** in 2001 being the most devastating terrorist attack in history – which has led many commentators to herald a new era of global terrorism and provoked the US president to declare a 'war on terrorism'. Whilst many terrorist groups such as the IRA have long had international links, the focus of their activities has tended to be within one nation and the ideological basis to be, similarly, related to the politics associated with that area. Al-Qaeda, on the other hand, makes global-scale claims about the nature of its political basis (the intervention of the Western countries in Islamic states around the globe) and also has always sought to undertake terrorist activity across the globe. Importantly, it is also in effect a global organization as opposed to a regional or national one with membership comprised of cells across the global Islamic diaspora.

At the global scale, this requires both a global-scale cause and a transnational community or network of activists willing to carry out terrorist acts. Islamic terrorism since the 1990s has provided both of these prerequisites and in that sense is a new development in world history. However, whilst the global scope in terms of targets and imagined identity of Islamic terrorism is unquestionable in the twenty-first century, the degree to which al-Qaeda represents an effective global-scale organization remains the subject of debate. Despite statements to this effect by US intelligence agencies after 9/11, commentators have subsequently questioned the coherence of al-Qaeda as an organization beyond regional or state-based autonomous cells.

Nevertheless, it is difficult to dismiss the argument that terrorism has thus become both globalized and bound into further globalizing transformations. **Nation-states** and supranational bodies such as the **United Nations** have responded to the perceived growing terrorist threat. In 1999 the UN Security Council unanimously called for better international cooperation in fighting terrorism and asked governments not to aid terrorists. A particular target has been state-sponsored terrorism with 'failing states' in the international system being linked to terrorism (Afghanistan 2001, Iraq 2003). Thus, the rise of global terrorism presents a wide range of new and difficult security challenges for states and other governance organizations that are likely to continue to dramatically change policies aimed at combating terrorism in future decades.

Further reading
Kegley, C. *The New Global Terrorism: Characteristic Causes* (London: Prentice Hall, 2002) [esp. Introduction]

GLOBAL WARMING

A specific aspect of climate change that is generally associated with increased planetary temperatures as a consequence of human activity. The term is widely confused with the greenhouse effect. Both occur as natural phenomena but are used most often to refer to the more specific effect of human-generated carbon dioxide and other gases being released into the atmosphere. These gases in effect act as an insulating layer on the planet and lead to more of the sun's radiation being retained. Scientific evidence from a range of historical data sources such as polar ice cores shows that with rising levels of (primarily) carbon dioxide over the last few centuries, there has been a warming of average temperatures across the planet. Furthermore, since the pace and absolute levels of carbon dioxide emissions have increased even more rapidly in recent decades, there is general consensus in the scientific community that this global warming process will continue and possibly accelerate through the twenty-first century. The major effects of this will be changing climates across the planet, with associated impacts on **agriculture** and other activities, as well as significant sea-level rises as polar ice caps and glaciers diminish. Therefore, whilst the Earth's climate has always been in a constant state of flux due to a variety of causes, human activity leading to contemporary warming is argued to be one of the most important aspects of contemporary global climate change.

The main source of carbon dioxide emissions is of course the use of fossil fuels: oil, coal and natural gas. Also important are the effects of global **economic growth** on natural environments such as forests that act as carbon sinks by absorbing atmospheric carbon dioxide and 'locking it' away in organic matter or solid deposits. Thus commercial deforestation and logging, often in less developed countries, are significant factors in producing global warming because they reduce the amount of carbon dioxide being removed from the atmosphere by trees. Other factors include the decline of oceanic algae and other micro-organisms that also absorb atmospheric carbon dioxide – a consequence of pollution.

Whilst there remain considerable disagreement about and differing models of the geographical effects of global warming, many scientists argue that its impact will be differentially experienced at the planetary scale. In particular, there is growing evidence that the most severe effects will be experienced disproportionately by the developing world where sea-level rise, desertification and other forms of environmental degradation are more likely and where governments have fewer financial resources to adopt preventative measures.

In the context of the **globalization** debate, global warming is thus an emblematic issue at the centre of theoretical and practical debates around political and **economic globalization**. The growth of the global economy and its rising demand for energy and other natural resources are the central forces leading to global warming, which nation-states are attempting to tackle through supranational organizations and agreements. Most important of these is the **Kyoto Treaty**, signed in 1997, which imposes agreed restrictions on levels of carbon emissions for the following decade. However, this attempt at global-scale regulation remains partial, with key countries, most notably the US, refusing to ratify or sign up at all. It seems likely that global warming will become an ever more central issue in future debates about globalization.

Further reading
Houghton, J. *Global Warming: A Complete Briefing* (Cambridge: Cambridge University Press, 2004)
Maslin, M. *Global Warming: A Very Brief Introduction* (Oxford: Oxford University Press, 2004)
Victor, D. *The Collapse of the Kyoto Protocol and the Struggle to Slow Global Warming* (Princeton, N.J.: Princeton University Press, 2004)

GLOBALISM

Manfred Steger, Professor of Global Studies at the Royal Melbourne Institute of Technology, defines the concept as 'a market ideology endowing the buzzword **globalization** with norms, values, and meanings that not only legitimate and advance neo-liberal interests, but also seek to cultivate consumerist cultural identities in billions of people around the world.' Globalism can thus be seen to be the word which seeks to capture how neo-liberal views of globalization add up to a comprehensive political ideology. Conceived as the dominant globalization project (amongst many possible ones), the goal of globalism is thus often associated with the negative aspects of contemporary globalization: the weakening of national sovereignty, the erosion of national identities and a global economy that serves the interests of investors and big business. John Saul in his book *The Collapse of Globalism* (2005) argues that this ideology has risen to become dogma since the early 1970s. He sums this dogma up as a faith that 'borderless commerce' – manifest as open, unfettered world 'trade' – will overcome restrictive government policies, grant peace, freedom and prosperity, and will last forever. Controversially, Saul argues that widespread belief in this dogma has now subsided and that national governments, groups and individuals are now reasserting their interests.

Setting aside Saul's arguments concerning globalism's dominance or otherwise, the concept's usage in the wider globalization debate remains problematic as many thinkers and commentators fail to adequately distinguish between globalism and globalization. Furthermore, not all commentators agree with the definition offered above. For example, Joseph Nye offers a contrasting theoretical distinction between globalism and globalization. He suggests globalism seeks to describe and explain nothing more than a world which is characterized by networks of connections that span multi-continental distances. In contrast, globalization is argued to refer to the increasing decline in the degree of globalism as a concept that focuses on the forces, the dynamism and speed of change. Thus, the contemporary period is characterized by a shift from 'thin' to 'thick' globalism which in effect refers to the intensity (in the terms of David Held and his co-authors) of interconnection. Globalization represents in this conceptual framework the process of getting from thin to thick globalism. Nye further argues that globalism can thus be divided into four dimensions – economic, environmental, military and socio-cultural – rather than the over-emphasis on the interconnection of economic activity emphasized in much discussion of globalization.

Overall, therefore, globalism is an unclear concept in current discussions of globalization. There appears to be a growing tendency to adopt the term as referring to the political ideology of neo-liberal globalization. In that way, it represents a key conceptual tool for untangling the conflated meanings of the concept of globalization itself – notably globalization as a political project as distinct from a wider abstract process or set of phenomena. Yet other meanings such as Joseph Nye's are being proposed and it remains to be seen whether a consensus develops.

Further reading
Nye, J. (2002) Globalism versus Globalization. *The Globalist*. Article available at: <http://www.theglobalist.com/DBWeb/StoryId.aspx?StoryId =2392>.
Saul, J. *The Collapse of Globalism*. (New York: Atlantic Books, 2005)
Steger, Manfred B., *Globalism: Market Ideology Meets Terrorism* (2nd edn; Lanham, MD: Rowman & Littlefield, 2005)

GLOBALIZATION
In the simplest sense, an umbrella concept that seeks to capture the growing interconnectedness and integration of human society at the planetary scale. David **Held** and Anthony **McGrew** argue, and many other theorists (such as Anthony **Giddens**, David **Harvey** or Manuel **Castells**) agree, that it can be usefully conceived as a process or a set of processes that embody a transformation of social relations and transactions which generate transcontinental or interregional flows

and networks of activity, interaction and power. From the theoretical perspective of David Held and his co-authors, this wider process can be divided up into four types of change. First, globalization involves a stretching of social, political and economic activities across political frontiers, regions and continents. This is in effect a growing extensity of human relations. Second, it suggests an intensification, or growing magnitude, of interconnectedness and flows of trade, investments, finance, culture etc. Third, they argue this growing extensity and intensity of global interconnectedness can be linked to a speeding-up of global interactions and processes as the evolution of worldwide systems of transport and communications increases the velocity of the diffusion of ideas, goods, information, capital and people. Fourth, and finally, all of these first three dimensions to globalization can be associated with a deepening impact such that the effects of distant events can be highly significant elsewhere and even the most local developments may come to have enormous global consequences.

For many theorists, globalization in general tends in fact to be defined in terms of sub-categories. The literature now commonly divides its discussion of globalization in general into different realms of human interactions: **economic globalization**, **political globalization**, **financial globalization**, **cultural globalization** etc. To some extent, these sub-concepts have now become an accepted framework for understanding what globalization 'is'.

However these kinds of approaches to defining globalization are not unproblematic. First, by defining globalization through a range of sub-concepts, there is a serious risk of compartmentalizing transformations in human affairs which are highly interrelated. Economic interrelatedness is hard to separate conceptually and empirically from its social, political and cultural aspects, and the same can be said of any 'sub-category' of globalization. Second, there is no clear agreement as to whether at its 'core' the concept of globalization refers to any singular identifiable thing. Because the word is used in so many contexts, critical commentators have questioned whether in fact it is so generalized an idea as to be meaningless. Third, use of the concept by much of the wider globalization literature continues to be criticized for being sloppy and ill-defined. In many instances, the term 'globalization' is used primarily as a synonym for the effects and development of a neo-liberal global capitalist economy of the last five decades. In that sense, it is commonly subject to a narrow interpretation and its usage can be highly misleading.

Further reading
Brawley, M. 'Defining Globalization', ch. 1 in *The Politics of Globalization* (New York: Broadview Press, 2003)
Held, D. and McGrew, A. 'Making Sense of Globalization', ch. 1 in *Globalization/Anti-globalization* (Cambridge: Polity, 2002)
See also the Introduction to this book.

GLOBALIZATION THEORY

The theorization of **globalization** as a concept, which is one of the most contentious questions that has arisen in the literature. Many contributors to the debate claim to offer a theoretical insight into or understanding of globalization, and there is certainly no form of globalization theory that represents a panacea for understanding all the diverse contexts in which the concept has been used. Most importantly, however, the idea of there existing one or more forms of globalization theory is itself problematic. This is because the concept of globalization theory implies that globalization offers an explanatory scheme for understanding the contemporary world. As Justin **Rosenberg** puts it, this undertaking 'is fraught with difficulties' since the term globalization itself is 'at first sight merely a descriptive category which denotes either the geographical extension of social processes' or possibly, as Anthony **Giddens** suggests, 'the intensification of worldwide social relations'. A theory of globalization in this sense can be an explanation of how and why worldwide social relations in their current form came about, but to be anything more than an empty circularity, this theory must fall back on some more basic social theory which can explain why the phenomena denoted by the term have become such a distinctive and salient feature of the contemporary world. Rosenberg's point is that globalization 'as an outcome' cannot be explained simply by invoking globalization as a process tending towards that outcome.

Whilst this premise may appear self-evident, the criticism holds considerable sway through much of the literature as many commentators do not address (or at least not adequately) the distinction between the descriptive term and the explanatory process. In that sense, a lot of globalization theory is vulnerable to the criticism that it is primarily 'theory-light' in so far as it never adequately distinguishes the concept of globalization from other possible social processes which can provide an explanation for the interrelatedness of the contemporary world.

However, a number of key contributions to the globalization litera-ture cannot be so easily dismissed. The more substantial attempts to develop globalization theories have followed largely in the tradition of classical social theorists, particularly **Marx** and Weber. Across sociology, politics, human geography and international relations a number of common epistemological threads can be identified amongst the various theoretical contributions. First, many place the (dialectical) process of **time–space distanciation** at the heart of glo-balization theory: the stretching of social relationships across time and space as the key distinguishing feature of globalization. Second, the transformation of institutions and organizations in relation to the individual experience as a consequence of 'high modernity' is also proposed as a key to theorizing contemporary globalization. For com-mentators such as Giddens and Ulrich **Beck**, the changing nature of organizations is producing new and distinct forms of intimacy, trust and risk in the world. Third, many theories of globalization also place the evolving nature of contemporary capitalism as a central explana-tory factor in understanding what globalization 'is'.

However, at least two pivotal problems remain for those who seek to develop a theoretical understanding of the contemporary world with globalization as the founding concept. First, there is the fundamental question of whether contemporary globalization as the integration of social relations can be meaningfully distinguished from earlier social processes. If globalization is simply a continuation and deepening of earlier social transformations, then there is no epistemological legiti-mation for developing distinctive globalization theories as opposed to using existing social theoretical frameworks and concepts. Second, given the grand claims of globalization as a broad concept, globaliza-tion theories themselves remain faced with the problem of whether one integrated theoretical framework can adequately capture the diversity of contexts for which globalization is used as a descriptive term. This again refers back to the issue of whether 'globalization' can ever be reduced to one phenomenon at all.

Further reading
Giddens, A. *Runaway World* (Cambridge: Polity, 1999)
Held, D., McGrew, A., Goldblatt, J. and Perraton, J. 'Introduction', in *Global Transformations* (Cambridge: Polity, 1999)
Mittelman, J. 'Globalization: An ascendant paradigm?', ch. 3 in *Whither Globalization? The Vortex of Knowledge and Ideology* (London: Routledge, 2004)

Rosenberg, J. *The Follies of Globalization Theory* (London: Verso, 2001)
Scholte, J. *Globalization: A Critical Introduction* (Basingstoke: Palgrave Macmillan, 2000) [esp. Introduction]

GLOCALIZATION

Attributed to Japanese origins, a concept that emerged in business jargon during the 1980s and was popularized by the British sociologist Roland Robertson in the 1990s. Literally, 'glocal' and 'glocalization' refer to the telescoping of the global and local scales to form a blend. The original business meaning related to micro-marketing: the tailoring and advertising of goods and services on a global or near-global basis to increasingly differentiated local and particular markets. Robertson, however, develops the concept in a social theoretical sense in order to conceptualize the relationship between the global and local scales and the wider experience of **globalization** as a spatio-temporal phenomenon. Robertson argues that glocalization in fact captures his view of what globalization 'is' in so far as he sees globalization as a process as an articulation of what he terms the global–local problematic. The concept is therefore a response to the perceived weakness of globalization as being cast in tension with **localization**. Rather, globalization needs to be conceived as involving the creation and incorporation of locality – a series of processes that themselves reflexively shape the compression of the world as a whole. Glocalization is thus a preferable concept to globalization as it has 'the definite advantage of making the concern with space at least as important as the focus on temporal issues'. The concept also helps with the issue of 'form' in Robertson's terms, that is, the form of globalization taken indicates how the compression of the world is structured. He sees glocalization as the current form of globalization, being related to an ideologically laden notion of world order. In other words, contemporary globalization is constituted through various forms of glocalization but, in a wider sense, other forms of globalization could be possible.

Further reading
Robertson, R. 'Glocalisation: Time–Space and Homogeneity–Heterogeneity', ch. 2 in Featherstone, M., Lash, S. and Robertson, R. (eds) *Global Modernities* (London: Sage, 1995)

GPNs *see* global production networks.

GRAY, JOHN

Gray's major contribution to the **globalization** debate is his book *False Dawn* (1997) in which he seeks to counter the hyperglobalist vision of globalization that emerged in the 1990s following **Fukuyama's** arguments about *The End of History*. Gray argues that unfettered global free market activity will not spawn a self-regulating utopia, but will lead to increasing social instability and economic anarchy. He contends that the 'free market' is in fact a rare phenomenon and that democracy and free markets are competitors, not partners. He expands these arguments through analysis of case studies including the collapse of the Mexican economy in 1994 and the development of capitalism in postcommunist Russia.

Further reading

Gray, J. 'What Globalization is Not', ch. 3 in *False Dawn: The Delusions of Global Capitalism* (Cambridge: Granta, 1997)

GREENPEACE

An independent non-governmental organization (NGO) whose stated mission is to campaign on global environmental problems using non-violent means and what it terms 'creative confrontation'. Founded in 1971 by a small group of activists seeking to protest against nuclear testing in the North Atlantic, Greenpeace has grown into a global-scale environmental organization with nearly three million members, and offices in over forty countries. Its major contemporary campaign issues are the protection of oceans and ancient forests, the phasing-out of fossil fuels and promotion of renewable energy, the elimination of toxic chemicals, the prevention of genetically modified organisms being released into the **environment**, an end to the nuclear threat and safe, sustainable trade.

Further reading

Wehler, R. *Greenpeace: The Inside Story: How a Group of Ecologists, Journalists and Visionaries Changed the World* (New York: Rodale Press, 2004)

GULF COOPERATION COUNCIL (GCC)

Officially the Cooperation Council for the Arab States of the Gulf, established in 1981, with the aim of promoting stability and economic cooperation among Persian Gulf nations. Its members are Bahrain, Kuwait, Oman, Qatar, Saudi Arabia and the United Arab Emirates (UAE). In 1991 the GCC joined with Egypt and Syria to create a regional peace-keeping force, and an **aid** fund was established to promote **development** in Arab states. The peace-keeping force was involved in the liberation of Kuwait in 1991. In 2003, the GCC members agreed to eliminate tariffs on trade between member nations and to establish common external tariffs. In this sense, the GCC is becoming more clearly a regional economic trading bloc with agreements now in place to establish a broader economic union (including a single market and currency) by 2010.

Further reading
For a strategic historical background, see <http://www.globalsecurity.org/military/world/gulf/gcc.htm>.
The International Monetary Fund also has a number of reports that offer perspectives on the trading bloc's economic position at present: <www.imf.org>.

HARVEY, DAVID

Approaching the concept from a geographical and Marxian perspective, David Harvey's main contribution to the **globalization** debate seeks to theorize what he terms the geographical-historical materialist development of (neo-liberal) capitalism. In his earlier work, he developed a theoretical account of the nature of globalization as a phenomenon in time and space, arguing that it could be understood as a dialectical process intrinsic to contemporary global economic development. His theoretical conception of globalization thus shares common ground with theorists such as Anthony **Giddens** and Ulrich **Beck**. However, more recently Harvey has argued that contemporary **economic globalization** is primarily a consequence of American **neo-liberalism** reaching a hegemonic position at the global scale. His recent analyses of globalization argue that with the end of the **Cold War**, American power and influence have grown still further and that there has been a shift from consent to coercion in the ways in which the US propagates neo-liberalist economic policies. He also argues, however, that there exist internal contradictions to the territorial logic of US power and that in order for new alternatives to be developed, the rest of the world needs to suppress anti-Americanism and concentrate on supporting political transformation from within the US itself.

Further reading
Harvey, D. *The New Imperialism* (Oxford: Oxford University Press, 2003)

HELD, DAVID

From the perspective of a political scientist, David Held has written extensively on **globalization** and **global governance**. With a number of political science co-authors, he has provided an important critical commentary on the development of the globalization debate over the last fifteen years. He and his co-authors argue the debate has been characterized by two major, opposing schools of thought: the hyper-globalists and the sceptics. The hyperglobalists group, argues Held, take the view that globalization has hollowed out the state and hollows out citizenship both at the level of global market forces and at the level of regional blocs like the **European Union**, and that this has circumscribed the range of choices of states. States become merely conveyor belts between citizens and market forces. In contrast, the sceptics regard this as a misunderstanding of the importance of institutions. For this school of thought within the globalization debate, political institutions can broker trade-offs, and political and democratic mandates still matter. Held, along with his co-authors, is a key proponent of a third approach to globalization which he terms a transformationalist perspective. This is a middle-ground position which seeks to reform political institutions so that they are better able to moderate the negative effects of neo-liberal **economic globalization**. Held's work has also been important in pro-viding a theoretical conceptualization of how globalization can be understood as a generalizable process. He argues that this can be done through a four-fold framework which examines the extensity of globalization processes across space, their intensity, velocity and impact.

Held has also made a series of contentious and provocative contri-butions that develop his arguments in the post **9/11** world. In particu-lar, he argues there is an urgent need for reform of global institutions. He sees the existing constitution of supranational political organiza-tions as entirely unsatisfactory, arguing that they will 'be forever burdened by the mantle of partiality and illegitimacy' and that they are not 'our institutions'. Rather, they are 'the tools of global capital and the petro-militarists in the White House and Pentagon'. Yet he is also pessimistic about even the possibility of what he terms 'suitable reforms' that would produce more accountable, democratic and progressive global governance. Whilst reform is needed, it remains impossible both in the present global political climate and also for the foreseeable future. He contends that all feasible attempts at reform will simply serve to actually legitimize, strengthen and extend the system of accumulation by dispossession.

In sum, David Held is an important contributor to thought on globalization, both in his work describing the nature of the conceptual debate and in his interventions in the increasingly heated debate about future policy approaches to it. His work is also significant in that, unlike many commentators, his arguments are grounded in detailed empirical analysis. From a critical perspective, there are many commentators who remain at odds with his middle-ground 'transformationalist' position, suggesting either that it entails unrealistic policy prescriptions or that, in the case of the **anti-globalization** theorists, offers little resistance to the proponents of neo-liberal economic globalization. However, in occupying the middle ground in the debate, Held's work remains significant in so far as it may be in a position to attract wider political support than those who adopt a more extreme stance.

Further reading
Held, D. *Global Covenant: The Social Democratic Alternative to the Washington Consensus* (Cambridge: Polity, 2004) [esp. Introduction]
Held, D., McGrew, A., Goldblatt, J. and Perraton, J. *Global Transformations* (Cambridge: Polity, 1999) [esp. Introduction]
Held, D. and McGrew, A. 'Making Sense of Globalization', ch. 1 in *Globalization/Anti-globalization* (Cambridge: Polity, 2002)

HINES, COLIN

In his book *Localisation* (2001), Hines offers what he argues is a manifesto to unite all those who recognize the importance of cultural, social and ecological diversity for the future – and who do not aspire to a monolithic global consumer culture. He seeks to challenge the claim that 'international competitiveness' is necessary to survive either as individuals or states and outlines what he sees as the destructive consequences of **globalization**. For Hines, the key problem is the lack of local knowledge and sensitivity to human societal development. He thus argues that local economies, local autonomy and local democracy can all be protected through global-scale action and institutions if the **aid** and trade rules are changed.

Further reading
Hines, C. *Localization: A Global Manifesto* (London: Earthscan, 2001) [esp. parts I and III]

HIRST, PAUL

Co-authored with Grahame **Thompson**, Paul Hirst's key contribution to the **globalization** debate is *Globalization in Question* (2nd edn, 2001). This contribution makes what is widely regarded as one of the most rigorous attempts to assess the phenomenon of 'globalization', articulating a sceptical viewpoint as to its extent. Hirst and Thompson define their engagement primarily as addressing the **economic globalization** that 'is the continued development of the international system of commercial liberalism'. They argue that this system remains essentially *inter*national, not truly global in nature, because it involves high levels of trade and investment between distinct national economies centred on major states. There are four major elements to this argument. The first is that, far from being engaged in a generalized process of globalization, **multinational corporations** are precisely that – *multi*national – in so far as they retain the bulk of their operations in their 'home' country. Second, they point to the novelty of the postwar growth in trade in the world economy. Using trade data from the mid-nineteenth century onwards, the book points out that postwar growth in trade was not historically unprecedented. Third, and in light of this, they argue that most trade occurs in regional trading blocs (the **European Union**, the **North American Free Trade Agreement** etc.) and does not in general occupy a global space. Fourth, Hirst (with Thompson) is highly critical of those who point to the decline of **nation-state**s. He has widely argued that the role of the state has been redefined upwards to the supranational level and downwards to local institutions. He points out that the world trading system started when state **sovereignty** was created and contemporary states remain a prerequisite for successful international trade. He thus emphasizes that contemporary economic integration is the result of the transformation of existing, and resilient, political and institutional structures.

A number of critical questions can be raised in response to Hirst's sceptical view of globalization. Whilst his and Thompson's empirical analysis was certainly a highly significant (and welcome) contribution to the 1990s debate, notably in response to the hyperglobalist business literature, their empirical analysis focuses on a certain set of transformations in the world economy as opposed to any others. First, they define firms as multinational on the basis of production figures without addressing the qualitative transformations associated with **organizational globalization** and the way in which production is organized at the global scale. There is in short more to the transnationality of firms than their critique engages with. Second, the 'death' of the nation-state is not a prerequisite for the validity of referring to globalization as multiple processes. On the contrary, a considerable segment of the literature argues that states themselves are an intricate part of contemporary globalization and that global economic and societal interrelatedness is mediated and facilitated through the state. Third, the analysis deliberately adopts a narrow economic definition of globalization and thus excludes many transformations that are increasingly conceived of as globalization processes. These include cultural and informational flows, as well as questions of global consciousness and identity. Overall, Hirst's contribution is important, and his untimely death in 2003 prevented further development and/ or response to his critics. Perhaps the most significant impact of his work was to bring a new wave of empirical rigour to what had been a largely abstract and rhetorical debate about globalization.

Further reading
Hirst, P. *How Global is Globalization?* (London: Goldsmiths College Press, 1999)
Hirst, P. and Held, D. 'Globalization: The Argument of our Time' (2002); debate accessible at <www.opendemocracy.net/debates>.
Hirst, P. and Thompson, G. *Globalization in Question: The International Economy and the Possibilities of Governance* (Cambridge: Polity, 1999; 2nd edn, 2001)

HIV/AIDS
The human immunodeficiency virus (HIV), one of two closely related retroviruses, responsible for the development of the disease AIDS

(acquired immuno-deficiency syndrome). The HIV viruses both progressively attack the human body's immune system and when this attack reaches an advanced stage, they are responsible for the development of full-blown AIDS. It can be many years before this stage is reached but it often leads eventually to death as the body becomes unable to fight off infections.

In the context of **globalization**, HIV/AIDS has become important as one of the key problems facing humanity at the global scale in the twenty-first century. Since 1983, when the virus was first isolated at the Pasteur Institute in Paris, AIDS has spread to reach the scale of a global epidemic. In 2004 the **World Health Organization** (WHO) estimated that between 39 and 44 million people were living with HIV/AIDS globally. Between 2.8 and 3.5 million people with AIDS died in 2004 alone, with around 60 per cent of those cases occurring in sub-Saharan Africa. All of these figures are projected to rise in the coming decade with levels of infection increasing in developed and developing countries alike.

HIV/AIDS has thus become a major issue in global **development**. Critics argue that both the global economy and supranational political structures and institutions are inadequate mechanisms to tackle the growing crisis created by the disease. Key points include the fact that there is a concentration of AIDS cases in developing countries (and Africa particularly) and that medical research expenditure is mainly in developed countries. Furthermore, most of the drugs that have been developed are in the hands of pharmaceutical **transnational corporations**. The majority of HIV/AIDS sufferers in developing countries cannot often afford these expensive drugs and critics argue that these TNCs are more interested in profit than in tackling the epidemic. It is further argued that the situation in Africa has become so bad because **aid** budgets have been insufficient to address the problem. Thus, the HIV/AIDS epidemic has become another battleground for the **anti-globalization movement**. Such issues were at the forefront of political and policy discussions of the fifteenth international conference on HIV/AIDS in Bangkok in July 2004 and the HIV/AIDS issue has been progressively rising up the international political agenda in recent years. There can be little doubt that it will become ever more pressing in the coming decades.

Further reading
UN Millennium Project *Combating AIDS in the Developing World* (London: Earthscan, 2005)

HOLOCAUST, THE

Nazi Germany's systematic genocide of various ethnic, religious, national and secular groups during the **Second World War**. It began in 1941 and continued until 1945. Whilst Jews across Europe were the main targets of the Holocaust, in what the Nazis called the 'Final Solution of the Jewish Question', other minority groups were also persecuted, tortured and murdered. The commonly used figure for the number of Jewish victims is six million, so much so that the phrase 'six million' is now almost universally interpreted as referring to the Jewish victims of the Holocaust. However, mainstream estimates by historians of the exact number range from five million to over six million. Other groups deemed 'undesirable' were the Slavs (Poles, Russians and others), the Roma, the Sinti and the disabled (mentally and/or physically). Taking all these other groups into account, the total death toll rises considerably. There are estimates of up to twenty-six million Holocaust victims in total. The Holocaust is important in relation to debates about **globalization** as it represents a key event that has propelled forward international initiatives to legislate against extreme **human rights** abuses. It is widely cited as a principal reason for the propagation of universal human rights and is also a central historical legitimation in arguments that the **sovereignty** of **nation-state**s should have agreed limits set by the global community. It has, of course, also had a profound impact on global political history in so far as it was a pivotal factor leading to the establishment of the state of Israel after the Second World War.

Further reading
Neville, P. *The Holocaust* (Cambridge: Cambridge University Press) [esp. Introduction and ch. 9]

HUMAN RIGHTS

The rights, conceived as universal, that belong to individuals by virtue of their being human, and encompassing civil, political, economic, social and cultural rights and freedoms based on the notion of personal human dignity and worth. Modern conceptions of human rights have their origins in the theory of natural law in Greco-Roman and early Christian writings, reflected in the Magna Carta of 1215. This was developed historically through the Enlightenment largely in European and American philosophical thought through the seventeenth and eighteenth centuries. Particularly important are the American Declaration of Independence (1776) and the French Declaration of the Rights of Man and the Citizen (1789). However, in the contemporary context, the benchmark statement of human rights is the **United Nations'** Universal Declaration of Human Rights (1948), which was the product of a commission set up in the aftermath of the horrific human rights violations that occurred during the **Second World War.**

The UN's thirty-article Universal Declaration introduced into the global-scale public realm the notion that rights are universal, inalienable and inherent to the well-being of an individual. In particular, the declaration limits the behaviour of the state by attributing certain responsibilities and duties of care with respect to its citizens. The main content of the declaration was made legally binding in **international law** by two covenants: the International Covenant on Civil and Political Rights (in force March 1976) and the International Covenant on Economic, Social and Cultural Rights (in force January 1976). A range of other UN conventions cover human rights including the Convention on the Prevention and Punishment of the Crime of Genocide (1951), the Convention against Torture (1984), the Convention on the Elimination of All Forms of Racial Discrimination (1969), the Convention on the Elimination of All Forms of Discrimination against Women (1981), the Convention on the Rights of the Child (1989) and the Rome Statute for the **International Criminal Court** (2002).

From the perspective of the debate on **globalization**, the extension of global-scale norms and enforceable conventions on human rights represents a key process of **political globalization** and the development of global citizenship. As such, the development of both the universal rights themselves and the impact of their enshrinement in international conventions have been controversial and contested. Two issues are of particular importance to the globalization debate. First, the notion that there are fundamental human rights has been resisted. It has been argued from a number of religious and cultural perspectives that the rights of the UN declaration remain Western-centric and amount to **cultural imperialism**. This ranges across, for example, political participation as not being part of certain African cultures or the tradition of arranged marriages in Islamic, Hindu-Buddhist and Confucian cultures. Second, the relationship of universal human rights to national **sovereignty** has been highly problematic. Where violations have occurred, the international community has sought to bring violators to account even where nation-states do not cooperate. In the most extreme cases, human rights violations are becoming increasingly cited as the reason for military conflict, notably in the wars in Kosovo, Afghanistan and Iraq. The opposing political argument is that where human rights are used to override national sovereignty, this is again an excuse for a (new) form of imperialism where powerful states attempt to impose their values, cultures and systems of governance on weaker ones.

Further reading
Brysk, J. (ed.) *Globalization and Human Rights* (Berkeley, Cal.: University of California Press, 2002)
Donnelly, J. *Universal Human Rights in Theory and Practice* (Ithaca, N.Y.: Cornell University Press, 2002)

HUNTINGTON, SAMUEL

Huntington is widely known for making one of the most influential and contentious contributions to contemporary understanding of global politics in the form of his 'clash of civilizations' thesis. Much debated, and widely misinterpreted, the thesis outlines a possible future world where there are 'great divisions among humankind and the dominating source of conflict will be cultural'. He argues that the contemporary world can be divided into seven current civilizations: Western, Latin American, Confucian, Japanese, Islamic, Hindu and Slavic-Orthodox. Africa exists as a marginal possible eighth, depending on how far one views the development of an African consciousness as having proceeded. For the most part, civilizations are defined on broad religious grounds.

In terms of the nature of global politics, Huntington argues that the end of the ideological confrontation between (capitalist) liberal democracy and communism means that future conflicts will occur along the borders between civilizations at the micro-level. At the macro-level, he predicts conflict occurring between states from different civilizations for control of international institutions and for economic and military power. In later work, Huntington developed this perspective in increasingly controversial ways. In particular, he and others such as Roger **Scruton** have focused on the argument that global conflict and politics will be cast in terms of the West versus the Rest. In the post **9/11** world, this has provoked a vigorous debate about whether the West and (especially) the Islamic world are destined for ongoing conflict.

Undoubtedly a favoured perspective for many right-wing American policy commentators, it depends to a large extent on the commentators' political viewpoint as to whether they see the clash of civilizations thesis as gross and unhelpful simplification or insightful analysis about the nature of global cultural interaction. The truth probably lies between these two poles. Huntington's arguments do offer some degree of insight into the nature of cultural generalizations about the contemporary world. They have also been important in countering a Eurocentric view of international relations and the development of globalization processes. However, like any generalized thesis, the approach has a number of significant flaws. Four important ones are identified here. First, in developing these generalized civilization categories, the thesis inevitably rides rough-shod over the complexity of internal differences within so-called civilizations. Second, there is no real justification in the clash of civilizations approach for cultural difference being more important than geopolitical reasons for conflict. Third, there is a problematic assumption that civilizations can be essentialized in a meaningful way. Whether on **religion**, social values or any other grounds, many theorists of **cultural globalization** would argue against the coherence of these 'real' features in the world (e.g. Arjun **Appadurai**). Fourth, in predictive terms, empirical analyses of civilizational conflicts from historical data provide no support for his arguments. Various commentators have found that in fact civilizational conflicts (by Huntington's definitions) were less, not more, common in the period 1989–2002. Furthermore, where civilizational conflicts did occur, it was more likely to be between, in Huntington's terms, 'culturally similar' civilizations.

Huntington is quick to reiterate criticism of those who have variously used his thesis as a shield for arguing that civilization identities will replace others, that nation-states will disappear, that each civilization is or will become a coherent entity or that there will not be internal conflicts. Yet overall in terms of understanding contemporary political or **military globalization**, Huntington's thesis appears to offer only a very partial and simplistic account of transformations many globalization commentators would argue are extremely complex. In many instances, however, its theoretical contributions have long since been superseded by the politicized popular debate it has provoked – much of which has been conducted in very crude, reductionist terms.

Further reading
Huntington, S. (1993) 'The Clash of Civilisations', *Foreign Affairs* 72, 3: 22–50
Said, E. *Reflections on Exile: And Other Literary and Cultural Essays* (London: Penguin, 2001)

HUTTON, WILL

A former British newspaper editor, Hutton has written extensively on **globalization** and in particular the relationship between the US and Europe. He argues that whilst many of the changes occurring in the contemporary world have their roots in the earlier postwar period, contemporary transformations in global society are 'all-encompassing and carry a new inevitability'. He suggests that current patterns of globalization have produced an interlocking between technological advances, a more aggressive capitalism and a political leadership that sees no alternative but to allow the process to continue. For Hutton, this is what is 'novel' in contemporary globalization and outweighs the importance of a continuation of the past. Overall, he adopts a balanced mid-ground position, seeing some of the consequences of these entwined processes as having positive outcomes and others negative ones.

However, aside from presenting a middle-ground commentary, Hutton's major contribution to the wider globalization debate is his arguments concerning the varieties of capitalism and in particular the contrasting values associated with the US and European versions. In *The World We're In* (2003) he argues that there is a risk that the future of globalization will be one modelled on an American neo-Conservative idea. He argues that since **9/11** and the arrival of the Bush administrations, the US has moved back towards a unilateralist position that could be its own and the rest of the world's undoing. Hutton argues that competing models for globalization are needed to address the limitations of the American model – for example, its poor approach to corporate governance and welfare provision. European societies offer a counter-balance and possible solutions but Europe needs to become politically united and to reform its currently problematic central institutions.

Hutton's position has come in for considerable criticism from both US and European commentators. Some right-wing US-based commentators argue that he fails to acknowledge the achievements of the neo-liberal approach and misrepresents the US as being simplistically unilateralist. In Europe others have questioned whether Hutton does offer a feasible blueprint for European **development**, especially given the ongoing difficulties being faced by many Eurozone economies in the last decade.

Further reading
Hutton, W. *The World We're In* (London: Jonathan Cape, 2003) [esp. Introduction, chs. 3 and 6]

ICC *see* International Criminal Court.

ICFTU *see* International Confederation of Free Trade Unions.

ICJ *see* International Court of Justice.

IFG *see* International Forum on Globalization.

ILO *see* International Labour Organization.

IMF *see* International Monetary Fund.

IMPERIALISM

First coined in the mid-nineteenth century to describe British global domination, the term, simply defined, is a policy of extending control or authority over foreign entities as a means of acquisition and/or maintenance of empires. This can be achieved either through direct territorial control or through indirect methods of exerting control over countries. The term is also used to describe the policy of a country in maintaining colonies and dominance over distant lands, regardless of whether the country calls itself an empire. Historically, the development of imperialism is important in earlier phases of globalization. The emergence and development of empires represent previous phases of societal integration, although it was not until the nineteenth century that this reached the global scale. Importantly, for Marxist theorists, imperialism is associated with Lenin's early twentieth-century definition as 'the highest form of capitalism'. This conceptual basis has been widely adopted amongst a number of left-wing commentators such as Michael Hardt and Antonio **Negri** who see contemporary globalization as corresponding to a new phase of imperialism (which they term **empire**). Perspectives differ as to the precise nature and locus of power and control in this view of globalization as an imperialist project. Hardt and Negri argue that the new 'empire' is not associated with one **nation-state** and resides in a diffused manner through the global capitalist and political elite. Others such as David **Harvey** associate contemporary imperialism more closely with US power in the post-**Cold War** era. Whilst classical conceptions of imperialism have a strong emphasis on the economic and political realm, the debate in relation to globalization has placed much greater significance on the cultural aspects of imperialism. Many suggest that US-led global capitalism equates to **cultural imperialism** as transnational firms and the global media propagate capitalist consumer values across the globe. Clearly, the degree to which contemporary globalization can be understood as imperialism is highly contested and critics argue that this approach oversimplifies the nature of power and control in the contemporary world.

Further reading
Hardt, M. and Negri, A. 'The Political Constitution of the Present', part I of *Empire* (Cambridge, Mass.: Harvard University Press, 2000)
Harvey, D. 'How America's Power Grew', ch. 2 in *The New Imperialism* (Oxford: Oxford University Press, 2003)

INTELSAT
A consortium founded in August 1964 as the International Telecommunications Satellite Consortium, with eleven participating countries. In 1973 the name was changed to Intelsat with eighty signatories, and there are now over 100 members. The consortium owns and manages a constellation of communications satellites to provide international broadcast services. Ownership and investment is distributed amongst members according to their respective use of the services, with investment shares determining each member's percentage of the total contribution needed to finance capital expenditure. The

organization derives revenue mostly from operating fees, with satellite services being available to any organization at the same rate. Intelsat is headquartered in Bermuda and has over 600 Earth stations in more than 140 countries.

Further reading
See the organization's website for more information: <www.intelsat.com>.

INTERNATIONAL CONFEDERATION OF FREE TRADE UNIONS (ICFTU)

An organization founded in December 1949, following a split within the World Federation of Trade Unions (WFTU). This centred on allegations that the WFTU was dominated by communists, and a large number of non-communist trade union federations including the US, Britain, France, Spain and Italy seceded to create the rival ICFTU at a conference in London. Originally representing around forty-eight million members in fifty-three countries, the ICFTU recruited new members from developing countries in Asia and then Africa. After the collapse of the communist states in Eastern Europe and of the Soviet Union, Confederation membership had reached one hundred million by 1992. The organization has continued to grow and takes on a central task of seeking to defend worker rights at the global scale.

Further reading
For more information see the ICFTU website: <http://www.icftu.org/>.

INTERNATIONAL COURT OF JUSTICE

The court established in 1945 under chapter fourteen of the **United Nations** Charter. It replaced the Permanent Court of International Justice and its statute repeats that of the former tribunal. The court consists of fifteen judges chosen from the UN General Assembly and Security Council, who have independent voting rights. Candidates are nominated by government-appointed national groups of **international law** experts. Nine judges constitute a quorum and questions are decided by a majority of the judges present. The court's permanent seat is The Hague, in The Netherlands, although it can undertake hearings elsewhere. All member states in the UN are automatically members of the ICJ, and if member states fail to comply with a court ruling, an appeal for assistance can be made to the Security Council. The court can pass judgement on certain disputes between states, and with the authorization of the General Assembly, it can also offer advisory opinions to any organ of the United Nations and/or its agencies.

Further reading
United Nations *The International Court of Justice: Questions and Answers about the Principal Judicial Organ of the United Nations* (New York: UN Press, 2001)

INTERNATIONAL CRIMINAL COURT (ICC)

A permanent international tribunal to prosecute individuals for genocide, crimes against humanity, and **war** crimes, as defined by several international agreements, most prominently the Rome Statute of the International Criminal Court (1998). The ICC represents a development from the **United Nations'** International Law Commission which convened tribunals on an *ad hoc* basis. It legally came into existence on 1 July 2002, having been ratified by sixty-six states. By late 2004, ninety-seven countries had ratified the Statute. Another forty-two states have signed but not ratified, including the US and Israel. Countries ratifying the treaty that created the ICC grant it authority to undertake trials and provides for ICC jurisdiction over offences committed on the territory of a state (including crimes committed on that territory by a national of a non-state party), by a national of a state, over crimes committed by any person when granted jurisdiction by the UN Security Council, and over crimes committed by nationals of a non-state party or on the territory of a non-state party where that non-state party has entered into an agreement with the court providing for it to have such jurisdiction in a particular case. The ICC can receive cases through one of four routes of referral: by a country member, by a country that has chosen to accept the ICC's jurisdiction, by the Security Council or if a three-judge panel authorizes a case initiated by the International Prosecutor.

The ICC is separate from the **International Court of Justice** (ICJ) which is a body to settle disputes between **nation-state**s. In February 2005 it announced plans to issue its first arrest warrants against leaders of the Lord's Resistance Army of Uganda and an unnamed militia leader in the eastern region of the Democratic Republic of Congo. It represents an important further development in attempts to create a more effective global-scale legal regime that is applicable to individuals who commit the worst crimes. Some states would like to add crimes such as 'aggression', 'terrorism' and '**drug trafficking**' to the list of crimes covered by the Rome Statute but this has so far been resisted on the grounds that these crimes were difficult to define, and that dealing with less serious crimes such as terrorism and drug trafficking would distract from the seriousness of the crimes the ICC was established to deal with. These may be added in future as amendments to the Statute but that cannot be done until the original has been in force for seven years.

Further reading
Schabas, W. *An Introduction to the International Criminal Court* (Cambridge: Cambridge University Press, 2004)

INTERNATIONAL DEBT
Debt between **nation-state**s. It has a long history as states have borrowed from both other states and commercial banks for several centuries. In the context of the contemporary globalization debate, however, it is the growth and geographical distribution of international debt since the end of the **Second World War** that is important. From the early 1970s, many developing countries borrowed large amounts of money from commercial banks in the **global North** (in part a response to the development of petrodollar and Eurocurrency markets at the international level). The stated goal was to use this money to invest in **development**, often through large infrastructure projects. However, in hindsight it appears many states used this debt to finance military hardware and that much money was siphon off through corruption. Certainly this debt did not succeed in boosting **economic growth** in many developing countries. In the early 1980s, when global economic conditions changed and interest rates increased, a debt crisis was provoked as states in Latin America, Asia and Africa found their repayments dramatically increasing. Led by Mexico, many defaulted on the loans and produced a risk of banking collapse amongst the lenders in the global North. The US government and **International Monetary Fund** intervened to prevent this, but the 1980s and 1990s saw a long phase of high levels of international debt with many of the world's poorest countries cutting welfare and social benefit programmes in order to service this debt. Through the 1990s

a growing political and popular movement has criticized supranational organizations such as the IMF and **World Bank** for the policies of structural adjustment they have encouraged and has argued for debt cancellation for the poorest countries. Commentators such as Noreena Hertz and Susan **George** have argued that this level of debt is not only unfair but is provoking global instability and requires urgent action by organizations such as the **G8** and national governments in the global North. Recent agreements made at the **Gleneagles** G8 Summit have undertaken some degree of debt cancellation for the poorest countries, and campaigning groups such as 'Make Poverty History' continue to press for further relief. International debt is also important within the global North in terms of the high degree of indebtedness of the US economy (the US is the world's largest debtor nation) and the potential problems this presents for future global economic development.

Further reading
Heertz, N. *IOU: The Story of Debt* (New York: Perennial, 2003)

INTERNATIONAL FORUM ON GLOBALIZATION (IFG)

A policy think-tank that adopts a broadly critical analysis of the impacts of **economic globalization**, describing itself as 'a North–South research and educational institution composed of leading activists, economists, scholars, and researchers'. It was founded in 1994 as a global-scale organization aiming to provide a critique of the hegemonic free market and neo-liberal model being prosecuted by the **Bretton Woods institutions** and other international bodies. The IFG is run by a board of key citizen movement leaders who form the hub of a **global network** of several hundred associates representing regions throughout the world on a broad spectrum of issues. Many of the board members are major contributors to the literature critical of current forms of **globalization** (for example, Walden **Bello**, Vandana **Shiva** and Martin **Khor**). The main focus of the forum is to promote global social justice and environmental sustainability through alternative approaches to global **development**. Its main objective is to provide activists and campaigners in these areas with critical thinking and frameworks that inform campaigns and activities 'on the ground'.

Further reading
See the IFG website: <http://www.ifg.org/>.

INTERNATIONAL LABOUR ORGANIZATION (ILO)

A specialized agency of the **United Nations** with the remit of dealing with labour issues. It is another international organization seeking to align standards and practices at the global scale. The ILO was founded in 1919, emerging from the negotiations of the Treaty of Versailles. It was initially an agency of the **League of Nations** and became a UN body after the demise of the League and the formation of the UN at the end of the **Second World War**. The organization seeks to strengthen worker rights, improve working and living conditions, create employment and provide information and training opportunities. ILO programmes include the occupational safety and health hazard alert system and the labour standards and **human rights** programmes. Historically, one of the functions the ILO has performed has been the establishment of international standards for workers' conditions, which have then become the basis for trade union and other activism in individual countries.

The ILO is advocating a fundamental declaration on worker rights but since conventions need government support to be adopted, this remains an objective rather than a reality. In the past, even when governments have voted for specific conventions, many have ended up not ratifying it. For instance, after ten years, the Part-Time Work Convention, adopted in 1994, had been ratified by only ten countries. On the other hand, a group of eight 'fundamental' conventions have had far wider recognition. These have all been ratified by a majority of the member states, and are known as the international labour standards. With the ratification of a convention comes a legal obligation to apply its provisions. Governments are required to submit reports detailing their compliance with the obligations of the resolutions they have ratified. Every year, the International Labour Conference's Committee on the Application of Standards examines a number of suspected breaches of ILO labour standards. Cases can cover all areas of policy and practice, e.g. freedom of association, discrimination, child labour and maternity protection.

Further reading
For more information see the ILO website: <http://www.ilo.org/>.

INTERNATIONAL LAW

The legal relationships that have been developed and formalized between states or between persons or entities in different states.

The development of international law is a key theme in relation to **political globalization** and the development of new forms of **global governance**. Historically, whilst international laws have existed for a long time between states and groups of states by mutual consent, the emergence of a more developed system of international law was prompted by the twentieth-century experience of two world wars. The experience of the wars led to an acknowledgement that international governance could not rely on the balance of power if the most extreme acts of violence against humanity were to be prevented.

In the post-**Second World War** period the **United Nations** has overseen the development of a new international legal regime through the **International Court of Justice** (ICJ) and the International Law Commission (ILC). The formation of the UN also opened a means for the world community to enforce international law upon members that violate its charter. The UN has, in theory, the power to enforce international law through sanctions and military force. In reality, many international laws are ignored or not enforced. However, David **Held** and his co-authors argue three important transformations are identifiable in recent decades: the extension of the scope of international law beyond being solely between states; its extension beyond political and geopolitical affairs to the regulation of economic, social, communication and environmental matters; and the questioning of whether the only true source of international law is the consent of states and the acceptance of new sources such as the 'will of the international community'. With the formation of the **International Criminal Court** (ICC), although still not ratified by all states, the trend continues to be one of progressive deepening and strengthening of a global-scale legal regime.

Further reading
Shaw, M. *International Law* (Cambridge: Cambridge University Press, 2004) [esp. ch. 1]

INTERNATIONAL MONETARY FUND (IMF)

A product of the agreement reached at the United Nations-sponsored Monetary and Financial Conference in Bretton Woods, New Hampshire, USA, in July 1944. It came into existence in May 1946. Together with the other two **Bretton Woods institutions**, the **Bank for International Settlements** and the **World Bank**, the original purpose of the IMF was to provide a 'bank' for **nation-states** in order to support postwar reconstruction of the (capitalist) world economy. The organization's prime responsibility is to manage the global financial system and to provide loans to its member states to help alleviate balance of payments problems. In the immediate postwar period, the main role of the IMF was therefore to stabilize countries' currencies in relation to each other under the Bretton Woods system of fixed exchange rates. The IMF is thus not like a commercial bank in that its loans come from a pool of money from which countries can borrow when they need to stabilize their currencies quickly. All loans from the IMF must be paid back within five years, in contrast to the World Bank, which offers longer-term loans. Over the last fifty years it has (controversially) increasingly taken on the remit of 'helping' states who are experiencing serious economic difficulties. It now describes itself as 'an organisation of 184 countries, working to foster global monetary cooperation, secure financial stability, promote high employment and sustainable **economic growth** and reduce poverty'. Only a small handful of UN member states do not participate, including North Korea and Cuba.

Within the **globalization** debate, the IMF is seen as a key supranational institution that has propagated and encouraged neo-liberal **economic globalization**. In the later part of the **Cold War** period, the way in which the IMF did this became more explicit. In particular, during the Latin American 'debt crisis' of the early 1980s, when a range of developing states defaulted on their debts to Western commercial banks, the IMF played a key role in brokering a solution to the crisis, which involved setting policy conditionalities on countries asking for loans. These conditionalities sought to produce structural adjustment in domestic economies which often involved austerity programmes under which developing states were forced to cut spending on welfare programmes. The IMF was therefore blamed by critics for creating greater poverty and social inequalities in some countries. In the last couple of decades, the critique of the IMF's policy approach has been instrumental in igniting the **anti-globalization movement**. The movement has also argued with increasing ferocity that, through its policies, the IMF is apathetic or even hostile towards democracy, **human rights** and labour rights. Furthermore, authors such as Joseph **Stiglitz** have argued that the IMF has used its economic ideology as a shield for serving the vested interests of rich Western economies and big business.

There continues to exist a vigorous debate about these criticisms of the IMF. Certainly it seems likely that at the very least, as Stiglitz argues, the IMF has in the past adopted a high-handed and dogmatic approach. Furthermore, empirical evidence of its success is limited. Given that this institution was created to help stabilize the global financial system, it is significant that since 1980 over 100 countries have experienced a collapse in banking that reduced GDP by 4 per cent or more. This is far greater than at any point historically, and whilst it may be attributable to wider processes of **financial globalization**, many argue that the IMF's responsive approach is ineffective and that the institution is in urgent need of reform.

Further reading
Bird, G. *The IMF and the Future* (Cambridge: Cambridge University Press, 2002)
Danaher, K. *10 Reasons to Abolish the IMF and the World Bank* (New York: Seven Stories Press, 2004)
Stiglitz, J. 'The Promise of Global Institutions', ch. 1 in *Globalization and its Discontents* (London: Penguin, 1999)
Vines, D. and Gilbert, C. *The IMF and its Critics: Reform of the Global Financial Architecture* (Cambridge: Cambridge University Press, 2004)

INTERNATIONAL TELECOMMUNICATIONS UNION (ITU)

An organization founded as the International Telegraph Union in Paris in May 1865 with the original purpose of establishing standards and regulations for telegraph communication. Today it fulfils the same function for radio and all other forms of telecommunications and is the world's oldest international organization. The main tasks are standardization, allocation of radio spectrum (frequencies etc.) and organizing interconnection arrangements between phone calls. It is one of the specialized agencies of the **United Nations**.

Further reading
For more information see the organization's website: <http://www.itu.int/home/index.html>.

INTERNATIONAL TRADE

The development of more extensive international trade is a central element of argument concerning contemporary **economic globaliza-**

tion. Trade in the sense of the exchange of goods and services between people over distance has a long history. Great trading empires have arisen periodically ever since regular long-distance travel became possible, but international trade, by definition, only emerged with the establishment of the **nation-state**. The significance of international trade in the **globalization** debate, however, rests on the degree to which current levels indicate the validity of contemporary globalization as a novel and distinct feature of the world economy at present. In that sense, international trade has been a major focus of disagreement and argument about the extensity, novelty and prevalence of economic globalization.

For many commentators in the 1990s, one of the key indicators of globalization as a phenomenon was the emergence of global markets for goods and concomitant trade globalization. Trade globalization implies the existence of significant levels of interregional trade such that markets for traded goods function at a global level rather than primarily an interregional level. Global trade thus entails a system of regularized exchange of goods and service at the interregional level. In the postwar era, the development of international trade has been mediated through the **Bretton Woods institutions** which provided a basis for a multilateral trading order. In a conscious attempt to avoid the **protectionism** of the 1930s, the 1947 Havana Charter provided for an International Trade Organization to oversee the operation of the world trading system. This was abandoned by President Truman due to opposition from Congress, and the weaker General Agreement on Tariffs and Trade (GATT) was set up – a multilateral forum for negotiations on tariffs. After many successive rounds of negotiations over the next fifty years, the GATT was finally superseded by the more powerful **World Trade Organization** in 1995.

The GATT and the WTO were based on four main principles for international trade: non-discrimination (the **most favoured nation** principle), reciprocity (tariff reductions in one country should be matched by reductions amongst trading partners), transparency (the nature of trade measures should be clear) and fairness (practices such as dumping of goods below market price were deemed unfair).

Broadly speaking, the GATT and WTO regime has been successful in liberalizing trade in goods. Despite the rise of non-tariff barriers, in the postwar period trade grew more rapidly than world income. Commentators such as Paul **Hirst** and Grahame **Thompson** have questioned whether contemporary levels of trade are historically unprecedented, but the growing consensus is that the historical evidence at both world and country levels shows a trend towards higher levels of trade today than ever before. Whilst, therefore, much of the growth in international trade has been occurring at the inter-regional scale with the development of trading blocs such as the **European Union**, the **North American Free Trade Agreement** and the **Association of South-East Asian Nations**, there has also been a qualitative shift in the extension and deepening of global markets for both goods and services. Consequently, international trade remains a key driving force in the emerging global economy of the twenty-first century.

Further reading
Held, D., McGrew, A., Goldblatt, J. and Perraton, J. *Global Transformations* (Cambridge: Polity, 1999) [ch. 3]
Hirst, P. and Thompson, G. 'The Limits to Economic Globalization', in Held, D. and McGrew, A. (eds) *The Global Transformations Reader* (2nd edn; Cambridge: Polity, 2003)

INTERNET

A global-scale computer network linking together thousands of individual computer networks at military and government agencies, educational institutions, non-profit organizations, industrial and financial corporations of all sizes and commercial enterprises (called gateways or Internet service providers) that enable individuals to access the network. The Internet (commonly now just called the 'net') functions through a large number of protocols such as the File Transfer Protocol (FTP) which enables the transfer of information between computers in different networks. It is one of the most important features of technological **globalization** and the development of an increasingly global informational society in the twenty-first century. The most popular features of the Internet include electronic mail (email), discussion groups, online conversations (called 'chats'), leisure activities and games, information retrieval and electronic commerce (e-commerce).

The public information stored in the multitude of computer networks connected to the Internet forms a huge electronic library, but the enormous quantity of data and the number of linked computer networks also make it difficult to find where the desired information resides and then to retrieve it. A number of progressively easier-to-use interfaces and tools have been developed to facilitate searching. Among these are search engines that use a proprietary algorithm to search a large collection of documents for keywords and return a list of documents containing one or more of these words. An indicator of the prevalence and significance of the Internet in the contemporary world is the fact that the company that owns the market-leading search engine, Google, became the most valuable corporation in the world in 2005.

The Internet evolved from a secret feasibility study conceived by the US Department of Defense in 1969 to test methods of enabling computer networks to survive military attacks, by means of the dynamic rerouting of messages. From a small number of US government agency connections, it grew in the 1970s to include US universities and research organizations with defence contracts. In 1973 the first international connections were established with networks in England and Norway. A decade later, the Internet Protocol was enhanced with a set of communication protocols, the Transmission Control Program/Internet Protocol (TCP/IP), that supported both local and wide-area networks. Shortly thereafter, the US National Science Foundation (NSF) created the NSFnet to link five supercomputer centres; this became the main framework for the Internet. In 1995, however, the NSF decommissioned the NSFnet, and responsibility for the Internet was assumed by the private sector. Fuelled by the increasing popularity of personal computers, email and the World Wide Web (which was introduced in 1991 and saw explosive growth beginning in 1993), the Internet became a significant factor in the stock market and commerce during the second half of the decade. The Internet is becoming increasingly available to more and more of the global population through more and more media such as wireless technology and cellular phones. It is becoming the most important form of informational interconnectedness at the planetary scale.

Further reading
Naughton, J. *A Brief History of the Future: Origins of the Internet* (London: Phoenix, 2000)

INTERPOL

The world's largest police organization, established in 1923 and now with 181 member countries. Its purpose is to promote and facilitate cooperation between police forces in different countries and is particularly aimed at fighting crime organized or occurring at the international scale. The organization is funded by member-state contributions and governed by a General Assembly, with each member state having one vote on this body. Its core functions are the exchange of information between police organizations internationally, the maintenance of global databases of criminal activity and the provision of support for police operations requiring an international perspective.

Further reading
See the organization's website: <http://www.interpol.int/Default.asp>.

ITU *see* International Telecommunications Union.

JAMES, HAROLD

James, an economic historian, has made a significant contribution to understanding the historical nature of **economic globalization**. In *The End of Globalization* (2002) he argues that a process of 'deglobalization' is identifiable during the interwar period which represented an earlier phase of **globalization**. His work provides evidence for the two most common explanations for economic collapse between the wars: rising volume and volatility of capital flows triggered unsustainable booms and busts, and widespread fear of globalization provoked a social and political backlash. However, he also offers a third view: that people and institutions were overwhelmed by a globalized world's pressures and consequences. The key argument is that the institutions that handled economic integration were not only burdened by crises but also became the channels through which longstanding political resentment flowed. The result was a period of intense deglobalization through the Great Depression. His analysis of this deglobalization considers three main areas. First is banking and monetary policy. He suggests that between the wars structural weaknesses led to financial instability and banking failures, with hot money flows transmitting contagion from one country to another. Second, during the 1930s, trade and payments policies became ever more closely and inextricably entwined. What began with tariffs ended with trading blocs, bilateralism and exchange controls. Third, with regard to labour policy and international **migration**, he argues that the US immigration acts of 1921 and 1924, followed by growing restrictions elsewhere, led to increasing labour market pressures which lent impetus to calls for national economic polices, and in the notorious case of Germany added to pressure for '*Lebensraum*'.

James acknowledges today's widespread **anti-globalization** sentiment but concludes in his analysis that a similar phase of deglobalization is unlikely in the contemporary period. This is because an essential ingredient for 1930s-style economic nationalism is missing today: a respectable intellectual package of anti-globalist policy ideas and a successful national model, such as the Soviet Union or Hitler's Germany. His work is therefore most important, overall, in establishing both the similarities and differences between early twentieth-century globalization and the current period.

Further reading
James, H. *The End of Globalization: Lessons from the Great Depression* (Cambridge, Mass.: Harvard University Press, 2000) [esp. the Introduction]

KALDOR, MARY

Writing from an international relations perspective, Kaldor has long focused her theoretical contributions on the nature of **war**, its historical development and its implications for contemporary society. She has made important contributions in this respect to the **globalization** debate. In her book *New and Old Wars* (1998), she argues that, in the context of globalization, what we understand war to 'be' – that is war between **nation-state**s in which the aim is to inflict maximum violence – is becoming an anachronism. She points to the fact that in the post-**Cold War** era, whilst the threat of nuclear war receded along with the threat of large-scale interstate conventional war, millions of people died during the 1990s in wars in Africa, Eastern Europe and elsewhere and millions more have become **refugees** or displaced persons. Her proposition is that war has been replaced in the era of contemporary globalization with a new type of organized violence, which she calls *new wars*, which could be described as a mixture of war, organized crime and massive violations of **human rights**. The actors involved are both global and local as well as public and private. These wars are fought for particularistic political goals using tactics of terror and destabilization that are theoretically outlawed by the rules of modern warfare. An informal criminalized economy is built into the functioning of the new wars, and political leaders and international institutions have been helpless in the face of the spread of these wars mainly because they have not come to terms with their logic. Importantly, Kaldor argues that these new wars are treated (inappropriately) either as old wars or else as anarchy. The recent US-led conflicts in Afghanistan and Iraq are cited as key examples of this misguided response to new wars. In contrast, she argues that there is a need in the contemporary era for a cosmopolitan political response to these wars, in which the monopoly of legitimate organized violence is reconstructed on a transnational basis and international peace-keeping is reconceptualized as cosmopolitan law enforcement.

This approach also has implications for the reconstruction of civil society, political institutions and economic and social relations. In *Global Civil Society* (2003), she develops her arguments for a developing **global civil society** as the means to move beyond war as a way of managing global affairs. With civil society no longer confined to the borders of the territorial state, it is now possible for a wide range of non-state actors to link up with other like-minded groups in different parts of the world and to address demands not just to national governments but to global institutions as well. She argues that this opens up new opportunities for human emancipation.

Further reading

Kaldor, M. 'Introduction', in *New and Old Wars: Organized Violence in a Global Era* (Cambridge: Polity, 1998)

Kaldor, M. 'Globalization, the State and War', ch. 5 in *Global Civil Society: An Answer to War* (Cambridge: Polity, 2003)

KEANE, JOHN

A political theorist, Keane's major contribution concerns the issue of an emergent **global civil society** (or otherwise). In his book *Global Civil Society* (2003) he contends that historical attempts to build global civil societies have always failed, drawing on examples from Christianity, Islam, ancient and more recent empires and Soviet-style socialism. Thus, the development of a contemporary global civil society needs to be understood in relation to these past failures. He argues that in the current phase of **globalization** a global civil society is developing that is not being imposed from above by one hegemonic group or another. In analysing a range of civil society movements, he argues that global, regional and national interconnected networks of widely differing non-governmental organizational configurations typify modern civil society. Consequently he suggests that global citizenship is developing as a 'cross-border mentality' where new groups are creating transnational social spaces from where they can challenge the powers that be, whether governmental or corporate. Keane argues that these movements share a mutual respect for diversity, compromise and connectivity. He also suggests that the development of this global civil society is the consequence of a complex interplay of civil society movements with their societal counterparts. Governments and the corporate sector have played a major role in the evolution of civil society. Thus, although he acknowledges that the dynamics between civil society, governments and corporate business are often contradictory, Keane urges all players not to be discouraged in working towards a new **global system** of governance. In his view what is needed is bold new democratic thinking for a new world governance system – an 'unprecedented world polity' – which he terms 'cosmocracy'. This is an evolving and dynamic system. Overall, his analysis is an optimistic one that seeks to counter the view that the form of contemporary global civil society is being imposed on the rest of the world by the **global North**. However, as with other theorists in this area, his analysis could be criticized for idealizing the democratic nature of many civil society organizations.

Further reading
Keane, J. 'Unfamiliar Words', ch. 1 in *Global Civil Society* (Cambridge: Cambridge University Press, 2003)

KELLNER, DOUGLAS

A critical social theorist and philosopher, Kellner has focused on theoretical understandings of contemporary society and he is well known for his work on postmodern philosophies and theoretical perspectives. In discussing **globalization**, he develops what he terms a critical theory of globalization which aims to distinguish between 'progressive and emancipatory features and oppressive and negative attributes'. He suggests that globalization signifies both continuities with the past, with modernity and modernization, as well as novelties of the present and the already here future. It must therefore be seen as a complex and multidimensional phenomenon that involves different levels, flows, tensions and conflicts. This in turn necessitates a transdisciplinary social theory to capture its contours, dynamics, trajectories, problems and possible futures. As a consequence, Kellner wants a rearticulation of the concept in order to address its contradictions and ambiguities. He argues that to understand globalization critically it is important to see it simultaneously as the product of technological revolution and global capitalist restructuring. In that sense he represents another voice arguing against the economic or technologically centred perspectives of much of the literature.

Further reading
Kellner, D. *Media Spectacle and the Crisis of Democracy: Terrorism, War, and Election Battles* (New York: Paradigm, 2005)

KEOHANE, ROBERT

As Professor of International Affairs at Princeton, Keohane's major contribution to the **globalization** debate has focused on questions of state **sovereignty** and **global governance** in the contemporary era. Keohane is largely concerned with the impact of contemporary globalization on the nature of world politics. In this respect, he argues that one of the key issues is the way sovereignty has been fundamentally transformed. He argues that this has arisen through a variety of mechanisms including the rise of supranational institutions such as the **International Monetary Fund** and the **United Nations**, the development of regional blocs such as the **European Union** and the evolution of the global economic system. Sovereignty has thus changed in meaning and it no longer enables effective supremacy over what occurs within territories. Whilst others have made this point, Keohane considers in depth what this new kind of sovereignty entails. He suggests that it confers on states, under conditions of 'complex interdependence', a legal authority that gives them a grip on the transnational process. This grip extends, for example, to multinational investment, world ecology or the movement of migrants. Sovereignty, in the context of contemporary globalization, has thus become a bargaining resource for a politics characterized by complex **global networks**.

Keohane argues that the central implication of this shift in the nature of sovereignty is the need for a new kind of transnational world order. He conceives this as essentially requiring a new form of multilateral transnational democracy at the international level. This requires, in effect, the reconstruction of liberal-pluralist democracy at the supra-state level. However, Keohane contends this needs to be without the complications of electoral politics. Instead, he suggests a vibrant transnational civil society should channel its demands to the decision makers whilst also making them accountable for their actions. International institutions thus become arenas within which the interests of all states and the agencies of civil society are articulated and through which consensus is negotiated and legitimated. Such a view has many commonalities with other commentators on **cosmopolitan democracy** but whether its ideals are achievable in practice is debatable. It could be argued that Keohane's prescription lacks sufficient consideration of power inequalities in world politics and it is questionable whether sufficient transnational consensus and transparency are ever likely to be achieved.

Further reading
Keohane, R. and Nye, J. 'Realism and Complex Interdependence', ch. 10 in Lechner, F. and Boli, J. (eds) *The Globalization Reader* (Oxford: Blackwell, 2004)

KERNAGHAN, CHARLES

The Director of the National Labor Committee, a US-based NGO that campaigns for worker rights and fairer trade, Kernaghan is an active commentator and campaigner on the 'underside of **globalization**'. His contribution has been to point to the exploitation of low-skill workers in developing countries as manufacturing jobs in industries such as textiles have increasingly shifted out of the advanced industrial economies such as the US. Much of his focus has been on 'sweatshops' in Latin America and Asia. In this context, he has argued that there is a need for global standards and rules to govern worker rights and that **transnational corporation**s need to be held accountable by governments in the wealthier countries. He sees contemporary **economic globalization** as having unleashed a race to the bottom over who will accept the lowest wages, the least benefits and the worst conditions. He argues that this needs to be redressed urgently if globalization is ever to produce anything resembling social justice in the twenty-first century.

Further reading
Kernaghan, C. *Bangladesh: Ending the Race to the Bottom* (New York: Diane Publishing, 2004)

KHOR, MARTIN

The director of a Malaysia-based think-tank, the Third World Network, Martin Khor has made a series of policy-based contributions that offer a critique of **economic globalization** from a **development** and developing-country perspective. Most of his arguments are laid out in his book *Rethinking Globalization* (2001) where he underlines the heterogeneous nature of **globalization** and argues that in its contemporary phase, the phenomenon has failed to deliver peace and prosperity to the world, and in particular to trade, finance and investment liberalization. His work is concerned to make policy proposals on how poor countries can start benefiting from the global economy. At the centre of this is the view that poor countries need to take action to change global economic policies determined by powerful international economic agencies dominated by the rich countries. Khor's work is important in highlighting the obstacles faced by poor countries under globalization. Three issues are emphasized: trade, policy-making and the nature of the international financial system. In all of these dimensions of contemporary globalization, Khor suggests that the poorer countries remain at a severe disadvantage.

Overall, Khor has argued on several occasions that the current system of globalization needs to be fought. He suggests that it amounts to a phase of re-colonization and that there needs to be a serious redistribution of power in favour of the poorer nations if the twenty-first century is to produce a **global system** that produces social justice. For him, as for other commentators such as Susan **George**, one of the key priorities thus has to be a re-**democratization** of the supranational institutions that are seeking to manage the contemporary world.

Further reading
Khor, M. *Rethinking Globalization: Critical Issues and Popular Choices* (London: Zed Books, 2001) [Introduction and ch. 1]

KLEIN, NAOMI

The publication of her most widely read book, *No Logo* (2000), pushed Naomi Klein into the position of one of the leading commentator-critics of **globalization** in the West. Klein comes from a journalistic background and her arguments in *No Logo* – a book that arose from the Web-based movement of the same name – rest on investigative rather than strictly academic research. She argues that contemporary globalization is for the most part a project perpetrated by **transnational corporation**s to further their own interests and profits. *No Logo* also highlighted the exploitative conditions under which many Western-branded consumer goods are produced in less developed countries where manufacturing workers are paid very low wages in poor conditions, whilst substantial profits are made by the TNCs owning the brands. Her attack was also directed at the advertising and marketing strategies of these firms aimed at selling products to young people.

Subsequently, she turned her attention to more specific examples of what she sees as the negative impacts of **economic globalization** in the less-developed world. A second book, *Fences and Windows* (2002), argues that the neo-liberal policies of institutions such as the **International Monetary Fund** and to a lesser extent the **World Bank** were behind the dramatic economic collapse of the Argentine economy. In echoing others such as Joseph **Stiglitz**, Klein's work has had a huge impact on the popular perception of globalization although it can be argued that *No Logo* itself places too great an emphasis on the power of advertising and marketing at the expense of the underlying political economic conditions which have produced such a global geography of manufacturing production.

Further reading

Klein, N. 'Consumerism versus Citizenship: The Fight for the Global Commons', Conclusions in *No Logo* (London: HarperCollins, 2000)

Klein, N. *Fences and Windows: Despatches from the Frontlines of the Globalization Debate* (London: Flamingo, 2002) [a selection of articles forms the chapters]

KORTEN, DAVID

In his important contribution to the **globalization** debate, *When Corporations Rule the World* (2nd edn; 2001), David Korten offers a critique of contemporary **economic globalization** and the power that **transnational corporations** now possess. He argues that economic globalization has concentrated the power to govern in **global corporations** and financial markets and detached them from accountability to the human interest. The book contends that this shift in power in the global economy has had devastating human and environmental consequences because the TNCs have been successful in their efforts to reconstruct values and institutions everywhere on the planet to serve their own narrow ends. In this key popular text amongst critics of neo-liberal economic globalization, Korten sees the mobilization of people in the resistance of the **anti-globalization movement** as an attempt to reclaim political and economic power from these elitist corporate forces. He also presents a proposed policy agenda for restoring democracy and rooting economic power in people and communities.

In a later book, Korten broadens the scope of his arguments to cover the nature of the new global capitalism more generally. He argues that there is a gap between the benefits promised by neo-liberal economic globalization and the world that has emerged, which is one of insecurity, inequality, social breakdown, spiritual emptiness and environmental destruction. He argues this can be traced back to the development of philosophical and scientific thought on economic values that have their roots in a conception of nature embedded in the story told by Newtonian physics of a clockwork universe in which life is an accident and 'consciousness an illusion'. For Korten, this has led to the creation of competitive, individualistic and materialistic societies grounded in a Hobbesian philosophy that there is no moral purpose to life and therefore good is merely that which brings pleasure and evil that which brings pain. His vision of a better future thus relies on enabling people to free the creative powers of individuals and societies through the realization of a radical democracy, the local rooting of capital through stakeholder ownership and a restructuring of the rules of commerce to create 'mindful market' economies that combine market principles with a culture that nurtures social bonding and responsibility. His arguments are well informed in a philosophical sense, but such a perspective might be criticized for its own idealism in so far as, like many alternatives, the practical mechanisms by which these transformations are to occur are only loosely elaborated.

Further reading
Korten, D. 'Prologue: A Story for the Third Millennium', in *The Post-corporate World: Life after Capitalism* (New York: McGraw Hill, 2000)
Korten, D. 'Corporate Colonialism', part III in *When Corporations Rule the World* (2nd edn; San Francisco, Calif.: Berrett-Kochler Publishers, 2001)

KYOTO TREATY

An attempt to lay out a set of procedures and mechanisms to start the process of delivering on the objective of the United Nations Framework Convention on Climate Change (UNFCCC), Article 2 is 'to stabilise greenhouse gas concentrations in the atmosphere at a level that would prevent dangerous anthropogenic interference with the climate system'. The UNFCCC protocol was drafted and signed by most of the world's nations in the early 1990s, coming into force in 1994. The Kyoto Treaty, drafted in 1997 and coming into force in 2005, aims at reducing levels of greenhouse gas emissions to below the level that would otherwise have occurred.

The Kyoto Treaty built on the legacy of the UNFCCC in setting out legally binding emissions reduction targets and mechanisms aimed at cutting the cost of curbing emissions. At the heart of the treaty lies a set of legally binding emissions reduction targets for industrialized countries (the so-called Annex 1 countries). These reductions amount to a total cut among all Annex 1 countries of 5.2 per cent from 1990 levels by the first commitment period (2008–12). The total cut is shared unequally, so that each Annex 1 party has its own individual emissions reduction target. These individual targets were decided upon in Kyoto (after intense negotiation) rather than through any formal allocation principle. They allow some nations such as Norway, Australia and Iceland actually to increase their emissions relative to 1990 because of the particular historical or prevailing economic or energy technological circumstances of these nations. **European Union** nations will also take advantage of a scheme under the Protocol, known as a bubble, to redistribute their collective 8 per cent reduction target amongst themselves.

The Kyoto Treaty remains a highly controversial measure both in terms of its goals with respect to climate change and in terms of its status in international politics. In particular, the refusal by the US Government to sign up to it casts doubt on the overall effectiveness of this attempt by the global community to tackle climate change, since the US accounts for over 25 per cent of all greenhouse gas emissions. Furthermore, a number of scientists have cast doubt on how effective the treaty will be in arresting anthropogenic global warming. The reductions the treaty requires are modest and are unlikely to do much more than slow down, rather than arrest, climate change.

With regard to the wider **globalization** debate, the treaty is highly significant in that it represents a key development in global political interconnectedness. As a first attempt, however modest, to manage global climate at the planetary scale, the kinds of agreements and inter-state arrangements that the treaty instigated were unprecedented. Consequently, in terms of the nature of **political globalization**, it represents a novel and important development in the contemporary world and in the evolution of supranational organizations, law and interaction. By some it is seen as a provisional model for further future supranational protocols and agreements which would develop and strengthen global-scale political governance.

More recently, the US government has moved its position and announced in 2005 its own intentions to tackle global warming in an alternative approach to Kyoto that focuses on voluntary reductions in gas emissions. Other non-signatory countries such as Australia have also announced similar policy intentions. However, at the supranational scale, the initial negotiations for the successor agreement on emissions after Kyoto expires in 2012 began in 2006.

Further reading
Victor, D. *The Collapse of the Kyoto Protocol and the Struggle to Slow Global Warming* (Princeton, N.J.: Princeton University Press, 2004) [esp. chs 1 and 5]

LANDMINES BAN

There now exists a network of more than 1,400 organizations scattered across 90 countries that are working towards a global ban on the production, sale and use of landmines. It is estimated that between fifteen and twenty thousand injuries are caused by unexploded landmines and other ordnance each year, and whilst this is a global problem, it affects people in the poorest countries most. In that sense, the global ban campaign is a major example of the development of a transnational issue-based political movement that is aiming to generate global-scale regulation.

Further reading
Williams, J. and Goose, S. 'The International Campaign to Ban Landmines', in Cameron, M. (ed.) *To Walk Without Fear: Global Movement to Ban Landmines* (Oxford: Oxford University Press, 1998)

LASCH, CHRISTOPHER

Lasch (1932–1994) was a prolific social historian who wrote on a range of topics concerning the nature of mass culture and political elites. Although he died in 1994, before the term **'globalization'** became widely circulated, many have subsequently turned to his work and found relevance in his arguments about the development of American culture and the emergence of a 'new elite' in the US (and elsewhere) that have lost their national ties and sense of communitarianism. In many ways, this argument has much in common with those who have subsequently discussed the emergence of a **transnational capitalist class** (such as Leslie **Sklair**) or a global social core. Lasch thus offers an important contribution to sociocultural understandings of the emergence of this group and its implications for democratic values and practice. A range of his other (earlier) works have also been adopted by contemporary globalization commentators, especially concerning cultural values and the notion that neo-liberal globalization is inevitably 'progressive'.

Further reading
Lasch, C. 'Introduction: The Democratic Malaise', in *The Revolt of the Elites and the Betrayal of Democracy* (New York: W. W. Norton, 1996)

LEADBEATER, CHARLES

A freelance journalist and think-tank associate, Leadbeater argues that the pessimists (ranging across critical academics, the **anti-globalization movement** and left-wing politicians) have over-emphasized the negative effects of **globalization** as a broad process and that what is needed is 'more globalization, not less'. Whilst accepting that there are some downsides to globalization in general, Leadbeater argues that the pessimists have failed to appreciate the broader tide of positive outcomes that contemporary globalization has produced (greater choice and freedom, prosperity, cultural richness, sharing of knowledge). His argument draws upon academic and political writing but its sweeping, generalized style leaves it open to criticism of insufficient engagement with the complexity of the positive/negative aspects of globalization.

Further reading
Leadbeater, C. 'More Globalization, not Less', Preface to the 2nd edn of *Up the Down Escalator: Why the Global Pessimists are Wrong* (London: Penguin, 2002)

LEAGUE OF NATIONS

An international organization that is seen as the forerunner to the **United Nations**. Founded at the Paris Peace Conference in 1919, it is thus considered an important stage in the historical development of global structures of political governance. The League's goals included disarmament, preventing war through collective security, settling disputes between countries through negotiation and diplomacy, and improving global welfare. The League had three principal organs: a secretariat (headed by the General Secretary and based in Geneva), a Council and an Assembly, and many agencies and commissions. Authorization for any action required both a unanimous vote by the Council and a majority vote in the Assembly. The diplomatic philosophy behind the League represented a fundamental shift in thought from the preceding century. The old philosophy, which had grown out of the Congress of Vienna (1815), saw Europe as a shifting map of alliances among nations, creating an equilibrium of power maintained by strong armies and secret agreements. Under the new philosophy, the League was a new form of international government, charged with settling disputes between individual nations in an open and legalist forum. The impetus for the founding of the League came from Democratic US President Woodrow Wilson, despite the fact that, along with many other countries, the US never joined.

The League lacked an armed force of its own and so depended on the Great Powers to enforce its resolutions, which they were often very reluctant to do. After a number of notable successes and some early failures, the League ultimately proved incapable of preventing aggression by the fascist states in the 1930s. The onset of the **Second World War** made it clear that the League had failed in its primary purpose – the avoidance of any future world war. The **UN**, founded to replace it after the **Second World War**, inherited a number of agencies and organizations founded by the League, as well as seeking to absorb a number of lessons from the League's failures.

Further reading
Ostrower, G. *The League of Nations: From 1919–29* (New York: Avery, 1997)

LEGRAIN, PHILIPPE

A former employee of the **World Trade Organization** and a journalist, Legrain has made his main contribution to the **globalization** debate in his book *Open World: The Truth about Globalization* (2002). Adopting a centre-left perspective, Legrain argues for a middle-ground position on contemporary (mostly economic) globalization. The book makes a lengthy defence of the benefits of **economic globalization**, criticizing commentators from the **anti-globalization** position such as Naomi **Klein**. Legrain argues that 'the beauty of **globalization** is that it can free people from the tyranny of geography' in offering new possibilities for international and global cooperation and cultural intermingling. Legrain thus rejects the anti-globalization argument that governments are losing control to transnational firms, and that branding is taking over our lives.

His approach has much in common with other commentators on the so-called British progressive Left such as Anthony **Giddens** and Will **Hutton**. He also argues for an international neo-Keynesian model for the future development of a more managed globalization. However, whilst well informed, he has been criticized for operating at a relatively superficial level and of idealizing the positive effects of globalization. His argument certainly lacks the economic and political theoretical basis of other similar contributors such as Will Hutton.

Furthermore, the analysis of the negative effects of globalization, especially in the less-developed world, is very limited. It is also hard to view his assertions in relation to the cultural benefits of globalization as anything other than utopian and simplistic in suggesting that most of the global population increasingly define themselves rather than let others define them. Overall, the book retains a sense of being under-theorized and selectively anecdotal – characteristics common to much popular commentary on globalization.

Further reading
Legrain, P. 'Free to Choose: What Kind of Globalization do We Want?', Introduction in *Open World: The Truth about Globalization* (London: Abacus, 2002)

LIVE8
A series of pop concerts staged across the globe that were aimed at promoting the need for international policy measures to tackle African poverty. Timed to coincide with the **G8** Ministerial Conference at **Gleneagles**, Scotland, in July 2005, concerts were staged in London, Edinburgh, Philadelphia, Berlin, Paris and Rome as part of a popular campaign for 'complete debt cancellation, more and better **aid** and trade justice for the world's poorest people'. Whilst undoubtedly important in propelling key questions of global **development** into the popular imagination across the **global North**, it is debatable to what extent the concerts were important in themselves in achieving the political concessions at the summit meeting. Furthermore, left-wing commentators such as George **Monbiot** have argued that the project allowed vested corporate interests and political leaders to gain credence at a time when they deserved closer scrutiny and criticism. Although a number of artists donated record sales profits, the events certainly could be criticized for enhancing the commercial interests of record and media companies without generating any direct financial benefit for the world's poorest people they purported to be concerned with helping.

Further reading
The website for this event remains online at: <http://www.live8live. com/>.

LOCALIZATION

In the broadest sense, the concept often taken as the polar opposite process to **globalization** (critiques of the binary opposition of global/ local notwithstanding). However, localization's increasingly widespread usage within the globalization debate relates to its deployment by **anti-globalization** commentators as an alternative to the current trajectory of global interconnectedness. Colin **Hines** and Tim Lang argue that this concept presents a desirable reverse process to globalization by discriminating in favour of the local scale. Depending on context, this 'local' may be part of a **nation-state**, the state itself or even a regional grouping of states. They argue that at the heart of localization is 'a rejection of today's environmentally and socially damaging subservience to the shibboleth of international competitiveness'. In its place, localization is about prioritizing local production and the protection and diversification of local economies (and communities). The process can thus act to create greater social cohesion, reduce poverty and inequality, improve livelihoods, social infrastructure and environmental protection. Localization in this form is not therefore the polar opposite of globalization as it is not about restricting the flows of that sort of information, technology, trade, investment, management and legal structures that themselves further localization. For many in the anti-globalization camp, localization is therefore a concept at the core of reconceptualized paths for global economic **development**. However, whilst a number of initiatives have been made around the globe, it remains questionable as to whether achieving significant localization is possible.

Further reading
Hines, C. *Localisation: A Global Manifesto* (London; Earthscan, 2000) [select chs from parts II and III]

MAI *see* Multilateral Agreement on Investment.

MANDER, JERRY

The President of the **International Forum on Globalization**, Mander's main contribution has been to offer environmentally grounded criticism of contemporary **economic globalization**. He co-authored *The Case against the Global Economy* (2001) with Edward Goldsmith. Like many '**anti-globalization**' critics, he has argued that the global economy, and especially **transnational corporation**s, are not leading to progressive development of global society. His ongoing focus, however, has been the environmental and ecological impacts of the developing global economy. He argues that contemporary economic globalization is not 'inevitable nor evolutionary' and that it is not in 'people or the planet's interests to continue'. Instead, he argues, with others in the environmental movement, what is needed is *relocalization* in order to achieve truly **sustainable development** in the twenty-first century.

Further reading

Mander, J. 'Technologies of Globalization', ch. 3 in Goldsmith, E. and Mander, J. (eds) *The Case against the Global Economy* (London: Earthscan, 2001)

MARCOS, SUBCOMANDANTE

Whilst not technically its leader, Marcos is the chief spokesperson for the **Zapatistas** (EZLN) in southern Mexico. He is a central figure in the foundation and development of the **anti-globalization movement** from the **global South** and was an active participant in the uprising in Chiapas, Mexico, in 1994. To a large extent, Marcos's innovative use of the **Internet** and global media was responsible for the international publicity and support from leading intellectuals that the Zapatistas gained. As well as (probably) penning a considerable part of the EZLN's declaration against the Mexican government (and the **North American Free Trade Agreement**), Marcos has subsequently written on the ideological foundations to their critique of the developing neo-liberal global economy. Grounded in Marxian analysis, he argues that the **globalization** of markets is eroding borders for speculation (of all forms) and crime, and that the process multiplies the impact of this for most people. He also points to new borders being created within **nation-state**s and suggests **neo-liberalism** does not produce one integrated global state but rather fractures states into many smaller ones. He sees this as going hand in hand with increased militarization at the state level and an increase in state repression as political elites, such as those in Mexico, use repressive power to impose neo-liberal institutions. Most importantly, in much of what he has written Marcos called and continues to call for a **global network** of rebels across five continents – a global resistance movement – to confront this neo-liberal and top-down path for global **development**. Grounded in the real lives and experiences of some of the world's poorest communities, Marcos's criticisms of state actions, policies and the playing out of neo-liberalism in reality remain powerful and hard to ignore, even for those who would not agree with his ideological position.

Further reading
Marcos, S. 'Tomorrow Begins Today', ch. 56 in Lechner, F. and Boli, J. (eds) *The Globalization Reader* (Oxford: Blackwell, 2004)

MARX, KARL

One of the key nineteenth-century political economists and philosophers, Marx made an enormous impact on world history and social scientific thought. The relevance of his work to the contemporary **globalization** debate is consequently also considerable. Hard to summarize briefly, at least four major points are worth emphasizing. First, Marx's theorization of capitalism as a system of production and exchange continues to provide the basis for a number of Marxist schools of thought that have spawned theories of globalization. Notable amongst these are Immanuel **Wallerstein**'s **world systems analysis**, theories of underdevelopment and imperialist approaches to globalization. More widely, a large tract of contemporary commentary is grounded in a Marxian lexicon of concepts such as capitalist processes, class, social justices and inequality; the concept of **empire** held by Antonio **Negri** and Michael Hardt is, for example, strongly grounded in Gramscian Marxism. Second, Marx's theoretical arguments concerning the impetus for expansion in capitalism provide an explanatory framework that contemporary commentators continue to draw upon in analysing patterns of trade and investment, global financial flows and governance in the global economy. Critiques of the instability brought about by **global financial integration** and financial crises, such as David **Harvey**, for example, commonly draw on Marxist theories of capitalist crisis. Third, since the end of the **Cold War** and the so-called 'triumph of capitalism', Marx's arguments concerning the collapse of capitalism appear defunct. A number of commentators account for the relatively unchecked rise of neo-liberal

economic globalization as being related to the weaknesses in Marxian-inspired political economic thought. Fourth, however, the **anti-globalization movement** continues to draw on various forms of Marxism as the foundation for its intellectual and conceptual critique of contemporary globalization. Most **anti-globalization** commentators couch their critiques in the terms of social injustice and worker exploitation and in this way, whilst much of the literature only makes references to Marxian thought at the margins, his ideas remain behind key underlying dimensions to the globalization debate.

Further reading
Kellner, D. 'Theorizing globalization' (unpublished, 2003); this paper, available on Douglas Kellner's website, gives a good view of Marx's relevance: <http://www.gseis.ucla.edu/faculty/kellner/essays/theorizingglobalization.pdf>.

MASSEY, DOREEN

Massey, a human geographer, is concerned with how we theorize **globalization** as an abstract concept in relation to two issues: power relations and space–time. She suggests that as **globalization theory** has developed, three major ways of imagining the relationship between space and society are identifiable. First, there is modernity's story of space divided up into parcels and of an assumed isomorphism between spaces/places and cultures/societies. Second, there is the currently hegemonic notion of the space of flows which is the space of the 'story of unfettered globalization'. She argues that both of these conceptualizations of space are deficient because they annihilate their spatiality, losing the autonomy of spatial differences by their discursive arrangement into temporal sequences. Rather, she proposes a third way to understanding space/society that offers a better approach to the phenomena captured in the concept of globalization. This imagines the spatial realm as 'a sphere of juxtaposition or co-existence of distinct narratives which are the product of power-filled social relations'. She argues for the usefulness of place as a concept to capture where these social relations can best be captured. This approach thus avoids seeking to understand spatial differences through a temporal logic as current theories of globalization tend to do.

Further reading
Massey, D. 'Imagining Globalization: Power-Geometries of Space–Time', ch. 2 in Brah, A., Hickman, M. and Mac an Ghaill, M. (eds) *Global Futures: Migration, Environment and Globalization* (New York: St Martin's Press, 1999)

MCA *see* Millennium Challenge Account.

McDONALDIZATION

A term coined by George **Ritzer**, referring to the process of rationalization that is occurring in his view across all dimensions of contemporary societies. Ritzer defines it as the process by which 'the principles of the fast food restaurant are coming to dominate more and more sectors of American society as well as the rest of the world'. **McDonald's** represents the 'archetype' for this societal transformation, but McDonaldization affects many aspect of society: education, work, healthcare, travel, leisure, dieting, politics and the family. It is thus hypothesized as a wider societal process. By rationalization, Ritzer is referring to a process defined by the classical sociologist Max Weber who examined the institutionalization of formal rationality in organization form and rules and regulations within nineteenth-century bureaucracies. McDonaldization embodies rationalization around four major areas: efficiency, calculability, predictability and control.

Further reading
Ritzer, G. 'An Introduction to McDonaldization', ch. 1 in *The McDonaldization of Society* (London: Sage, 2000)

McDONALD'S

A restaurant chain that combines efficient working practices with rationalized food production processes through an essentially Fordist approach to food production. Founder Ray Croc opened the first McDonald's restaurant in Des Plaines, Illinois, in 1955, and although Croc's innovations gained ground only gradually in the early days of the company, in effect they led to the development of fast food. Set up as a franchise operation and widely copied, McDonald's developed a series of standardized icon food products with the corporation providing quality assurance, marketing and product development. Since the 1970s McDonald's has extended its operations to the global scale and now operates in 119 countries through over thirty thousand local restaurants. It is an emblematic symbol of the cultural clothing of contemporary **economic globalization** and the products of **transnational corporations**. It has also been the target of resistance from the **anti-globalization movement** in relation to the impact of its contract arrangements on **agriculture** and the **environment**.

Further reading
Love, M. *McDonalds: Behind the Arches* (New York: Bantam Press, 1995)

MCGREW, ANTHONY

A British professor of International Relations, McGrew's work on **globalization** is wide ranging. A co-author of the significant *Global Transformations* (1999), McGrew is a contributor to commentary and analysis produced on the globalization debate in this book (see the discussion in the introductory chapter). However, he has made a wide-ranging set of more specific contributions concerning international politics, **anti-globalization** and transnational democracy. McGrew argues that four distinctive theoretical approaches to transnational democracy can be identified. First, liberal internationalism aims to promote the reform of the world order so that international institutions facilitate **free trade** and relatively unfettered markets. McGrew suggests this is a technocratic and Western-centric perspective that fails to acknowledge power relations properly. Second, he identifies radical democratic pluralism which eschews the reformism of liberal internationalism in favour of direct forms of democracy and self-governance. This is essentially a 'bottom-up' approach to transnational democracy. Third, he discusses **cosmopolitan democracy** which he suggests is more focused on the institutional and political conditions that are necessary for effective democratic governance. This is characterized by a principle of autonomy for both individuals and collectivities, to be upheld through the development of a cosmopolitan democratic law that McGrew argues is an enormously ambitious agenda for reconfiguring **global governance** and the world order. Fourth, he identifies deliberative or discursive democracy, which is more concerned to focus on the possibilities for democratizing the governance that does exist in the international system rather than the government that might. McGrew argues that there are serious problems with many of these models for transnational democracy and that it is not clear whether any are an appropriate response to the impact of globalization. However, in his work with David **Held**, it is in a developing form of cosmopolitan social democracy that McGrew sees the potential for a more progressive and socially just global order. McGrew in particular sees scope in the future development of Europe and the **European Union** as offering a major opportunity for advancing this approach.

Further reading

McGrew, A. 'Models of Transnational Democracy', ch. 43 in Held, D. and McGrew, A. (eds) *The Global Transformations Reader* (2nd edn; Cambridge: Polity, 2003)

MERCOSUR (Mercado Común del Sur)

An economic common market (regional trading bloc) that began operating in the southern cone of South America in 1995. The trading zone includes Brazil, Argentina, Uruguay and Paraguay and its purpose is to promote **free trade** and movement of goods and peoples, skills and money, between these countries. Bolivia, Chile, Colombia, Ecuador, Peru and Venezuela all have associated member status. The combined GDP of the member nations is more than one trillion dollars a year and there are more than 220 million consumers in the market. In December 2004, MERCOSUR merged with the Andean Community trade bloc (CAN) to form the South American Community of Nations. The latter is more closely modelled on the **European Union**.

In the wider context, MERCOSUR incorporated political as well as purely economic objectives. The founder states, and others in South America, saw the formation of the bloc as a bulwark against the encroachment of the US in the region through the Free Trade Area of the Americas (FTAA) or the development of bilateral treaties. However, MERCOSUR was significantly weakened by the collapse of the Argentine economy in 2002 and some have argued that the Bush administration's refusal to bail out Argentina was influenced by its desire to undermine the trading area.

Further reading
Rafael, A. and Porrata-Doria, J. *Mercosur: The Common Market of the
    Southern Cone* (Durham, NC: Carolina Academic Press, 2005)

MFN *see* most favoured nation.

MICROSOFT

Arguably the most successful and influential software company in
the world. It has certainly played a key role in shaping the nature
of technological **globalization** and the development of the **Internet**.
It was founded in 1975 by Bill Gates and Paul Allen, and the combination of Microsoft's software and Intel's hardware pioneered the
PC and revolutionized the computer industry. The company's
Windows operating systems have become the *de facto* global standard
on the desktop, and major contenders in the server arena. Particularly
important in this has been the company's marketing and licensing
methods with its Internet Explorer browser becoming dominant in
the industry (although it has also been accused of anti-competitive
practices in relation to this). However, its other software is equally
important to this global dominance, with Microsoft Office, for
example, the most successful application suite in history in terms of
global sales.

Further reading
Bank, D. *Breaking Windows: How Bill Gates Fumbled the Future of Microsoft*
    (New York: Simon & Schuster, 2001)

MIGRATION

In its simplest sense, the movement of people and their temporary
or permanent geographical relocation. The movement of people is
possibly the most ubiquitous form of **globalization**. People have always
been on the move and even in ancient times moved great distances.
The reasons behind these movements are numerous but the com-
monest certainly include migration as a consequence of **war** when
victorious armies have swept into new territories and existing populations have fled; the enslaved being torn from their homes and relo-
cated to the lands of the enslaver; the unemployed and under-employed

moving in search of work; the persecuted seeking asylum; and the curious travelling and exploring. However, in the contemporary period, globalization commentators have argued that migration has become more widespread, involving far greater numbers of people and forms of movement than in the past.

David **Held** and his co-authors define migration in the context of contemporary globalization as the 'movement of people across regions and between continents, be they labour migrations, diasporas or processes of conquest and colonisation'. They maintain that the academic literature supports the argument that contemporary patterns of migration are more geographically extensive than what they term the great global migrations of the modern era (European imperialism, the world wars), although on balance they are slightly less intensive. However, also important to the distinctiveness of migration in the contemporary period is the evidence of far greater enmeshment across national borders. Western European states, for example, have acquired their most multi-ethnic character to date. Elsewhere in the literature, theorists such as Leslie **Sklair** also point to new and distinctive forms of migration: for example, temporary migrations of global business travellers, the growth of global tourism and (sometimes enforced) migration of low-skilled workers, including a growing proportion of women (see the work of Barbara **Ehrenreich**).

Contemporary global and regional migrations are also argued, in the context of the globalization debate, to have significant implications for the autonomy and sovereignty of **nation-state**s. Held and his co-authors point to five major arguments. First, the flow of illegal and undocumented migrants, economic and non-economic, demonstrates the limited capacity of many nation-states to secure independently their own borders. Second, those states that have extended surveillance of their borders have been unable to stem the flow of illegal migrants. A considerable literature, for example, discusses the failure of the **European Union** and member states to contain illegal in-migration, despite a growing raft of policy initiatives in recent decades. Third, such growth of international attempts to control or coordinate national policies with respect to migrations demonstrates a recognition of the changing nature of state autonomy and **sovereignty** and the necessity of increasing transborder cooperation in this area. Fourth, in the realm of economic and cultural policy, migration has transformed the domestic political milieu with new patterns of alliances reshaping political interests. The rising profile of national identity as a political issue in many states is seen as a key example. Fifth, migration has altered the kinds of policy options open to states and the balance of costs and benefits that those policies bear.

Further reading
Held, D., McGrew, A., Goldblatt, D. and Perraton, J. 'People on the Move', ch. 6 in *Global Transformations* (Cambridge: Polity, 1999)
Koslowski, R. (ed.) *International Migration and Globalization* (London: Routledge, 2005)
Papastergiadis, N. *The Turbulence of Migration: Globalization, Deterritorialization and Hybridity* (Cambridge: Polity, 1999)

MILITARY GLOBALIZATION

The process and patterns of military interconnectedness that transcend the world's major regions as reflected in the spatio-temporal and organizational features of military relations, networks and interactions. Commentators often distinguish between global militarization and military globalization. David **Held** and his co-authors suggest that global militarization, in contrast, refers to a generalized process of military build-up which can be measured by increased levels of total world military expenditures, armaments or armed forces. They argue that these two kinds of processes may, at specific historical periods, be highly correlated because specific phases of global militarization appear to be associated with distinct phases of military globalization. They cite the example of the 1980s as an example where superpower rivalry underwent resurgence.

In this sense, military globalization is defined as a process which embodies the growing extensity and intensity of military relations amongst the political units of the world system. The concept therefore attempts to reflect both the expanding network of worldwide military ties and relations, as well as the impact of key military technological innovations (from steamships to reconnaissance satellites) which have reconstituted the world into a single geostrategic space over time. They argue that historically this process of time–space compression (see **time–space distanciation**) has brought centres of military power into closer proximity and potential conflict as the capability to project enormous destructive power across vast distances has proliferated. This has been accompanied by a simultaneous shrinking of military decision and reaction times, with the consequence that permanent military machines, along with their permanent preparation for **war**, have become an integral feature of modern social life.

Within this definition, three analytical facets of military globalization are proposed. First, there is the global reach of the war system which includes the geopolitical order and Great Power rivalry as well as conflict and security relations. Second, there is the arms dynamic through which military capabilities and armaments production technologies are diffused throughout the globe. Third, and finally, is the geo-governance of organized violence which embraces the formal and informal international regulation of the acquisition, deployment and use of military power.

Overall, the literature as summarized and developed by Held and his co-authors suggests that contemporary military globalization is a key contributor to the reconstitution of **sovereignty**, autonomy and democracy which is widely associated with **globalization** as an umbrella concept. Yet a number of problems with this set of arguments remain. First, the Held et al. perspective, as with other sub-concepts in the globalization debate, tends to represent military globalization as a largely independent dynamic or process in world society. Clearly, as Held et al. acknowledge, it remains heavily related to other dimensions of globalization (economic and **political globalization**). There is a risk therefore of placing too much emphasis on the role of military integration where others might argue that in some instances military integration is more a symptom than a proactive agent of societal integration in other areas.

Second, existing discussions of military globalization tend to offer a simplistic conception of the scalar development of military integration. The real history of military integration represents a more complex and spatially uneven set of patterns to military integration which is probably less coherent than the link made between larger states and greater military reach. Twenty-first century military engagements (Afghanistan or Iraq, for example) arguably present a more complicated and fragmented form of integration of military activity than simply the capacity of the US and other Western states as major military powers. This leads to a third point which is that military globalization may also be thought of as occurring 'from below' in terms of the global extensiveness of resistance and other small military organizations with nominally local military interests and scope but which in fact exhibit complex forms of global interconnectedness (in terms of everything from the sourcing of arms to the legitimation and presentation of the conflict in which they are engaged).

Further reading
Held, D., McGrew, A., Goldblatt, D. and Perraton, J. 'The Expanding Reach of Organized Violence', ch. 2 in *Global Transformations* (Cambridge: Polity, 1999)

Millennium Challenge Account (MCA)

A bilateral **development** fund announced by the US Bush Administration in 2002 and created in January 2004. The programme aimed permanently to increase US foreign **aid** funding by $5 billion by 2005 through a new government agency, the Millennium Challenge Corporation. Recipient countries are selected on a competitive basis through a set of sixteen indicators designed to measure a country's effectiveness at ruling justly, investing in people and fostering enterprise and entrepreneurship. During the first year, 2004, in which aid was donated, sixteen countries were announced as being eligible: Armenia, Benin, Bolivia, Georgia, Ghana, Honduras, Lesotho, Madagascar, Mali, Mongolia, Morocco, Mozambique, Nicaragua, Senegal, Sri Lanka and Vanuatu. Madagascar and Honduras were the first countries to receive actual funding. As of May 2005, Nicaragua, Cape Verde and Georgia also met the conditions and will receive aid. However, by the end of 2004 Congress had only provided $1.5 billion of the $2.5 billion the president had asked for. It is therefore likely that the objective of increasing US foreign aid by 50 per cent through the MCA will not be met. In the context of the **globalization** debate, the reception of the MCA has been mixed. Critics claim it amounts to a new kind of imperialism and represents another method of imposing neo-liberals' conditions on developing countries.

Further reading
See the White House website: <http://www.whitehouse.gov/infocus/developingnations/millennium.html>

MNC *see* multinational corporation.

Monbiot, George

A British journalist and prolific campaigner, George Monbiot is a strong critic of contemporary neo-liberal **globalization** and has written extensive critiques on the power of **transnational corporations**, debt, the **Bretton Woods institutions**, the **International Monetary Fund** and **World Trade Organization** and the nature of contemporary democracy. He is an important left-wing commentator who adopts a strongly critical position of global capitalism. Central to his contributions is the enduring argument that the development of global capitalism has not benefited the majority of the planet's population. He argues in a number of his books that corporations have become so powerful they now threaten the foundations of democratic government and that there is an urgent need to develop new forms of effective democracy at the global scale. Unlike many **anti-globalization** contributors, Monbiot has made a more detailed attempt to outline alternatives to the current trajectory of neo-liberal globalization. At the centre of this is a reformulated form of democracy where power is redistributed away from the increasingly unaccountable global political and business elite and **global corporations** are much more rigorously regulated.

Further reading
Monbiot, G. *The Age of Consent: A Manifesto for a New World Order* (London: Perennial, 2004)

MORLEY, DAVID

A cultural and media theorist, Morley has long been concerned with the relationship between the media, culture and **globalization**. In his earlier work with Kevin **Robins**, he examined how new satellite and televisual media are transforming identity in Europe and in particular the UK. His subsequent work has developed these ideas to argue that traditional notions of home, homeland and nation have been destabilized both by new patterns of **migration** and by new communications technologies. He argues that these new technologies routinely transgress the symbolic boundaries around both the private household and the **nation-state**. His work is thus concerned with exile, diaspora, displacement, connectedness and mobility in the context of contemporary globalization. Morley is perhaps best known in the globalization literature, however, for his idea of the 'home territory' in relation to national media cultures. He suggests that 'home territories' are media cultures whose 'translocal communicative connectivity' has been territorialized in such a way that national frontiers are the main borders of many 'communicative thickenings'. The process of 'thickening' of the national 'imagined community' is in part territorially bounded but also no longer exists in a pure form. Globalization is leading to communicative connectivity becoming more and more deterritorialized. The consequence is that in the contemporary era, the 'borders' of the 'imagined communities' we belong to do not necessarily correspond with the territorial borders. What home and home territory mean for people in today's world is becoming increasingly problematic. In this way, Morley offers an important insight into how the communicative connectivity of translocal media cultures is impacting on the nature of national cultures and identity.

Further reading
Morley, D. 'Introduction', in *Home Territories: Media, Mobility and Identity* (London: Routledge, 2000)

MOST FAVOURED NATION (MFN)

A key tenet of **free trade** agreements in the contemporary world. Put simply, it is a provision in a treaty or agreement which binds signatories to extend trading benefits equally to all those given to any third state. This is one of the essential principles underpinning **economic globalization**. In the postwar period, the GATT negotiations on free trade, which ultimately led to the establishment of the **World Trade Organization**, operated on the basis that international trade agreements should adhere to the MFN principle although since the **United Nations** Conference on Trade and Development in 1964, states have recognized in principle that the MFN rule should be relaxed to accommodate the needs of developing countries.

Further reading
Further information is available on the WTO website at: <http://www.wto.org/english/thewto_e/whatis_e/tif_e/fact2_e.htm>.

MULTILATERAL AGREEMENT ON INVESTMENT (MAI)

The (now postponed) treaty whose goal is to extend the deregulatory agenda of the GATT-**World Trade Organization** to economic sectors and aspects of the global economy not already covered by GATT-WTO rules. The MAI was negotiated through the **Organization for Economic Cooperation and Development**, and its primary goal was to do for capital mobility what GATT had done for trade in the postwar period. The intention was to produce an international treaty agreement which would compel signatory **nation-state**s to open virtually all sectors of their economies to foreign investment, treat foreign corporations the same as local companies and bar governments from altering these new investor rights. The treaty enshrined the principle that international corporate investors should be able to compete with local companies for all the world's resources, labour and consumer markets. Translated into **international law**, this would have meant a standard of national treatment, where governments would have had to treat foreign investors no less favourably than domestic investors. The MAI thus sought to give foreign corporations a right to invest in almost all sectors of nations' economies (with the exception of national security industries). Had it been implemented, it would have represented a large step forward in the direction of global investment liberalization and neo-liberal **economic globalization**.

However, after several years, the MAI negotiations were finally postponed indefinitely in 1998. Growing opposition to the treaty ultimately led to stalemate. Critics of the MAI argued that it was flawed, most notably that despite the need for corporate accountability in the international economy, the MAI contained no binding obligations on corporate investors. It was therefore seen as an undesirable shift in power towards the interests of global capital and **transnational corporation**s at the expense of national governments and local communities. The MAI agenda has not disappeared in the context of trade and investment liberalization, but there are no current plans to reinitiate negotiations.

Further reading
A series of articles are available on the global policy website: <http://www.globalpolicy.org/socecon/bwi-wto/indexmai.htm>.

MULTILATERALISM
The concept of multiple countries working in concert. Most contemporary international organizations are multilateral in nature, for example, the **United Nations** and the **World Trade Organization**. Historically, the main proponents of multilateralism have been the so-called 'middle powers' such as Canada and the Nordic countries. Larger or dominant states such as Britain in the nineteenth century,

or the US in the twentieth, often act unilaterally. The concept is extremely important in debates surrounding the nature of military and **political globalization** and the emergence in the twenty-first century of new forms of global-scale governance.

Formalized multilateralism developed in nineteenth-century Europe after the end of the Napoleonic Wars where the great powers met to redraw the map of Europe at the Congress of Vienna. This produced the Concert of Europe – a group of great and lesser powers that would meet to resolve issues peacefully. Conferences such as the Conference of Berlin in 1884 helped reduce Great Power conflicts during this period. The concert system was destroyed by the **First World War**. After the war, the **League of Nations** represented a new, ultimately unsuccessful, multilateral effort to prevent another conflict of similar scale. After the **Second World War**, an array of multilateral organizations emerged. In addition to the **Bretton Woods institutions**, others range from the **World Health Organization** to the **International Court of Justice**.

In the post-**Cold War** period, many commentators argue that **globalization** is producing increasingly multilateral forms of **global governance**. However, this is far from unproblematic. In the post-Cold War era, and especially since **9/11**, the actions of the US in Iraq (2003) and on issues such as the **Kyoto Protocol** and the **International Criminal Court** have been argued to show the continued US tendency towards **unilateralism**. More recently, commentators have also argued that Russia is again showing similar tendencies in its dealings with its post-communist near neighbours in central Asia. Whilst multilateralism is thus seen as the ideal mode for global governance, it is questionable whether contemporary political globalization is producing a truly multilateral world.

Further reading
Sewell, J. (ed.) *Multilateralism in Multinational Perspective: Viewpoints from Languages and Literatures* (Basingstoke: Palgrave Macmillan, 1999)

MULTINATIONAL CORPORATION (MNC)
In the strict sense, a company that produces goods or markets services in more than one **nation-state**. Such a company may also be called a multinational enterprise (MNE). However, both terms are used to cover a wide range of forms that multinational business can take. In the narrowest form, the enterprise controls and manages subsidiaries

in a number of countries outside its own base country. The classic MNC therefore has separate operations in each country that are for the most part discrete from each other. This applied to the first true MNCs which emerged in the first decades of the twentieth century and were mostly US-originated firms. In the contemporary world, however, MNCs are increasingly entwined in complex **global production networks** and the distinction between them and the more recent **transnational corporations** (TNCs) is often poorly defined.

Further reading
Morgan, G., Kristensen, P. and Whitley, R. (eds) *The Multinational Firm: Organizing across Institutional and National Divides* (Oxford: Oxford University Press, 2001) [esp. ch. 1]

NAFTA *see* North American Free Trade Agreement.

NAIRN, TOM
Professor of Nationalism and Cultural Diversity at the Royal Melbourne Institute of Technology, Melbourne, Australia, Nairn has written extensively on national and international politics. In a series of articles on the relationship of America to contemporary **globalization**, he argues that globalization should not be equated with Americanization. His contention is that the onrushing process of globalization will render America just another country in the wider context and that conflicts in recent years such as the Iraq war should be seen not as a war about oil or as a response to Osama Bin Laden (in contrast to commentators such as David **Harvey**). He suggests that Iraq was a war concerned with globalization itself as the US seeks to militarize the economic domination it enjoyed in the 1990s. As with other commentators, he sees the progressive path for global **development** in the twenty-first century as requiring the reconstruction of democratic nationalism where the positive aspects of global interconnectedness can be incorporated into a revitalized form of nationalism. These themes are central to his book *Global Matrix* (2005) (with Paul James), where he is critical of those who argue globalization is leading to the demise of the **nation-state** (for example, Kenichi **Ohmae**). He also argues that the rise of **(global) terrorism** is not a consequence of violence arising from below, but a consequence

of state-led policy at the global scale and of the wider experience of interconnectedness by individuals across the planet.

Further reading
Nairn, T. and James, P. *Global Matrix: Nationalism, Globalism and State-terrorism* (London: Matrix, 2005)

NATION-STATE

A territorially bounded political unit inhabited predominantly by a people sharing a common culture, history and language. David **Held** and his co-authors point out that nation-states are distinguishable from early forms of political-territorial governance (kingdoms, empires, city-states etc.) as 'political apparatuses, distinct from both ruler and ruled, with supreme jurisdiction over a demarcated territorial area and are backed by the claim to a monopoly of coercive power within that territory'. The concept is often used interchangeably (although incorrectly) with the idea of a nation. However, a nation can exist without a territorial or institutional form: for example, the concept of the Black diasporic nation. The nation-state has progressively become the dominant form of territorial-political governance in the contemporary world, with most people on the globe now living in one, even if they do not personally identify with that state. The rise of the nation-state and its spread around the globe as a common form of governance is a central aspect of **political globalization**.

The earliest nation-states, in the contemporary sense, have their origins in the developing forms of political-territorial governance in Western Europe from the sixteenth century onwards. The Treaty of Westphalia in 1648 is seen as a key early moment in the demarcation of these territorial states. However, recognizable modern nation-states were only fully achieved during the nineteenth century. In the twentieth century, and especially in the aftermath of the **Second World War**, the number of nation-states has proliferated.

With regard to contemporary **globalization**, one of the key debates has been the extent to which the nation-state has suffered a decline in its **sovereignty** and its wider power and relevance in the world. Some commentators have argued that the nation-state is coming to an 'end' as the dominant political-territorial form in a globalized world. This is linked to a series of factors including the rise of **transnational corporations**, integrated global financial markets and the growing power and proliferation of supranational political bodies.

Others argue that this has been overstated, but it is certainly true that nation-states have seen their role change dramatically over recent decades.

Further reading
Held, D., McGrew, A., Goldblatt, J. and Perraton, J. 'The Territorial State and Global Politics', ch. 1 in *Global Transformations* (Cambridge: Polity, 1999)

NATO *see* North Atlantic Treaty Organization.

NEGRI, ANTONIO

An Italian intellectual and political activist, Negri's major contribution to the **globalization** debates is his book *Empire* (2000) with Michael Hardt. A longstanding Marxist thinker, Negri regards contemporary **economic globalization** as an imperial undertaking that in effect fits into a Marxian understanding of the continued expansion of capitalism to the global scale. He remains firmly anti-capitalist in his stance and argues there is a need for a more democratic, non-capitalist means of economic **development** in order to achieve social justice at the global scale. Negri's work (like Hardt's) is strongly influenced by Gramscian Marxism, which in essence sees the locus of capitalist power and influence in the socio-political and cultural realms as well as the economic. *Empire* is thus concerned to argue that there exists a new form of imperialism, not centred on any one **nation-state**, but located in the emergent **transnational capitalist class**.

Further reading
Hardt, M. and Negri, A. 'Globalization as Empire', ch. 10 in Held, D. and McGrew, A. (eds) *The Global Transformations Reader* (Cambridge: Polity, 2000)

NEOCOLONIALISM

A term that came into wide usage in the post-**Second World War** period, particularly with the decolonization of Africa, the Caribbean and other former imperial possessions by Western European states. Neocolonial theorists, many arguing from a Marxist perspective, contend that whilst the European colonial powers might have formally ceded control of their colonies, they were still exercising control and were dominating less powerful countries through indirect means including economic, financial and trade policies. In the 1970s, key neocolonial theories include Gunder Frank's conception of dependent **development** and Immanuel **Wallerstein**'s core–periphery theorization of the world capitalist system. Critics of these theorists argued that neocolonialism discourse presents a one-sided account of late twentieth-century development because less wealthy and powerful countries have benefited from investment and **economic growth** instigated through Western countries' relationships with them.

In this sense, the concept continues to be a relevant and commonly cited term in the context of early twenty-first-century **globalization**. **Anti-globalization** commentators have argued, in criticizing the policies of the **Bretton Woods institutions** such as the **International Monetary Fund** and **World Bank**, that these supranational bodies replicate neocolonial relations between richer and poorer countries (and class segments in global society). From a theoretical perspective, Antonio **Negri** and Michael Hardt have offered an updated account of how the contemporary global economy replicates neocolonial relations through their Gramscian-Marxist concept of empire. This shifts the terms of reference for neocolonial relations in the contemporary world into a postnational sphere where **transnational corporations**, the **transnational capitalist class**, political elites and supranational institutions join nation-states as the dominating forces.

Further reading
Hardt, M. and Negri, A. 'Passages of Sovereignty', part II in *Empire* (Cambridge, Mass.: Harvard University Press, 2000)
Young, R. *Postcolonialism* (Oxford: Blackwell, 2000) [see part I]

NEO-LIBERALISM
The contemporary variant of a theoretical perspective which argues at core that free market competition among businesses with limited state regulation is the best way to foster **economic growth**. One of the most widely used terms in the **globalization** debate, it is a contested concept in so far as there are a variety of different schools of thought propagating different versions of neo-liberal policy. However, Susan **George** has argued that neo-liberalist policies at an international or

global level have concentrated on three fundamental points: **free trade** in goods and services, free circulation of capital and freedom of investment.

The prefix 'neo-', meaning new, is used to denote an ideological perspective that has taken shape over the last thirty years. Yet liberalism as a social philosophy has a much more longstanding history. Emerging through the early modern period, liberalism represented by the late eighteenth century a fairly coherent philosophical perspective. A number of its basic principles are important to contemporary neo-liberalism. First, liberalism entailed a belief that the form of society should be an outcome of processes which involve all members of society – the market being perhaps the best example of such a process. Second, interference and intervention in these processes were undesirable and would lead to unethical outcomes. Thus liberalism entails a rejection of any design or plan for society. Third, liberty is (arguably) the most important value in society which outweighs ethical value judgements about what is good or bad. Liberty itself represents 'freedom' in that sense, and whilst seeing all participants as equal, it places limited significance on consent. Fourth, classic liberalism rejects the idea of external moral values, seeing the social world as composed of competing opinions. The processual interplay of this market for opinions leads to the 'truth' in a practical sense. From a contemporary perspective, classic liberalism is often attributed in economic terms to the eighteenth-century economist Adam Smith although this has also produced a vigorous debate as to what extent Smith's original arguments concerning liberal free markets do or do not align with neo-liberalist thought.

Contemporary neo-liberalism retains many aspects of these philosophical viewpoints. In essence, it encapsulates the ideological perspective which dominates contemporary **economic globalization** through the remaining **Bretton Woods institutions**. In a historical sense, the election of Reagan and Thatcher in the US and UK respectively during the early 1980s marked the ascendancy of neo-liberal ideas in domestic politics. Both governments implemented typical neo-liberal policies: for example, deregulation of capital movements, privatization of state-owned industries and withdrawal of state intervention in society. Through the 1980s and 1990s, the **International Monetary Fund** and **World Bank** adopted a similar ideological stance in their approach to encouraging economic growth in developing countries. Loans and **aid** were often offered on the condition of 'opening up' national economies to global markets and global flows of investment in conjunction with privatization programmes. This has led some commentators from the **anti-globalization movement** to argue that contemporary **economic globalization** is nothing more than a value-neutral shield concept behind which to hide a deeply politicized political project (neo-liberalism).

Further reading
Chomsky, N. *Profits over people: Neoliberalism and the Global Order* (New York: Seven Stories Press, 1998)
Harvey, D. *A Brief History of Neoliberalism* (Oxford: Oxford University Press, 2005)

NEW WORLD ORDER

The term referring to dramatic changes in the balance of power in the international sphere. The term was first widely used by US President Woodrow Wilson in the period just after the **First World War**, with particular reference to the formation of the **League of Nations**. It was suggested that the First World War, as the 'war to end all wars' between the so-called Great Powers, had been a powerful catalyst in international politics and that the world would not be able to operate as it once had. The term fell from usage with the failures and subsequent collapse of the League and was used very little after the **Second World War** during the formation of the **United Nations**. During the 1970s and 1980s, UN agencies began again to refer to the 'new international economic order' in relation to aims around redistributing wealth to less-developed countries. However, in the context of the contemporary **globalization** debate the term has been redeployed by a range of commentators since the end of the **Cold War**. In the early 1990s, US President George H. W. Bush suggested that a new world order was emerging with the collapse of communism and that order would see a new era of unprecedented international cooperation through the United Nations. The post-Cold War world order saw the US as the only remaining superpower and a shift in alignments between **nation-states**. For example, the extension of the **North Atlantic Treaty Organization** pact to regions in Eastern Europe, former communist states seeking to join the **European Union** and the growth of regional trading blocs in Latin America, Africa and Asia fall within the scope of this shift.

Yet events in recent years, coupled with the developing nature of globalization, have shifted conceptions of a new world order from the positive perspective of the early 1990s. In the aftermath of **9/11**, the US is argued by many to have adopted a more unilateralist approach to foreign policy and the Bush administration has been highly critical of the UN as a forum for effective **global governance**. Critics of neo-liberal **economic globalization** (for example, George **Monbiot**) have also recruited the term in a negative light to characterize the dominatory nature of key groups and ideologies within contemporary economic globalization that include transnational firms, global financial markets and the global business elite. This use of the term under contemporary globalization shifts its meaning into a postnational theorization where the emerging new world order is heavily criticized for its lack of democratic accountability and dogmatic adherence to market ideologies. Thus, in the current globalization debate, the precise nature of the new world order has become a key focus for the debate about the nature of power and control in the increasingly interconnected twenty-first-century world.

Further reading
Two contrasting positions:
Kagan, R. *Paradise and Power: America and Europe in the New World Order* (New York: Atlantic, 2004)
Monbiot, G. *The Age of Consent: A Manifesto for a New World Order* (London: Perennial, 2004)

NORTH AMERICAN FREE TRADE AGREEMENT (NAFTA)

An agreement that came into force on 1 January 1994, the stated aim of which was to promote greater levels of trade, and thus **economic growth**, between the three signatories: the US, Mexico and Canada. NAFTA represents another supranational pillar of contemporary neo-liberal **globalization** which is founded firmly in **free trade** theory. The agreement itself follows the ideological underpinnings of the GATT-**World Trade Organization** approach in that it reduced tariffs and other barriers to goods and services between the three signatory countries whilst seeking to provide consistent and transparent rules for the trading environment. Importantly, the agreement also places great emphasis on the provision of a stable regional basis for investment between signatory states. It does also in principle enshrine a commitment to sustainable **development**, employment growth and the protection of workers' rights. However, from the outset critiques from the Left argued that the agreement would not produce even economic development, would not necessarily boost employment in the US and Canada or lift Mexico out of its less-developed economic status.

Politically therefore, NAFTA has been and continues to remain controversial. The Zapatista uprising in the poor southern Mexican state of Chiapas was timed to coincide with the agreement's implementation, with the negative economic impacts that NAFTA would have on the large number of poor smallholder farmers being a key impetus. The **Zapatistas** argued that NAFTA was an unfair agreement which would increase wealth inequalities and which exemplified the way that the agreement's neo-liberalist ideology favoured vested corporate interests.

Theorists of globalization have interpreted the agreement differently in the context of wider **economic globalization**. It has been taken, along with other trading blocs, as evidence of growing regionalization rather than globalization of economic activity. However, others such as David **Held** and his co-authors and Manuel **Castells** argue, on the basis of studies of interregional trade, that trade regionalization is complementary to and has grown alongside interregional trade.

Academic critics from a variety of disciplines have to a large extent supported the critical voices. After ten years of NAFTA opponents argue that it has failed to achieve its stated beneficial objectives of job creation and increased economic prosperity. Instead, they cite a race-to-the-bottom in wages, job losses in the US and a driving-down of environmental standards. Some academic commentators support the claims of the **anti-globalization movement** to a degree in arguing that NAFTA has served the interests of large corporations at the expense of small firms and individuals. However, as with wider arguments about the underpinnings of the WTO free trade agenda, it is difficult to make strong overall claims as to whether the agreement has been successful or not (in GDP terms at least) because of the lack of possible measurements of the counter-factual regional economy without NAFTA. It is certainly true that NAFTA represents only one distinct interpretation of free trade ideology and the last decades have seen other developing countries in the Americas seeking to form different types of trading agreements, such as the Central American Free Trade Area (CAFTA) and the Free Trade Area of the Americas (FTAA) in the Caribbean. Many see these agreements as fairer, more socially progressive and better for the long-term benefit of the populations in LDCs.

Further reading
Smith, P. and Chambers, E. (eds) *NAFTA in the New Millennium* (Alberta: University of Alberta Press, 2002)

NORTH ATLANTIC TREATY ORGANIZATION (NATO)

An organization established under the North Atlantic Treaty in 1949 by Belgium, Canada, Denmark, France, Great Britain, Iceland, Italy, Luxembourg, the Netherlands, Norway, Portugal and the US. Greece and Turkey entered the alliance in 1952, with West Germany (now Germany) entering in 1955 and Spain in 1982. After the end of the **Cold War**, a number of former communist states of Eastern Europe also sought membership. In 1999 the Czech Republic, Hungary and Poland joined, with Bulgaria, Estonia, Latvia, Lithuania, Romania, Slovakia and Slovenia following in 2004. This brings the current membership to twenty-six. NATO has its headquarters in Brussels, Belgium.

The NATO treaty represented one of the major Western counter-measures against the threat of aggression by the Soviet Union during the Cold War and its key aim was to safeguard the freedom of the North Atlantic community. Considering an armed attack on any member an attack against all, the treaty provided for collective self-defence in accordance with Article 51 of the **United Nations** Charter. The treaty was also designed to encourage political, economic and social cooperation.

Since the early 1990s, with the collapse of the Soviet Union and the Warsaw Treaty Organization, NATO's role in world affairs has changed, and former heavy deployments of US forces in Europe have been substantially reduced. Many Eastern European nations initially sought NATO membership as a counterbalance to Russian power. They were first offered membership along with Russia in the more limited Partnership for Peace (1994). The Partnership engages in joint military exercises with NATO. NATO is not required to defend Partnership for Peace nations from attack. In 2002 NATO and Russia established the NATO–Russia Council, through which Russia participates in NATO discussions on many non-defence issues.

NATO's post-Cold War role has increasingly concentrated on extending security and stability throughout Europe, and on peace-keeping efforts in Europe and elsewhere. NATO air forces were used under UN auspices in punitive attacks on Serb forces in Bosnia in 1994 and 1995, and the alliance's forces were subsequently used for peace-keeping operations in Bosnia. NATO again launched air attacks in 1999, this time on Yugoslavia (now Serbia and Montenegro) in the aftermath of the breakdown in negotiations over Kosovo. In 2003 NATO forces also assumed command of the international security force in the Kabul area in Afghanistan.

However, NATO's future remains unclear. The membership of many NATO nations in the increasingly integrated **European Union** has led to tensions within NATO between the US and those EU nations, particularly France and Germany, who want to develop an EU defence force, which necessarily would not include non-EU members of NATO.

Further reading

Sloan, S. *NATO, the European Union, and the Atlantic Community: The Transatlantic Bargain Challenged* (London: Rowman & Littlefield Publishers, 2005). Also see the organization's website: <http://www.nato.int/>.

OECD *see* Organization for Economic Cooperation and Development.

OHMAE, KENICHI

Coming from a business and management background, Ohmae's major early contribution to the **globalization** debate was *The Borderless World* (1990) where he presented what David **Held** and his co-authors termed a hyperglobalist world where **nation-state**s became less relevant and **global corporation**s, technological change and information flows were the bedrock of global integration that was transforming the globe for the better. During the 1990s he elaborated this positive, if not utopian, thesis in *The End of the Nation State* (1996). Here he contended that nation-states had become obsolete and that five 'great forces' – communication, corporation, customers, capital and currencies – have usurped the economic power once held by them. Ohmae continues to be a major proponent of the potential benefits of contemporary forms of **economic globalization**. In *The Next Global Stage* (2005) he makes the case that regardless of whether individuals, states and firms like it or not, they must increasingly act on a global stage. In this sense, he is one of the key proponents of the positive effect that the developing global economy can have, although critics argue he presents a blinkered and idealistic view of the activities of **transnational corporations**.

Further reading
Ohmae, K. 'The End of the Nation State', ch. 26 in Lechner, F. and Boli, J. (eds) *The Globalization Reader* (2nd edn; Oxford: Blackwell, 2004)

ORGANIZATION FOR ECONOMIC COOPERATION AND DEVELOPMENT (OECD)

An international organization of thirty full member states, founded in 1961. Most of these states correspond to the wealthier countries of the **global North** and their pledge through the OECD is to work together to promote their economies, to extend **aid** to less developed nations and to contribute to the expansion of world trade. The OECD superseded the Organization for European Economic Cooperation which was set up in 1948 to coordinate the Marshall Plan for European economic recovery following the **Second World War**.

As an international organization of these richer developed countries, the OECD has played an important role in furthering the emergence of contemporary **economic globalization**. In particular, in recent decades it has kept up the pressure to reduce trade restrictions and to liberalize the international **foreign direct investment** (FDI) regime. Membership of the OECD requires governments to abide by explicit codes and standards with respect to foreign investments which involve according 'national treatment to international investors' and enacting 'transparent, liberal and stable foreign investment rules'. The OECD was also an important source of pressure for the **Multilateral Agreement on Investment** in the late 1990s as it sought greater harmony and transparency in FDI and its regulation. The role of the OECD has recently also come in for greater criticism from the **anti-globalization movement** and less-developed nations, in particular for failing to practise what it preaches in terms of transparency and for protecting the interests of its members to the cost of the **global South**.

Further reading
See the organization's website: <www.oecd.org>.

ORGANIZATION FOR SECURITY AND COOPERATION IN EUROPE (OSCE)

An international organization established as the Conference on Security and Cooperation in Europe (CSCE) in 1973, with the aim of promoting East–West cooperation in the context of the **Cold War**. Its headquarters are in Prague in the Czech Republic. The OSCE's best-known action was at a 1975 meeting in Helsinki, Finland, where acts, commonly known as the Helsinki Accords, were ratified. The accords were signed by every European nation (except Albania, which did so later), the US and Canada. The OSCE is responsible for reviewing the implementation of those accords. Since the end of the Cold War, it has also aimed to foster peace, prosperity and justice in Europe. There are now 55 OSCE members, including all European nations, all former republics of the Soviet Union, along with the US and Canada.

Further reading
See the organization's website: <http://www.osce.org/>.

ORGANIZATIONAL GLOBALIZATION

The concept of the internal processes of change occurring within organizations which are leading to their greater extensiveness at the planetary scale. The term has most commonly been applied to **transnational corporation**s, although it could also be relevant to political, civil society or other organizations that are restructuring themselves. The processes that organizational globalization refer to are associated with a transformation of organizational form and structures that create a new arrangement of responsibilities and collective practices. In general this often is associated within TNCs with a shift from a territorially based form of the organization towards a functionally based one. Thus, **multinational corporation**s have historically organized themselves to manage business activity within discrete geographical areas: districts, sub-national regions, **nation-state**s and supranational regions. In that sense, senior managers and decision-makers held strategic responsibility and control functions over geographical territories. Organizational globalization entails a shift towards these responsibilities and functions being coordinated at the global scale with, for example, divisions and key positions referring to functions rather than territorial spaces.

However, the term can be taken at a more general level to refer to any change in organizational form which leads to greater cross-border extensiveness. Most TNCs have undertaken such a strategy in order to enhance competitiveness and profitability as they enter new markets and extend their operations to more and more countries. The way in which a specific organization seeks to carry out organizational globalization is highly variable and there is no one model for understanding the effectiveness of different strategies geared to generating greater 'organizational globality'.

Further reading
Kristensen, P. and Zeitlin, J. 'The Making of a Global Firm', ch. 9 in Morgan, G., Kristensen, P. and Whitley, R. (eds) *The Multinational Firm: Organizing across Institutional and National Divides* (Oxford: Oxford University Press, 2001)

OSCE *see* Organization for Security and Cooperation in Europe.

POLITICAL GLOBALIZATION
In one sense, the closer integration and interrelatedness that is developing between governmental and other political organizations. In many ways it has become the core interest of International Relations as a subject discipline and much of the existing literature focuses on contemporary transformations to the **nation-state** and the nation-state system at the global scale. However, the sub-concept is also used to refer to new forms of political interaction beyond the organizational scales of states and suprastate bodies. In that sense, the literature on new social movements (NSMs), grassroots politics and **global civil society** also engages with another dimension of political globalization.

With regard to the nation-state, Jan **Scholte** argues that contemporary political globalization is most strongly characterized by the radical transformation the contemporary period of intensified **globalization** has produced in states and their nature. Current political globalization in this theoretical story is primarily the processes that have produced the breakdown of the so-called **Westphalian model**. Named after the Peace of Westphalia of 1648, the Westphalian model was primarily a description of a world divided up territorially between sovereign nation-states which interacted with each other in an 'international system'. Each state was solely responsible for and governed its parcel of territory. Many commentators see the key dynamic of contemporary political globalization as being the multiple dimensions to the breakdown and/or dissolution of this world order. Whilst the institutional apparatus of states survives (and in fact is larger, stronger and more intrusive than ever before), the core principle of Westphalian territorial **sovereignty** is no longer operative. Political globalization has in this sense removed the ability of national governments to effect changes in their nominally sovereign territories. Contemporary states are unable by themselves to control (or conversely to exist) without global companies, trade, finance, security arrangements and so on.

Political globalization as a concept therefore applies to the multitude of actors and processes which are bound into these new forms of interconnectedness. Scholte offers a fourfold framework for theorizing the nature of what he terms post-sovereign governance in the contemporary era. First, political globalization has a substate level as a considerable growth in links has developed between substate authorities which bypasses national governments. Second, globalization has led to a shift in governance upwards to suprastate organizations. Whilst permanent multilateral institutions have been around since early in the twentieth century, their number, size and influence have increased dramatically. Third, Scholte argues that another dimension of political globalization is the development of **global governance** functions by market institutions. Fourth, the role of the non-governmental political globalization has also led to the development of a global civil society sector spanning non-formal political actors which as, often small organizations, have developed highly extensive global-scale linkages. Whilst useful, however, this typology also serves to emphasize how political globalization, as with other sub-concepts in the lexicon of globalization, is blurred across the economic, cultural or other forms of globalization.

Further reading
Baylis, J. and Smith, S. (eds) *The Globalization of World Politics* (Oxford: Oxford University Press, 2001) [esp. Introduction]
Scholte, J. *Globalization: A Critical Introduction* (Basingstoke: Palgrave Macmillan, 2000)

POP MUSIC

Either an abbreviation of the wider category of popular music, or a sub-genre of it. It is the sub-genre that has received most attention and can arguably be defined in a broad sense by the presence of a hook (catchy melody) and a fashionable music production technique. The key issue in relation to the **globalization** debate is the development of pop music as a global-scale cultural phenomenon. Contemporary pop music increasingly draws on a wide variety of musical traditions that originated in different geographical regions but which have become hybridized. Commercial pop music is also now marketed worldwide and retailed through the placeless global spaces of shopping malls and airports. In that sense it is often cited as a notable example of the interrelationship between economic and **cultural globalization** processes.

Further reading
Frith, S. 'Pop Music', ch. 4 in Frith, S., Straw, W. and Street, J. (eds) *The Cambridge Companion to Pop and Rock* (Cambridge: Cambridge University Press, 2004)

PROTECTIONISM
An economic policy of promoting favoured domestic industries through the use of high tariffs and other regulations to discourage imports. A number of historical variants of this policy have included mercantilism, where trade policy is aimed at maximizing currency reserves by running large trade surpluses, and also import substitution where targeted imports are replaced by local manufactures in order to stimulate local production. Protectionism was a national economic policy approach widely adopted by more developed countries in the early decades of the twentieth century as they attempted to shield domestic industries from overseas competition. Many commentators argue that it was an important factor in exacerbating the severity of the Depression in the 1930s, with tariff measures such as the Hawley-Smoot Tariff Act (1930) in the US further stifling investment and undermining business confidence.

The post-**Second World War** period has been dominated by international attempts severely to limit national protectionism and to free up global trade. The GATT negotiations, now continued through the **World Trade Organization**, aimed to remove tariff barriers and open up domestic markets to international competition. Despite this, many countries still maintain tariff barriers to protect some industries, and the elimination of such barriers remains a contentious political and diplomatic issue. In recent rounds of trade negotiations from the 1980s, questions of protectionism have moved beyond primary commodities and manufactures to services. In the current **Doha Development Round**, critics of contemporary **economic globalization** have also sought to counter what they argue is a dogmatic adherence to anti-protectionism that has in fact tended to favour more developed countries. Less developed countries point, for example, to the continued protection Europe and the US give to their agricultural industries, which is the sector where less developed nations have most to gain from freer trade.

Further reading
See Jagdish Bhagwati's definition online: <http://www.econlib.org/library/ Enc/Protectionism.html>.

REFUGEES
People who flee (or in some cases are expelled) from their home country or country of their nationality to escape real or imagined danger and are unwilling or unable to return. Refugees are often seeking to escape war or punishment for their political affiliations. Early examples of mass dislocations include the expulsion of the Jews and the Moors from Spain in the fifteenth century, the flights from religious persecutions in Europe to the New World in the sixteenth and seventeenth centuries and the exodus of the émigrés in the French Revolution. Before the twentieth century there was little or no systematic attempt to help refugees, although some groups did offer help on a private basis. The problem of refugees has become more acute since the beginning of the twentieth century as a consequence of global integration. With warfare shifting to the global scale, and greater access to mass transportation, more and more people have become refugees over the last century. In the aftermath of the **First World War**, a number of international organizations were founded to assist refugees. During the 1930s, Hitler's accession to power in Germany (1933), his annexation of Austria (1938) and Czechoslovakia (1939) and the persecution of Jews led to significant movements of refugees. The Republican defeat in Spain (1939) and anti-Semitic legislation in Eastern Europe added to the overall problem. Many asylum governments attempted

to return refugees to their country of origin and they were often forbidden to work and sometimes imprisoned. Some progress was achieved with the establishment of a permanent committee for refugees in London after a conference of thirty-two nations held in France in 1938.

The **Second World War** created unprecedented numbers of refugees and in its aftermath the **United Nations** took on a leading responsibility for the estimated eight million displaced people with the formation of the UN Relief and Rehabilitation Administration (UNRRA), later the International Refugee Organization. In the latter part of the twentieth century, the numbers of refugees continued to grow with major contributory events including the Partition of India (1947), the Arab–Israeli War (1967) and the Vietnam and Cambodian civil wars. Africa has continued to experience mass movements of refugees in recent decades through wars, poverty and famine. By the 1990s there were close to seven million refugees in Africa, including 4.5 million displaced Sudanese. The break-up of the former Yugoslavia also displaced more than one million people in Eastern Europe in the late 1990s. The world's international refugee population was estimated to be about sixteen million by 1999. Many governments continue to refuse asylum to refugees and the hardships that refugees endure have devastating effects on the well-being of both individual refugees and nation-states.

Further reading
Ouseley, H., Kushner, A. and Knox, K. *Refugees in an Age of Genocide: Global, National and Local Perspectives during the Twentieth Century* (London: Frank Cass, 1999)

RELIGION
A phenomenon whose relationship to the **globalization** debate is becoming increasingly complex. Initial engagements with the concept of religion focused on the rise of religious fundamentalism as a localized response to the processes of globalization. For example, Peter Beyer distinguishes between religious movements that defend sociocultural particularism and those that support the change towards a pluralistic world order in which different traditions coexist. Conservative anti-systemic movements, such as Islamic fundamentalism, react against global trends that threaten old identities.

Whilst their desired public impact remains limited and localized, liberal movements such as religious environmentalism, by contrast, aim to infuse world culture itself with ultimate meaning. They may contribute resources for dealing with residual problems that secular systems cannot address. In the context of contemporary globalization processes this suggests that religious actors and beliefs will be more prominent in discourse about the globe than in institutions shaping actual global relations. A number of commentators thus concurred with Beyer that various contending versions of a global civil religion will develop in contrast to traditional religions which are conceptualized primarily as cultures that serve individuals.

However, as the globalization debate has developed, religion has become an increasingly central topic in theorizations of cultural and **political globalization** more generally. At least four areas can be identified where religion intersects with the concept of globalization in more than just the terms of a response by cultural groups in given areas. First, the rise of global consciousness, as a dimension of globalization, is novel and is bound into the development of religions. Many religions have been naturally expansive from a historical perspective and are thus bound into the development of a wider global consciousness. Second, religion is a prime medium and example of the development of cultural heterogeneity or **'glocalization'** as Roland Robertson terms it. Third, globalization fundamentally alters religious power relationships in organizational and scholarly terms. Pentecostals in Africa and Brazil share resources with those in the US. The fate of the Anglican Church in the UK lies with its African majority. Fourth, globalization highlights 'religious' processes that extend far beyond church life. For example, one can analyse **human rights** in light of the Durkheimian notion that religion gives us a symbolic meaning to social life.

Overall, Frank Lechner argues that in the study of religion, globalization has come to indicate both a set of substantive issues and a change in perspective. The issues concern the historical role of religious values and institutions in fostering a new **global system**, the actual religious content of the current debates about world order, and the future role of religiously inspired actors as significant players in globalization. He further argues that the change in perspective also entails a new way of thinking about religion because it questions notions of secularization as something that affects individual societies. Furthermore, it also leads to a realization that apparently localized, ethnocentric religious conservatives are also engaged in a global discourse and that attempts to link religion to a cohesive national culture bolsters solidarity. Recent examples include the diversification of different strands of Islamic fundamentalism into global religious-based political causes. The rhetoric of Osama Bin Laden and other Islamic militants increasingly makes references to and seeks to generate a global-scale religious cause that not only pits its values against specific nation-states, but also against the hegemonic notion of the secular modern state. Similarly, the imaginations of identity that Hindu nationalists in India seek to develop are referenced through global-scale conceptions of identity and the global situation of religious groups.

Further reading

Beyer, P. *Religion and Globalization* (London: Sage, 1994)

Lechner, F. 'Global Fundamentalism', ch. 41 in Lechner, F. and Boli, J. (eds) *The Globalization Reader* (Oxford: Blackwell, 2004)

RITZER, GEORGE

The proponent of the **McDonaldization** thesis, Ritzer is an American sociologist who famously developed Max Weber's arguments about the rationalization of bureaucracies and applied it to contemporary American and global society. More recently, he has extended the remit of his argument to **globalization**. In *The Globalization of Nothing* he in effect develops a theoretical perspective on the relationship of global capitalism and its associated forms of consumption to the wider phenomenon of globalization. By 'nothing' he identifies four forms that are characteristic in contemporary globalization: non-places (shopping malls, Las Vegas casinos), non-things (global branded goods), non-people (low-skilled workers in fast food, telemarketing) and non-services (ATMs, **Internet** retailing). He identifies a variety of ways in which these non-forms are proliferating around the world as a consequence of globalization.

Further reading

Ritzer, G. *The Globalization of Nothing* (London: Sage, 2004) [esp. chs 4, 5 and 7]

ROBINS, KEVIN

A British cultural geographer, Robins has contributed to debates around **globalization** that focus on the impact of greater global inter-connectedness on identity, in particular in relation to the development of new forms of global media. Writing with David **Morley** in the mid-1990s, Robins argues that the development and restructuring of global media are leading to a crisis identity that is ramifying into and undermining national cultures in complex ways. More recently, his attention has turned to the 'encounters' that globalization produces between cultures. He argues that whilst many have highlighted how globalization produces 'third cultures' or 'the creolization of global culture' through a creative process of hybridization, it also produces tension and collision. He sees the impact of globalization on our apprehension of the world as transformative in sharply contrasting ways. For Robins, particular cultures and identities are being revalidated in ways that 'provoke new senses of orientation and disorientation' that give rise to 'new experiences of both placeless and placed identity'. The effect of this is to call into question old certainties and existing hierarchies of identity. He suggests that **cultural globalization** can thus be understood in at least three important ways. First, it is as a process whereby the frontiers and divisions between different cultures are dissolved. Second, is the way in which cultural globalization promotes cultural encounter and interaction. Cultures are transformed by the incorporations they make from the other cultures in the world. Third, the contradictory nature of a rejection of cultural globalization and its encounters in a reassertion of traditional or fundamental values. Robins argues that closures from global culture are themselves an expression of globalization as these identities seek to position and assert their distinctiveness in a new global space.

Further reading
Robins, K. 'Encountering Globalization', ch. 20 in Held, D. and McGrew, A. (eds) *The Global Transformations Reader* (Cambridge: Polity, 2000)

RODRIK, DANI

A prolific contributor to debates on global economic integration, Rodrik is a professor of International Relations at Harvard who has made sustained arguments questioning the aggregate benefits of neo-liberal **economic globalization**. In *Has Globalization Gone too*

Far? (1997), he argues that the most serious challenge for the world economy in the years ahead lies in making **globalization** compatible with domestic social and political stability. He suggests there is a serious risk that international economic integration will contribute to domestic social disintegration. Rodrik points to three sources of tension between globalization and society: the growing power imbalance between unskilled workers and owners of capital or high skills, the intensifying conflict between different domestic norms and institutions in the international setting and the declining ability of governments to provide social insurance for their citizens. All of these factors, he argues, could lead to social disintegration. However, he argues that disintegration can be avoided if both advocates and adversaries of globalization are more realistic and less dogmatic and labour organizations acknowledge that trade has both benefits and consequences, thus toning down protectionist rhetoric. He also suggests that a huge role must be played by national governments who must continue to promote social insurance.

Rodrik's earlier contributions were largely focused on the US and the effects of globalization on the developed North, with an emphasis on the US. More recently, however, he has turned his attention to the plight of developing countries. He has argued that there is a need to make 'globalization's rules friendlier to poor nations' but that this is difficult whilst leaders of the advanced countries continue to 'dress up' policies championed by special interests at home as responses to the needs of the poor in the developing world. He thus adopts a largely pragmatic view of how globalization needs to evolve to prevent the creation of social fissures. This entails the need for the developed world to provide room for poor nations to develop their own strategies of institution-building and economic catch-up. Part of the onus, he suggests, also is on developing nations, who will have to stop looking to financial markets and multilateral agencies for the recipes of **economic growth**.

Further reading
Rodrik, D. *Has Globalization Gone too Far?* (New York: The Institute for International Economics, 1997)

ROSENAU, JAMES
An international relations theorist and political scientist, Rosenau's main contributions to the **globalization** debate have centred on issues

of **global governance** and more recently the role of the individual in the growing complexity of global relationships. With regard to global politics and governance, Rosenau has argued at length that contemporary globalization has produced 'governance without government'. At the international scale, **nation-state**s represent only one 'channel of control'. The emerging form of global governance therefore has literally millions of control mechanisms driven by different histories, goals, structures and processes. World politics has always been anarchic, and global governance is therefore an outcome of many actors who are constantly evolving. The important point is that governance is taking place despite the fact it cannot be attributed to a single actor or a small group. He does acknowledge, however, that **political globalization** is producing 'an upsurge in the collective capacity to govern'. This will never produce a single coherent government order, but rather a continuous dynamic of new governmental forms.

In his book *Distant Proximities* (2003), Rosenau argues that the phenomenon of globalization has 'outgrown' the concept of it. He argues that the concept has become 'insufficient' to organize understanding of world affairs. This is not based on the same arguments of earlier critics who suggested globalization had become merely a buzzword or was based on vague assertions. From Rosenau's perspective, existing globalization theories do offer a series of empirically grounded processes and structures. Rather his proposition is that the dynamics and wider consequences of these currently identified processes require a much more nuanced set of theories. His argument is that beyond globalization as a concept are a set of conceptual tools that supplement the existing analytic tools used to probe globalization and can add considerable insight into the state of the world in the twenty-first century. In essence, the main approach he advocates appears to be an (almost dialectical) analysis of an endless series of distant proximities where the forces pressing for greater globalization interactively play themselves out. The rise of these distant proximities distinguished the current epoch and leads Rosenau to propose a new concept, 'fragmegration', to capture the 'nature, processes and structure' of the dynamics of distant proximities at every level of the community. In particular, this aims to shift theorization onto the scale of individuals.

These kinds of arguments echo theorists such as Doreen **Massey** in the geographical literature, discussing distance, proximity and the relationships of different scales in theorizing globalization, and Rosenau's work is undoubtedly important in both developing these ideas and pushing this kind of conceptual discussion into political science. However, a number of critical questions can be identified in the context of the wider debate. First, to what extent does Rosenau's conceptual approach really transcend the existing analytical tools? It can be argued that many of his concepts and his polarities are primarily based around those already identified in the debate (coherence–incoherence, integration–disintegration etc.). Second, and following on, it is questionable as to what extent these polarized dualisms are effective in capturing the complexity of greater societal integration. If scalar dualism (global–local) has been criticized in the literature to an increasing extent, then whether Rosenau's list of polarizations adds anything new is questionable. Third, his arguments about how distinctive an epochal shift 'frag-megration' represents are vulnerable. Whilst he convincingly illustrates the increasing complexity of global relationships, the degree to which these define the current era as distinct requires further exploration.

Further reading

Rosenau, J. *Along the Domestic–Foreign Frontier: Exploring Governance in a Turbulent World* (Cambridge: Cambridge University Press, 1997)

Rosenau, J. and Singh, J. (eds) *Information Technologies and Global Politics: The Changing Scope of Power and Governance* (New York: State University of New York Press, 2002)

Rosenau, J. *Distant Proximities: Dynamics beyond Globalization* (Princeton, N.J.: Princeton University Press, 2003)

ROSENBERG, JUSTIN

An international relations theorist, Rosenberg's major contribution is to philosophical and theoretical understandings of globalization. His book *The Follies of Globalisation Theory* (2001) engages with the developing theoretical frameworks for understanding globalization that emerged during the 1990s. Notably, he engages in depth with the epistemological basis for globalization theories developed by Jan **Scholte** and Anthony **Giddens**. His main argument is that 'the very idea of globalization as an explanatory schema in its own right is fraught with difficulties' because the term is, at first sight, simply 'a descriptive category'. His argument is that globalization theory is itself thus contradictory because 'globalisation as an outcome cannot be explained simply by invoking globalisation as a process tending towards this outcome.'

Rosenberg's critique of globalization theory in general centres on three key issues. First, he argues that it jettisons a vital resource for understanding exactly the spatio-temporal phenomenon it deems so significant – namely, seeking to move beyond the classical social theory of Karl **Marx** and Max Weber – and ends up fetishizing spatial categories over all others. Second, he suggests that globalization theory conflates the general issue of relations between societies with a specific historical form of those relations caricatured as the Westphalian system. Third, he sees globalization as an obstacle rather than an aid to producing what is needed in international relations theory: 'a genuinely social theory of the international system'. For Rosenberg then, 'globalization theory' is a deeply problematic theoretical edifice that is full of contradictions and is built upon precarious foundations in terms of existing social theory. His contribution thus represents an important 'brake' on the headlong propulsion of globalization to the centre of contemporary social theories.

Further reading
Rosenberg, J. 'Introduction: The Problem of Globalisation Theory', ch. 1 in *The Follies of Globalisation Theory* (London: Verso, 2001)

ROY, ARUNDHATI

Indian writer and winner of the 1997 Booker Prize for Fiction for her novel *The God of Small Things*, Roy has subsequently campaigned and written extensively against corporate **globalization**. The novel itself explores themes prevalent in debates about **cultural globalization** in its story of a family's history between several continents and the way that individual cultural identity and experience are shaped by global interconnectedness. As a critic of **transnational corporations**, Roy has argued that the US's wars in Afghanistan and Iraq are clearly motivated by and linked to its economic interests and supports this by pointing to the links between specific corporations, the US government and business interests across the Middle East. She has also been a vocal critic of the view that global economic **development** is leading to a reduction in poverty. She points to the growing disparity between rich and poor, citing the 1990s 2.5 per cent ten-year growth in global GDP against the increase of 100 million people living in poverty. She argues that 'free market' neo-liberal policies are brazenly protecting Western markets and have historically been used to force developing countries to lift their trade barriers, thus reinforcing the ongoing process by which the poor are getting poorer and the rich richer. She has also argued that this non-transparent, unjust and greed-driven emergent global economic system is doomed to failure in the twenty-first century because it will inevitably produce greater and greater resistance as a very small global elite gains more and more power. Overall, whilst important in highlighting the (many) failings of corporate globalization, Roy's contribution is one that sees TNCs as almost entirely a negative force in contemporary global development and, as such, it is vulnerable to criticism that it presents a selective, one-sided and simplistic representation of the impacts of corporate activity. As with other critics, the strong rhetoric presents a view of a highly coherent (almost conspiratorial) world where corporations, states, supranational institutions and the media all act to the detriment of the (poor) majority. Such a position implies a degree of global coherence and consistency that has to be questionable.

Further reading
Roy, A. *An Ordinary Person's Guide to Empire* (Cambridge, Mass.: South End Press, 2004)

RUGMAN, ALAN

Writing from a business and management perspective, Rugman has argued that broadly defined **economic globalization** is a myth and that its meaning for business was misrepresented during the 1990s. His main critical argument is to point to the strong continuation of regional patterns of productive and marketing activity amongst **transnational corporation**s and the influence of regional economic trading blocs on that pattern. He emphasizes the role of the trading bloc triad (broadly the **European Union**, the **North American Free Trade Agreement** and the **Association of South-East Asian Nations**) but his analysis assumes a rather narrow definition of **globalization** that does not take account of the wider societal integration processes with which the concept is associated.

Further reading
Rugman, A. 'Introduction', in *The End of Globalization* (London: Random House, 2001)

Sassen, Saskia

A professor of Urban Planning at Chicago and also at the London School of Economics, Sassen is important to the **globalization** debate around two major threads. First, her book *The Global City* (2nd edn, 2001) outlined a series of important theoretical arguments about the development of a global-scale urban system. Sassen originally proposed that three cities had emerged by the early 1990s as key nodes in the global economy: London, New York and Tokyo. As a consequence of ongoing economic globalization and technological development in information and communications, she argues that these cities have taken on distinctive new functions as centres of command and control, as global market centres and as the prime locations for new advanced service industries. Her work has also been equally interested in the impact of these changes on the physical built environment and social form of cities. By the second edition of her book, Sassen had revised the concept of the global city to encompass increasingly the degree to which all cities around the globe are taking on aspects of these functions in a globalized network. Second, her work has also addressed the issue of **transnationalism**, transborderness, **denationalization** and the global movements of people. In that sense, Sassen's more recent ideas have been concerned with the impact of globalization on political organization as well as identity, community and social groups. In particular, she has argued that understandings of what have been conceived as national, supranational and subnational institutions and organizations need rethinking.

Further reading
Sassen, S. 'Overview', ch. 1 in *The Global City* (2nd edn; Princeton: Princeton University Press, 2001)

Scholte, Jan

Writing from the perspective of international relations, Scholte has made a series of important conceptual and critical contributions to understandings of **globalization** and to **globalization theory**. In *Globalization: A Critical Introduction* (2nd edn, 2005), Scholte argues that earlier stages of the globalization debate produced five general conceptions: globalization as internationalization, as liberalization, as universalization, as westernization and as **deterritorialization**. He argues that the first four have become largely redundant and that it is as a process of deterritorialization that the concept is historically distinctive in the contemporary era. For Scholte, therefore, globalization is a phenomenon in the world that is characterized by deterritorializing processes. He calls these processes different things in various spheres of human life: the 'global', 'supraterritorial', 'transworld' or 'transborder' social spaces. The dynamics of 'globalization' thus involve several of the core forces of modern social life: rationalist knowledge, capitalist production, automated technology and bureaucratic governance. In this context, Scholte goes on to argue that contemporary globalization has propelled several important shifts in primary social structures. The growth of supraterritorial spaces has encouraged the emergence of new forms of capitalist production, multilayered and more diffuse governance, greater pluralism in the construction of the community and an increased questioning of rationalist knowledge. Globalization is thus producing 'an intricate interplay of continuity and change in the social order'.

For Scholte this has a series of policy implications. Primarily, it involves the development of an academic critique that has similar threads to the **anti-globalization movement**. Neo-liberal globalization is flawed in Scholte's eyes in so far as it has, to date, increased insecurity, inequality and democratic deficits. He therefore advocates a different kind of globalization because the phenomenon 'is very much what we make it'.

Overall, Scholte offers an impressive critical overview of the globalization debate which he has subsequently updated. However, similar lines of critical engagement are applicable to those that can be applied to other generalist globalization theorists. Namely, that in dealing at the broad systemic level, both the analysis of 'what is happening' and that of 'what can be done' in policy terms conflate a large number of more complex and heavily politicized issues that in reality are hard to understand adequately through such a broad approach. Furthermore, as with theorists such as Anthony **Giddens**, the foundation of globalization as a universally applicable phenomenon grounded in the process of deterritorialization remains potentially problematic.

Further reading
Scholte, J. 'What is "Global" about Globalization?', ch. 4 in Held, D. and McGrew, A. (eds) *The Global Transformations Reader* (Cambridge: Polity, 2000)

SCRUTON, ROGER

A British political philosopher, Scruton has offered theoretical arguments concerning **globalization**, its relationship with **religion** and the emergence of **global terrorism**. He argues that globalization does not merely mean the expansion of communications, contacts and trade around the globe but that it is more importantly defined by 'a transfer of social, economic, political and juridical power to global organisations'. These organizations are not located in a particular sovereign jurisdiction and are governed by no particular territorial law. He sees the growth of these organizations negatively, as a 'regrettable by-product of our addiction to freedom'. Global terror networks are thus a consequence of this process and, in the case of al-Qaeda, of the specific interactions of developing global consciousness and certain interpretations of Muslim theology.

Further reading
Scruton, R. 'Introduction', in *The West and the Rest: Globalization and the Terrorist Threat* (London: Continuum, 2002)

SEATTLE

The city in Washington State, US, where the **World Trade Organization** convened trade negotiations in November 1999. The intention was to launch the new 'millennial round' of international trade negotiations, but the meeting was quickly overshadowed by massive and controversial street protests outside the hotels and convention centre. Seattle was thus the key event heralding the emergence of the so-called '**anti-globalization movement**' in the more developed world. Lower estimates put the crowd at over 40,000 and it may have been over 100,000 at some points. This display of mass protest dwarfed any previous demonstration against leader summits or meetings of the **Bretton Woods institutions**. It became clear in the aftermath that a large number of organizations had been involved in the planning of this demonstration, including NGOs, trade unions, student groups and religious-based groups. The coalition of participants was certainly only loose and many different campaign interests were represented. The main general focus of the protest was that **economic globalization**, as propagated by the WTO, favoured wealthy nations and people at the expense of the poor majority, especially in the developing world. The demonstration itself included direct action by a number of groups to make their point, including the setting up of road blocks and invasions of roads and highways. A number of groups vandalized retail outlets and signs of major **transnational corporations** (for example, **McDonald's** and Nike) and the protest did at times involve violent clashes with riot police. Over 600 people were arrested but few were formally charged and the city authorities in Seattle accepted there had been a considerable degree of 'inappropriate policing' during the event. Seattle set the precedent for subsequent mass protests in Genoa and on May Day around the globe in the following years.

Further reading
Thomas, J. *The Battle in Seattle: The Story Behind and Beyond the WTO Demonstrations* (London: Fulcrum, 2003)

SECOND WORLD WAR
A global armed conflict (1939–45) that involved the majority of the world's countries and every inhabited continent. Virtually all countries that participated in the **First World War** (1914–18) were involved, and it is estimated that around fifty-seven million people died as a result of the war, with the scale of destruction and human suffering having no historical precedent. In that sense, it has been described by historian Eric Hobsbawm as a 'global human catastrophe'. It was certainly the most extensive and expensive armed conflict in the history of the world. The start of the war is debatable. Generally taken as 1 September 1939 in Europe when Germany invaded Poland, historians have also argued that it began earlier in Asia in 1937, with the Japanese invasion of China on 7 July (the start of the Second Sino-Japanese War), or even the 1931 Japanese invasion of Manchuria. A number of commentators have gone further to argue that the two world wars are one conflict separated only by a 'ceasefire'. The causes of the war are complex and still subject to debate but factors commonly mentioned are the terms of the settlement in the Treaty of Versailles (1919), the Great Depression (early 1930s) and the rise of nationalism and militarism. Fighting occurred across the Atlantic Ocean, in Western and Eastern Europe, in the Mediterranean Sea, Africa, the Middle East, in the Pacific and South-East Asia, and it continued in China. In Europe, the war ended with the surrender of Germany on 8 May 1945 (VE Day), but it continued in Asia until Japan surrendered on 15 August 1945 (VJ Day) as a consequence of the nuclear strikes on Hiroshima and Nagasaki by the US.

The Second World War is important in understanding **globalization** both in terms of its global extensiveness and the way in which **nation-state**s became increasingly interwoven in military terms, and also equally in terms of the global-scale geopolitical map and forms of international governance that emerged in its aftermath. The trans-national organization of **war** had never achieved as full or effective an expression as it did during the Second World War (and it was very hard for any nation or society on the globe to remain unaffected). After the war, however, the bipolar **Cold War** world that emerged was also populated by reformed and new supranational institutions (the **United Nations**, the **European Union** and the **Bretton Woods institutions** that have been instrumental in shaping contemporary globalization). In the First World, the role of these supranational institutions in promoting international **free trade** and free markets was very much an important ideological aspect of the arguments that emerged as a consequence of the war concerning how future global-scale conflict could be avoided.

Further reading
Keegan, J. *The Second World War* (London: Penguin, 2005)

SEN, AMARTYA

Nobel prizewinner in Economics and **development** economist, Sen is well known for both his academic and policy contributions to the **globalization** debate. His major contribution has been consistently to criticize the tendency to see globalization as either simply Westernization or Americanization and to conflate the process of market-led **economic globalization** with its outcomes. He argues that globalization is a historical process that has offered 'an abundance of opportunities and rewards in the past and continues to do so'. In that sense, he offers a mid-ground position between the poles of neo-liberal support for and the **anti-globalization movement**'s opposition to contemporary economic globalization. He argues that (economic) globalization has the potential to offer very great benefits and that the key issue is therefore the question of how these benefits can be shared out fairly. In that sense, he sees the central issue of contention as not being globalization (conceived as generalized historical process), nor the use of markets as institutions, but rather the inequity in the balance of institutional arrangements. He is thus a proponent of the urgent need for institutional reform at the supranational and national scale which he sees as the main inhibitors of 'fairness' in distributing the benefits of globalization to the global poor.

Sen has argued in this light that the essential debate around globalization should 'not be ultimately about the efficiency of markets or about technology, but about the inequality of power'. He makes three major points in this respect. First, he suggests that the key problem with contemporary globalization is that 'inequalities are monumental in the world today both in economic affluence and political power'. Globalization is a positive force in terms of human contact and the movement of ideas, knowledge and understanding but it is power inequalities that present the problem. Second, he sees economic globalization as a major source of potential (and often actual) advancement of living conditions but that the circumstances where it produces maximum benefit for the poor do not currently exist. This is not an argument against economic globalization, but for a better division of its benefits. He emphasizes that the success of globalization should not be measured in terms of whether the poor are getting a little richer. Third, he argues that the market economy is just one institution amongst many and that other institutional mechanisms exist for shaping the form of globalization. He therefore argues that information technology, the **Internet** and media can be used positively to create forms of globalization that generate social justice.

Sen's contribution to globalization literature is extensive and cannot be summarized in its totality here. However, his position has inevitably attracted criticism. Three main areas are identifiable. First, commentators from the anti-globalization movement suggest his mid-ground position is idealistic and that he underestimates the power of the vested interests of global capital to maintain the status quo. Second, from a policy perspective his work has been regarded as being limited in terms of prescriptions for change. Third, some have argued he has misrepresented the anti-globalization movement and their goals in tackling market-led economic globalization. Overall, most critics tend to reflect the political viewpoint they are writing from and, in a sense, Sen's middle-ground position is unacceptable to both proponents and opponents of globalization.

Further reading
Sen, A. *Development as Freedom* (Oxford: Oxford University Press, 2001)
Sen, A. 'How to Judge Globalism', *The American Prospect* (2002) 13, 1: Jan 1–14

SHAW, MARTIN

Approaching the **globalization** debate from an international relations perspective, Shaw argues that globality as a concept corresponds to a growing sense of worldwide human commonality as a practical social force that arises from political struggle not technological change. He proposes two main concepts in this context. First is the idea of an unfinished global democratic revolution from the post-**Second World War** period. Until the end of the **Cold War**, democratic revolution was directed against the anti-democratic approach of the communist Second World, but since the end of the Cold War this opposition has disappeared. Yet democratic struggle continues and now has to address non-state or suprastate bodies. Second, and related, is the relationship of the global Western state to this democratic struggle. Shaw sees that the rise of democratic principles is imperfectly captured in contemporary Western states and thus the global state becomes the arena of conflict in which democratic values need to be fought for. In his 'global theory', he therefore represents a key critic of simplistic analyses of the nature of states and the 'national' and 'international' scales in the contemporary era.

Further reading
Shaw, M. 'Introduction: Globality in Historical Perspective', in *Theory of the Global State: Globality as an Unfinished Revolution* (Cambridge: Cambridge University Press, 2000)

SHIPMAN, ALAN

A journalist and commentator, Shipman's *The Globalization Myth* (2002) represents a popular and journalistic response to the campaigns and arguments forwarded by many in the **anti-globalization movement**. He argues that whilst the anti-globalization movement is right to criticize aspects of contemporary **globalization**, the prescriptions and alternatives proposed 'are almost always misguided and inappropriate'. He joins other popular 'pro-globalization' commentators in arguing that many dimensions of globalization have been beneficial and that the future should be about political debates concerning what kind of globalization is desirable rather than opposing it. In particular, he is highly critical of the anti-globalization call for relocalization as an alternative, pointing to the fact that the global economy and **transnational corporation**s are responsible for considerable increases in global economic output and raising material living standards across the world. His conception of calls for **localization**, however, is rather narrow when compared to that of commentators such as Colin **Hines**. Shipman's version of localization is one which is conflated with a caricatured defensive isolationism and the reassertion of borders. This is also not the interpretation currently being deployed by many of the anti-globalization critics such as Jerry **Mander**. Overall, Shipman is a defender of a liberal and free market global economy but at times his analysis is more rhetorical than well supported by examples, and his perspective glosses over many of the more serious critiques concerned with **neo-liberalism** and the dominance of TNCs.

Further reading
Shipman, A. 'Planetary Spin', introduction to *The Globalization Myth* (London: Icon Books, 2002)

SHIVA, VANDANA
A radical Indian intellectual and longstanding environmentalist and campaigner, Shiva has made a major contribution to the **globalization** debate with her various critiques of modernity, science and technology and the power structures in global capitalism that are disenfranchising people from nature and control over natural resources. A particular focus of her specific campaigns has been women, especially those in poor and developing countries. In the late 1980s she wrote extensively on new forms of resistance to the negative environmental impacts of the activities of **transnational corporations** – a key case study was the Chipko resistance movement to corporate logging in north India. During the 1990s her attention broadened out to cover what might be described as the negative impacts of **economic globalization** and TNCs on global natural resources. She has sought to highlight the disempowering and anti-democratic nature of developing international legal agreements on intellectual property as TNCs have begun to patent biological material often identified in the flora or fauna of the world's poorer countries. Shiva argues that this is a dangerous and unjust development as global corporate interests in effect are stealing and creating large profits from the common biological inheritance on planet Earth. From her perspective, the Western-inspired and unprecedented widening of the concept of intellectual property does not in fact stimulate human creativity and

the generation of knowledge. Instead, she contends it is being exploited by TNCs to increase their profits by means of the age-old knowledge of the world's farmers and at the expense of the health of ordinary people, especially the poor. A similar argument is echoed in her later book on the 'water-war' of the twenty-first century. She points to the progressive privatization by the multinationals of communal water rights and argues that whilst drought and desertification are intensifying around the world, corporations are aggressively converting free-flowing water into bottled profits. She again points to the growing corporate and capitalist control over a key natural resource through the erosion of communal water rights, the international water trade and industrial activities such as damming, mining and aquafarming. The main argument once more is that this represents a destructive process which is disenfranchising the world's poor as they are stripped of rights to a precious common good. She calls for a movement to preserve water access for all and offers a blueprint for global resistance based on examples of successful campaigns.

Overall, Shiva has made a considerable number of radical contributions that are heavily critical of the social and environmental consequences of economic globalization. However, she does at times offer sweeping critical generalizations about the activities of TNCs and has been criticized for conveying a polarized representation of the **development** process in poorer countries and being unnecessarily 'anti-state'.

Further reading
Shiva, V. *Stolen Harvest: The Hijacking of the Global Food Supply* (London: Zed Books, 2001)
Shiva, V. *Water Wars: Pollution, Profits and Privatization* (London: Pluto Press, 2002)

SKLAIR, LESLIE
A British sociologist, Sklair has made a number of important contributions to the **globalization** debate. In *Sociology of the Global System* (1998), he proposes a theoretical framework for understanding globalization based around the development of transnational practices. He posits that in effect globalization can be understood as a global (social) system which operates at three levels, knowledge about which can be organized into three spheres: the economic, the

political and culture-ideology. Each sphere is typically characterized by a representative institution, a cohesive set of practices and is organized and patterned. Sklair sees capitalist globalization as the dominant form of globalization in the present era but in his more recent work argues that alternative forms of globalization are available that avoid the worst negative effects of the current form. His emphasis on transnational practices has also led him to theorize what he argues is an emergent **transnational capitalist class** grouping at the global scale. In many ways, there are parallels between Sklair's idea of the transnational capitalist class and Antonio **Negri** and Michael Hardt's arguments about where power resides in the contemporary world – captured in the concept of **empire**.

Further reading
Sklair, L. 'Sociology of the Global system', ch. 9 in Lechner, F. & Boli, J. (eds) *The Globalization Reader* (2nd edn; Oxford: Blackwell, 2004)

SOROS, GEORGE

Leading financier turned commentator, Soros has made a number of contributions to the **globalization** debate which are focused on considering how supranational institutions such as the **International Monetary Fund** should be reformed in the coming decades. He argues that the international financial system needs better regulation and could be much better implemented to assist poorer countries. In his view the **Bretton Woods institutions** have been effective in creating wealth, but they have failed in providing other public goods. His contention is that, ironically, the right-wing free market fundamentalists and the **anti-globalization movement** are both fighting towards the same undesirable goal: destroying these international institutions. He offers a series of specific measures which he sees as presenting significant improvement in the effectiveness of the Bretton Woods system in encouraging global **development**. A key idea he develops in depth is for the IMF's Special Drawing Rights (SDRs) to be used to fund aid.

Further reading
Soros, G. *On Globalization* (Oxford: Public Affairs, 2002) [esp. Introduction and Conclusion]

SOVEREIGNTY

The supreme authority in a political community, usually expressed in terms of control over an area of territory. However, ideas of sovereignty have a long history of development stemming from works of classical antiquity by thinkers such as Plato. The sixteenth-century French lawyer Jean Bodin is generally attributed with producing the first modern theory of sovereignty. In his *Six livres de la république* (in English as *Six Bookes of a Commonweale*) (1576) Bodin asserted that the prince, or the sovereign, has the power to declare law. Thomas Hobbes later furthered the concept of monarchical sovereignty by stating that the monarch (or king) not only declares law but creates it. This gives the sovereign absolute power both moral and political. Hobbes also asserted that the king derives his power from a populace which has collectively given up its own former personal sovereignty and power and placed it irretrievably in the king. In the development of **nation-state**s, sovereignty has for the most part subsequently translated from the authority of an individual to a state. A sovereign state is thus one that is free and independent and in its internal affairs has undivided jurisdiction over all persons and property within its territory.

In debates about **globalization**, the nature of sovereignty has become a key issue. The sovereignty of a nation-state has thus been asserted through international agreements since the Treaty of Westphalia in 1648. This 'Westphalian' conception of sovereignty enshrines the right of a state to conduct its economic life without regard for its neighbours, to increase armaments without limit, for no other nation to be able to rightfully interfere in its domestic affairs and to be able in its external relations to enforce its own conception of rights and declare **war**. However, in the contemporary phase of globalization, many commentators argue that this form of sovereignty is being eroded and/or is becoming anachronistic. Nation-states are losing power over their economies and societies to a range of other actors: **transnational corporation**s, supranational bodies such as the **European Union** or **North American Free Trade Agreement** or to integrated global markets and other networks of actors. Commentators such as Kenichi **Ohmae** have even argued that contemporary globalization has produced the end of sovereignty as it has been understood to date. However, others argue that globalization has produced a positive and progressive reconstitution of sovereignty into new forms. Whichever perspective is adopted, however, there can be little doubt that in the twenty-first century the nature of sovereignty is changing rapidly.

Further reading
Keohane, R. 'Sovereignty in International Society', ch. 13 in Held, D. and McGrew A. (eds) *The Global Transformations Reader* (2nd edn; Cambridge: Polity, 2003)

STIGLITZ, JOSEPH

Former Chief Economist at the **World Bank** and Nobel Prize-winner for Economics, Stiglitz has made a series of key contributions to the wider debate about **globalization** in relation to **development** and the governance of the global economy. In *Globalization and its Discontents* (1999) he argues that the model of **economic globalization** propagated through the 1980s and 1990s is failing to work with respect to lifting large proportions of the global population out of poverty. Stiglitz suggests that the **Bretton Woods institutions** have largely failed to achieve the goals they were founded for because of a combination of poor communication, mismanagement, inflexibility, political interference and misguided ideological dogma. His critique is particularly trenchant given his position at the top of one of these key institutions, and his arguments have had a wide audience and significant political impact. Stiglitz is not, however, aligned with the left-wing and anti-capitalist perspective of much of the **anti-globalization movement**. His mid-ground position is that economic globalization and the global economy can be powerful mechanisms for development and greater welfare and prosperity if better managed and regulated. He argues that the Bretton Woods institutions, and in particular the **International Monetary Fund** and **World Trade Organization**, are in urgent need of reform. He suggests that greater transparency and a fairer form of governance within the WTO, that includes developing nations, can produce the kind of globalization that benefits the majority of the global population. His proposed reforms focus in particular on the need better to regulate financial markets with improved regulation, risk management and safety nets. He also argues strongly for a reformed trading regime and debt forgiveness to assist developing countries. In his later book, *The Roaring Nineties* (2003), he also hones this critique towards the neo-liberalist American style of capitalism that produced the 1990s boom/bust cycle. Again, his argument, in what is broadly a neo-Keynesian stance, is for the need to regulate global capitalism more effectively.

Further reading

Stiglitz, J. 'The Promise of Global Institutions', ch. 1 in *Globalization and its Discontents* (London: Penguin, 1999)

Stiglitz, J. 'Globalization: Early Forays', ch. 9 in *The Roaring Nineties* (New York: Norton, 2003)

SUSTAINABLE DEVELOPMENT

A concept of which the most widely cited definition stems from the **United Nations'** Brundtland Commission (1987): '**development** that meets the needs of the present without compromising the ability of future generations to meet their own needs'. The important shift in environmental thought that came with the Commission's report was a move away from the earlier focus on growth versus the **environment** to the potential complementarity of **economic growth** and the environment. This conception of sustainable development as 'ecological modernization' has become the mainstream arena of discussion in relation to **globalization** and the language of ecological modernization has been incorporated into much of the stated policy of leading governments and international organizations such as the UN and the **World Bank** in the last couple of decades. In this sense, from the perspective of the key proponents of contemporary global economic development, sustainability is a central goal which is being addressed.

However, sustainable development cast as ecological modernization has forced many radical environmentalists to disown the concept. Critical commentators such as Vandana **Shiva**, Martin **Khor** and Edward Goldsmith, many associated with a wider '**anti-globalization**' perspective, contest whether ecological modernization is producing or is in future likely to produce truly sustainable development. They point to continuing (and accelerating) environmental degradation across the globe, as well as to a wide range of activities perpetrated by **transnational corporation**s, that are unsustainable. This critique suggests that the early twenty-first-century global economy is still focused on growth at the expense of the environment and that as it grows, an ever larger proportion of the Earth's natural resources are being exploited. The destruction of tropical rainforest, species extinction, increasing mineral exploitation, sub-Saharan desertification and the depletion of marine life are only a few of the major areas of this global environmental degradation that are cited as the consequence of unsustainable global development. The prospect of whether or not (and how) sustainable development can be achieved at the planetary scale has thus become a key issue in international politics with an increasing proportion of high-level meetings (for example, **G8** summits and UN conferences) being absorbed by different aspects of this issue. It is likely to become increasingly central in future debates about the benefits and disbenefits of contemporary **economic globalization** in the coming decades.

Further reading
Elliot, J. *An Introduction to Sustainable Development* (2nd edn; London: Routledge, 1999) [esp. Introduction, chs 1 and 2)
Reid, D. *Sustainable Development: An Introduction* (London: Earthscan, 2004)

TCC *see* transnational capitalist class.

THIRD WORLD

A term coined by the economist Alfred Sauvy in 1952, which initially became widespread in the later 1950s to refer to countries within what was known as the 'non-aligned movement'. This was comprised of countries that were not part of either the **North Atlantic Treaty Organization** or the Warsaw Pact and sought to distinguish themselves from the postwar bi-polar superpowers (the US and the Soviet Union). Original members included Yugoslavia and India, but in subsequent decades the term has come to be more focused on less developed countries. It is used generically (but often loosely) to refer to all less developed countries, although commonly it is most often used to refer to the less wealthy countries in Africa, Asia and Latin America. However, since the end of the **Cold War** the relevance and usefulness of the term has diminished. Many commentators have argued that the Third World is increasingly problematic as a geographical term. In the context of contemporary **globalization**, there are increasing differences between many of the countries in the so-called Third World with, for example, a number of Latin American and Asian countries having achieved much higher levels of **economic growth** in recent decades than African states. The term has also been criticized for implying that countries within the Third World are isolated from the rest of the global economic system. In contemporary academic and policy discussions, the term has been largely superseded by the concept of the **global South**.

Further reading
Smith, B. 'The Idea of the Third World', ch. 1 in *Understanding Third World Politics: Theories of Political Change and Development* (2nd edn; Basingstoke: Palgrave Macmillan, 2003)

THOMPSON, GRAHAME

An international political economist, Thompson's major contribution is his joint book with Paul **Hirst**, *Globalization in Question* (1996). In this work, they contest the 'hyperglobalist thesis' that **(economic) globalization** has developed in the current period to unprecedented levels. Grounded in empirical analysis of international trade, capital and investment flows, the book argues that current levels of global economic integration are not historically unprecedented in a number of ways and that integration tends more to regionalization than true **globalization**. Thompson has subsequently published numerous contributions that follow on and develop this sceptical approach. In particular, he has focused on the nature and role of various forms of borders, boundaries and frontiers in relation to territories in the contemporary world. He has analysed the rise of corporate social responsibility (CSR) within **transnational corporations** and assessed what role 'global corporate citizenship' could play in twenty-first century global **development**.

Further reading
Hirst, P. and Thompson, G. 'Globalization – A Necessary Myth?', ch. 7 in Held, D. and McGrew, A. (eds) *The Global Transformations Reader* (2nd edn; Cambridge: Polity, 2003)

time–space compression *see* time-space distanciation.

TIME–SPACE DISTANCIATION

Arguably a key process underpinning the generalized concept of **globalization**. Anthony **Giddens'** contribution is particularly important in maintaining that this phenomenon is pivotal in understanding the experience of contemporary social life. He argues that the separation and standardization of time and space has brought about the new conditions 'under which time and space are organized so as to connect presence and absence'. This is what he terms a new type of 'time–space distanciation'. Whereas traditional societies are mainly integrated through co-presence of actors, Giddens suggests that modern societies are integrated through institutions stretching over time and space – through the mediate presence or absence of actors. This has several implications for the dynamism of modernity in the contemporary period. First, social activity becomes disconnected from the particular context of presence, and thus it opens up the manifold possibilities of change by breaking free from the restraints of local habits and practices. This represents a process of **deterritorialization** and reterritorialization. Second, it provides the mechanisms for the rational organization to connect the local and the global in untraditional ways. Third, time and space are recombined to form a genuinely world-historical framework of action and experience.

Theorists of globalization have adopted many aspects of this and other similar arguments concerning the contemporary experience of space and time. David **Harvey**, for example, refers to 'time–space compression', which he describes as a historical process by which 'the world has shrunk' over time proportionately to the increasing speed of transportation. In this analogy, the world in the 1960s was about one-fiftieth the size of the world of the sixteenth century because jet aircraft can travel at about fifty times the speed of a sailing ship. Furthermore, if people in one part of the world experience the same thing at the same time as others living elsewhere in the world, then Harvey argues that this is akin to them living in the same place. Space has been annihilated by time compression.

Many globalization theorists such as David **Held** and his co-authors or Ulrich **Beck** make significant use of time–space distanciation or compression as an underlying process which defines globalization in general. However, others such as Justin **Rosenberg** have questioned the coherence of generalized theories of globalization by arguing in part that the concept of time–space distanciation does not offer an adequate abstraction for understanding all aspects of the phenomenon.

Further reading
Giddens, A. 'The Globalizing of Modernity', ch. 2 in Held, D. and McGrew, A. (eds) *The Global Transformations Reader* (2nd edn; Cambridge: Polity, 2003)

Rosenberg, J. 'The Problem of Globalization Theory', ch. 6 in Held, D. and McGrew, A. (eds) *The Global Transformations Reader* (2nd edn; Cambridge: Polity, 2003)

TNC *see* transnational corporation.

TOBIN TAX

Proposed by the economist James Tobin in 1972, a suggested tax on all trade of currency across borders. This was supposed to put a penalty on short-term speculation in currencies. The proposed tax rate would be low, between 0.05 and 1.0 per cent. Tobin made his proposal in the light of President Nixon's announcement of US withdrawal from the Bretton Woods system of exchange rate management in order to promote international financial stability. Many commentators have argued that one country acting alone would find it very difficult to implement this tax and that it would be best implemented by an international institution. No action was taken during the 1970s and interest in the Tobin Tax was only reignited in the late 1990s with a proposal to create an association for the introduction of this tax, which was named ATTAC (Association for the Taxation of Financial Transactions for the Aid of Citizens). This organization sought to couple the original conception of the Tobin Tax as an economic tool for creating financial stability with a developmental goal. ATTAC's proposal was that the money raised from tax would be used to produce funds for **development** projects in the **global South**, allowing governments and citizens to reclaim part of the democratic space conceded to the financial markets. As a consequence of ATTAC, the Tobin Tax became a *cause célèbre* of the **anti-globalization movement**. Tobin himself, however, distanced himself from the ATTAC position in 2001, suggesting that financial stability was the key goal of the tax and it was not a means to halt neo-liberal **economic globalization**.

Overall, academic opinion remains divided as to whether the Tobin Tax would be beneficial or have negative impacts on **economic growth**. Proponents argue that its introduction would improve the economies of countries that are damaged by financial speculation and limit the worst excesses of neo-liberal **globalization**. Yet pro-globalization commentators argue that it would constrain economic globalization in damaging ways, resulting in lower growth and low flows of investment into developing countries. Interestingly, divisions on the virtues or otherwise of the Tobin Tax do not fall along conventional globalization and anti-globalization lines. George **Soros**, the multimillionaire financial speculator is unexpectedly amongst its proponents, while even commentators on the Left have expressed concern that a Tobin Tax might inhibit investment flows, and particularly global financial liquidity, to the detriment of all.

Further reading
Patamaki, H. *Democratizing Globalization: The Leverage of the Tobin Tax* (London: Zed Books, 2001)

TOMLINSON, JOHN

A UK-based professor of cultural sociology, Tomlinson contributes to the **globalization** debate with a focus on conceptions of culture. He argues that cultural issues are at the heart of the debate about globalization. Taking a social theory and cultural studies approach to the understanding of it, his proposition is that the modern world displays what he terms *complex connectivity* – the rapidly developing and ever-densening network of interconnections and interdependencies that characterize contemporary social life. He suggests that theories of globalization need to be concerned with both understanding the sources of this condition of complex connectivity and also interpreting its implications across various spheres. He distinguishes in particular between connectivity and proximity, arguing they are not the same thing. People and places are becoming more and more interconnected through new forms of proximity, but this does not mean they are becoming the same. In Tomlinson's view, globalization for most people is about staying in one place but experiencing the displacement that globalization brings to them. Importantly, he is therefore critical of arguments that globalization is leading to cultural homogenization and one **global culture**. Rather he suggests the world is becoming interconnected through ever more complex and numerous cultural flows. More recently, Tomlinson has turned this argument towards the issue of **cultural imperialism** to theorize the complex nature of power and relationships of domination through a cultural lens.

Further reading
Tomlinson, J. 'Cultural Imperialism', ch. 39 in Lechner, F. and Boli, J. (eds)
    The Globalization Reader (Oxford: Blackwell, 2000)
Tomlinson, J. 'Globalization and Cultural Identity', ch. 23 in Held, D.
    and McGrew, A. (eds) *The Global Transformations Reader* (2nd edn;
    Cambridge: Polity, 2003)

TRADE-RELATED ASPECTS OF INTELLECTUAL PROPERTY RIGHTS (TRIPS) AGREEMENT

An international treaty that sets down minimum standards for most forms of intellectual property regulation within all member countries of the **World Trade Organization**. It was added to the GATT at the end of the Uruguay Round in 1994. Specifically, TRIPS deals with copyright and related rights (i.e. the rights of performers, producers of sound recordings and broadcasting organizations); geographical indications (including appellations of origin); industrial designs; integrated circuit layout-designs; patents (including the protection of new varieties of plants); trademarks; and undisclosed or confidential information (including trade secrets and test data). TRIPS also specifies enforcement procedures, remedies and dispute resolution procedures. The obligations under TRIPS apply equally to all member states although developing countries are allowed a longer period in which to implement the changes applicable to their national laws. States which do not adopt TRIPS-compliant intellectual property systems can be disciplined through the WTO's dispute settlement mechanism, which is capable of authorizing trade sanctions against non-compliant states. The agreement itself introduced intellectual property law into the international trading system for the first time, and remains the most comprehensive international agreement on intellectual property to date.

TRIPS has become increasingly controversial, particularly receiving criticism from NGOs, developing countries and the **anti-globalization movement**. TRIPS is seen to encapsulate much of what is unfair about contemporary **globalization**. A particular 'battleground' in this respect has been the production of cheaper **HIV/AIDS** drugs in Africa that were developed and patented by Western pharmaceutical companies. To date, there has been little moderation in the agreement itself although a number of states in the **global North** have sought to circumvent the restrictions imposed around products such as the HIV/AIDS life-saving drugs.

Further reading
Richards, D. *Intellectual Property Rights and Global Capitalism: The Political Economy of the TRIPS Agreement* (White Plains, N.Y.: M. E. Sharpe, 2004)

TRANSNATIONAL CAPITALIST CLASS (TCC)

A concept developed by Leslie **Sklair**, the existence of which is argued to be a central feature of contemporary globalizing economy and society. **Sklair** makes four propositions in relation to the TCC. First, he argues that this class is emerging based around those who work for **transnational corporation**s and that it is more or less in control of the processes of globalization. Second, the TCC is beginning to act as a transnational dominant class in some spheres. Third, the globalization of the capitalist system reproduces itself through the profit-driven culture ideology of consumerism. Global capitalism in this sense survives by persuading us that the meaning and value of our lives are to be found principally in what we possess, that we can never be totally satisfied by what we possess, that goods and services are best provided by the free market and that the generator of private profit lies at the heart of capitalism. Fourth, the TCC is working constantly to resolve two central crises: (i) the simultaneous creation of increasing poverty and increasing wealth within and between communities and societies (the class polarization crisis) and (ii) the unsustainability of the system.

Sklair's thesis is clearly grounded in a neo-Marxian theoretical framework and is supported through reference to a variety of case studies of TNCs and the actions of their employees. At a general level it is important in providing a theoretical way of thinking about the collective interests of a key group of actors in **economic globalization** but the stronger claims of the argument are more questionable. In particular, the coherence of this group and their ability/rationale for acting through anything resembling class interest is highly debatable.

Further reading
Sklair, L. 'Globalizating Class Theory', ch. 2 in *The Transnational Capitalist Class* (Oxford: Blackwell, 2002)

TRANSNATIONAL CORPORATION **(TNC)**

A term that came to the fore during the 1990s as arguably a successor term to **multinational corporation** (MNC) or multinational enterprise (MNE). Used to describe the world's largest firms, the concept of the TNC is one which remains ill defined and often used interchangeably with MNC or MNE and **global corporation**. However, within the academic literature there exists a theoretical basis for distinguishing the transnational from the multinational firm. This rests on the 'degree of globalness' or 'globality' that the firm as an organization exhibits. The argument of theorists such as Peter **Dicken** is that, during the 1990s, the largest firms in the global economy had extended their productive and business operations across so many national borders that they in effect straddled many national economies. The 'trans-' prefix thus denotes the cross-border nature of the operations and organization of these firms. Whilst various researchers have shown that the home or original economy of a firm continues to exert a strong influence on all aspects of that firm's production, management and culture, the transnational corporation is thus distinguished from the multinational one by the fact that its organizational form has taken on supranational characteristics. In particular, this is manifest in the development of globalized production and the global operation of high-order corporate functions. For example, automotive TNCs no longer manufacture all the components for an automobile in one national economy but rather components are made in a range of production locations across the global economy. Furthermore, many of the world's largest firms no longer duplicate many corporate functions in each country of operation – for example, management, research and development, marketing, advertising – but have organized these activities at the global scale. In that sense, these companies are not exclusively based in any one national economic space.

Transnational firms are argued by many theorists to be the key actors in **(economic) globalization** as their numbers and size continue to increase. Increasingly these very large firms dominate global markets in all sectors of goods and services and they account for an increasing proportion of total global output. For this reason, they are also seen as having eroded the ability of **nation-state**s to control economic activity within national territories as investment decisions about where to site production now fall to these corporations. The ability of TNCs to open and close productive operations, along with their ability to avoid regulation and taxes by shifting production to cheaper, less taxed and regulated locations, has led critical commentators to argue that they have become too powerful in the context of contemporary **globalization**. In recent years, they have certainly also become the target for campaigns, boycotts and protests by **anti-globalization** groups who see them as negative influences on democracy and the distribution of wealth.

Overall, however, excessively positive or negative claims about TNCs should be treated with caution since the term now refers to an increasingly large and diverse number of often very different firms. The existing globalization literature is often simplistic and sweeping in its criticisms or praise of TNCs, again reflecting the often polarized nature of the debate. In reality, there is a growing body of research that points to the complex relationship between TNCs as the key economic agents in the global economy and a range of other actors such as governments, regulatory bodies, institutions and consumers.

Further reading

Dicken, P. 'Placing Firms: Grounding the Debate on the Global Corporation', ch. 2 in Peck, J. and Yeung, H. (eds) *Remaking the Global Economy* (London: Sage, 2004)

Greider, W. 'Wawasan 2020', ch. 19 in Lechner, F. and Boli, J. (eds) *The Globalization Reader* (2nd edn; Oxford: Blackwell, 2004)

Jones, A. 'Rethinking the Transnational Firm', ch. 2 in *Management Consultancy and Banking in an Era of Globalization* (Basingstoke: Palgrave Macmillan, 2003)

TRANSNATIONALISM

A series of economic, sociocultural and political practices which transcend the territorially bounded jurisdiction of the **nation-state**. The concept thus describes a condition in which, despite great distances and notwithstanding the presence of international borders (and all the laws, regulations and national narratives they represent), certain kinds of relationships have been globally intensified and now take place paradoxically in a planet-spanning yet common – however virtual – arena of activity. It also is often associated with a process of **deterritorialization** in so far as increasing mobility and the development of communication have intensified transborder relations, leading to social and political mobilizations beyond boundaries and the development of global-scale identities. Stephen Vertovec argues that across the **globalization** literature, transnationalism refers to a set of variegated transnational phenomena which includes communities, capital flows, trade, citizenship, corporations, inter-governmental agencies, non-governmental organizations, politics, services, social movements, social networks, families, **migration** circuits, identities, public spaces and public cultures. He proposes six strands to the way in which **transnationalism** is used: to describe social morphology, as a type of consciousness, as a mode of cultural production, as an avenue of capital, as a site of political engagement and as a mode of reconstructing place/locality.

It is also worth noting, however, that transnationalism is also often used in more specific discussions of **political globalization** to refer to what might also be called 'transnational nationalism'. For example, in Islam the rhetoric of *Umma* – the worldwide unified Muslim community – reinterprets various forms of national diversity as one imagined 'political' community at the global scale. In this sense, this transnational nationalism takes form after nationalism and **nation-states** have become realities and extends state nationalism in new ways, producing exclusionist discourses based on national membership that is 'deterritorialized'. It does so without making claims on behalf of territorial self-determination. Thus, it fashions new power relationships with states and acts as a challenge to their territorially demarcated political identities.

Further reading
Vertovec, S. 'Conceiving and Researching Transnationalism', *Ethnic and Racial Studies* 22 (1999): 447–62
Have a look at the University of Chicago's transnationalism project site: <http://transnationalism.uchicago.edu/>.

TRIPS *see* Trade-related Aspects of Intellectual Property Rights Agreement.

UN *see* United Nations.

UNCHR *see* United Nations Commission on Human Rights.

UNESCO *see* United Nations Educational, Scientific and Cultural Organization.

UNHCR *see* United Nations High Commissioner for Refugees.

UNILATERALISM

One-sided action or relevant concern for only one party, a term generally used with reference to **nation-states'** policies in the international context. As such, unilateralism is an antonym for **multilateralism**. The debate over the relative merits and weaknesses of unilateralism as opposed to multilateralism is central in the ongoing debate about **political globalization**. In classical international relations theory, unilateralism may be preferred in those instances when it is assumed to be the most efficient – that is, in issues that can be solved without cooperation. However, a government may also have a principal preference for unilateralism or multilateralism. The **United Nations**, and before it the **League of Nations**, represent supranational institutions founded on the basis that multilateralism is the most desirable form of **global governance**.

During the **Cold War**, most attention focused on the degree to which the US and Soviet Union undertook a unilateralist approach in their foreign policy, although other countries such as China also acted unilaterally in a regional context on occasions. In the context of contemporary **globalization**, commentators argue that unilateralism represents a rejection of the essentially interconnected nature of twenty-first-century global politics. It has also been argued that unilateralism, aside from being misguided, is also becoming increasingly impossible as even the US becomes ever more interwoven in its affairs with the rest of the world. However, since the election of the first Bush administration in 2000, the US has adopted a much more unilateralist stance. The conflicts in Afghanistan and Iraq saw the US taking a unilateral approach which is also in evidence in other policy areas such as its refusal to sign up to the **International Criminal Court** or the **Kyoto Treaty**. More recently, in his second term President Bush appears to have had to moderate his strong unilateralist approach, which can be seen as evidence of the growing difficulties in true unilateral action in the contemporary world.

Further reading
Malone, D. and Khong, Y. *Unilateralism and U.S. Foreign Policy: International Perspectives* (New York: Lynne Reiner, 2002)

United Nations (UN)

A supranational institution that came into being after the **Second World War**, in many ways as a development of the earlier inter-war

League of Nations. The League itself had been an attempt to mitigate the circumstances that had produced the First World War and aggression between **nation-states**. However the League faded out in the years immediately preceding the Second World War as international political events made a mockery of its founding principles. The UN therefore represented at its foundation in 1945 an attempt to develop an international organization that overcame the flaws the Allies perceived to have existed in the League. The UN would give a much stronger position to the traditional great powers through the UN Security Council. Fifty-one states became members at its foundation; there are 191 member states now.

The Charter of the UN comprises a preamble and nineteen chapters divided into 111 articles. The Charter sets out three major purposes of the UN: the maintenance of international peace and security; the development of friendly relations among states; the achievement of cooperation in solving international economic, social, cultural and humanitarian problems. The UN as an institution has six main components: the General Assembly, the Security Council, the Economic and Social Council, the Trusteeship Council, the **International Court of Justice** and the Secretariat. There are a (growing) number of other bodies that function as specialized agencies of the UN but which are not specifically included in the Charter such as the International Bank for Reconstruction and Development (the **World Bank**) and the **World Health Organization**. The UN is headed by a Secretary General who transcends a merely administrative role by his authority to bring situations to the attention of the various UN organs, his position as an impartial party in conciliation and by his power to perform special functions entrusted to him by other UN organs.

The UN clearly represents a key supranational institution in the development of contemporary **globalization**. Its role has not evolved in practice as was envisaged at its inception, and it has also taken on new significance in the last fifteen years. During the **Cold War**, the UN's role was very much suppressed by the domination of the US and Soviet Union as superpowers. It played very much a secondary role in the major world crises: the Arab–Israeli Wars (1964 and 1973), the India–Pakistan War of 1971, and the **wars** in Vietnam and Afghanistan. With the end of the Cold War, however, the UN has taken on a much higher profile and multilateral role, largely in its peace-keeping function. During the 1990s, this was the case with the first Gulf War, the conflicts in Kosovo and Bosnia and in a number of African states including Angola, Mozambique, Sierra Leone and

Somalia. It also has taken on new supranational roles, particularly on the **environment** since the 1992 Earth Summit in Rio and in areas such as **human rights** and **development**. Yet the emergence of the UN as the central global supranational political institution still retains key weaknesses. Disagreement and dissent continue about the distribution of voting rights in the General Assembly and the Security Council between nation-states and the disproportionate influence of the major Western states. The UN was certainly criticized for being weak, reactive and slow in taking action in Kosovo, Rwanda and Somalia. Since the advent of the Bush administration, the US has again suppressed the role of the UN, notably in the case of Iraq. It therefore remains to be seen whether the UN can maintain the momentum of its revived role during the 1990s.

Further reading
Bowles, N. *The Diplomacy of Hope: The UN since the End of the Cold War* (London: I. B. Taurus, 2004)
Roberts, A., Kingsbury, B. and Ghali, B. *United Nations, Divided World: The UN's Roles in International Relations* (Oxford: Clarendon Press, 2003)
And the UN website: <www.un.org>.

UNITED NATIONS COMMISSION ON HUMAN RIGHTS (UNCHR)
The commission supervised by the Office of the UN High Commissioner for Human Rights, composed of representatives from fifty-three member states. It meets once a year in the spring for six weeks in Geneva. The Commission aims to examine, monitor and publicly report on **human rights** situations in specific countries or territories (known as country mechanisms or mandates) as well as on major phenomena of human rights violations worldwide (known as thematic mechanisms or mandates). Supporters in most democratic countries consider the work of the UNCHR and the UN High Commissioner for Human Rights, whom the Commission advises, as helpful for the worldwide human rights situation. Critics, notably the US, argue however that several of its members themselves have poor human rights records. The US was pushed out of the Commission in 2001 because it would not recognize the **International Criminal Court**, although it was readmitted in 2003.

Further reading
See the human rights section of the UN website: <www.un.org/rights>.

UNITED NATIONS EDUCATIONAL, SCIENTIFIC AND CULTURAL ORGANIZATION (UNESCO)

One of the specialized agencies of the **United Nations**, which has its headquarters in Paris. Its predecessor in the **League of Nations** was the International Committee for Intellectual Cooperation. Founded in 1945, UNESCO became an agency of the UN in 1946. It now has 190 **nation-state** members. The organization's policies are decided by the biannual general conference, attended by one representative for each member. UNESCO has an executive board with thirty-four members elected for three-year terms, and also a secretariat. The secretariat is headed by a director general and is charged with carrying out the organization's programme. National commissions or cooperating bodies of member states act as liaison between UNESCO and national educational, scientific, and cultural organizations. UNESCO's stated main objective is to further world peace by encouraging free interchange of ideas and of cultural and scientific achievements and also by improving education.

Further reading
See the UNESCO website: <www.unesco.org>.

UNITED NATIONS HIGH COMMISSIONER FOR REFUGEES (UNHCR)

A UN organization founded in December 1950 and headquartered in Geneva, Switzerland, that exists to protect and support **refugees** at the request of governments or the UN. It also assists in the return and resettlement process. It has offices in more than 120 countries and a staff in excess of 5000. It was awarded the Nobel Peace Prize in 1954 and 1981. UNHCR is mandated with leading and coordinating action to resolve refugee problems worldwide with a focus on the rights and well-being of refugees wherever they are. One of its main tasks is to try to ensure that anyone can exercise the right to seek asylum and find refuge in another **nation-state**, with the options of returning home voluntarily, integrating locally or resettling in a third country. By 2004 the agency had helped an estimated fifty million people.

Further reading
See the organization's website: <http://www.unhcr.ch/cgi-bin/texis/vtx/home>.

UNITED NATIONS SECRETARY GENERAL

The official appointed on a five-year term as the head of the **United Nations** Secretariat which is one of the principal organs of the UN. The UN Charter establishes that the Secretary General is appointed by the General Assembly on the recommendation of the Security Council. The Secretary General is described by the Charter as the 'chief administrative officer' of the UN. His or her role includes not only administering the Secretariat, but also speaking out on global issues and using his or her good offices to mediate disputes. From 1 January 1997, Kofi Annan has been the incumbent, beginning a second term in 2002. UN Secretaries General normally spend two terms in office and the position is supposed to rotate by geographic region.

Further reading
See the UN website for more information on the role of the Secretary General: <www.un.org>.

URRY, JOHN

A British professor of sociology, Urry has long been interested in the nature of capitalism and modernity. His key contribution to the **globalization** debate is his book *Global Complexity* (2003). Urry provides a far-reaching and radical engagement with how sociological theory is developed in a postnational world. He argues that many existing sociological theories are becoming obsolete because they are grounded in the investigation of bounded and organized capitalist societies. However, he is critical of attempting to theorize globalization in a singular sense. He argues that the global 'system' is less 'a coherent structure discernible by the sociologist than a tumult of unplanned processes and scattered centres of power'. Thus, there is no 'global centre of power' or 'global conspiracy' but the degree of complexity in contemporary society warrants a different approach to theorizing. For Urry, therefore, theoretical engagement with today's world requires an attempt to understand how global society is less a planned system than a complex product of millions of separate local decisions. He sees the current emergent order (such as it is) as structured through multiple interdependent organizations that are collectively performing the 'global'. In that sense, he is sceptical about the existence of globalization as one thing, arguing overall that contemporary global complexity teeters on the brink of chaos 'without a central "governor"'. He suggests that most analyses of globalization are flawed by their tendency to treat it 'as too unified and as too powerful'. In his view, **global system**s are always 'on the edge of chaos'.

Further reading
Urry, J. *Global Complexity* (Cambridge: Polity, 2003) [esp. chs 1 and 7]

WALLERSTEIN, IMMANUEL

In his major historical works examining the rise of the capitalist world system, Immanuel Wallerstein is seen by many as one of the key 'proto-**globalization**' theorists. Writing from a Marxian perspective, he proposed a theoretical framework during the 1970s called '**world systems analysis**'. Adopting a long historical perspective, the world systems approach seeks to theorize how capitalism has progressively become the dominant mode of organizing economic, political and cultural life at the planetary scale in the modern period.

Wallerstein identifies two main forms of social system. First, a mini-system is an entity that has within it a complete **division of labour** and a single cultural framework. He argues that such systems no longer exist but were a feature only in very simple agricultural or hunting and gathering societies. Second, in more recent times, there have only existed world systems which are defined simply as a unit with a single division of labour and multiple cultural systems. World systems therefore come in two forms: those with a single political system and those without, which Wallerstein terms 'world-empires' and 'world economies' respectively. In his analysis, world economies have been historically unstable structures leading either towards disintegration or conquest by one group and hence transformation into a world empire. Examples of such world empires include the pre-modern Roman, Chinese or Egyptian civilizations. He distinguishes these from the nineteenth-century empires, such as Great Britain or France, that were not world empires but **nation-state**s with colonial appendages.

Within this framework, Wallerstein contends that since the seventeenth century, one world system based on capitalism has become 'global in scope'. Wallerstein thus frames a Marxian view of the development of a single capitalist world economy along geographical lines. At the global scale, he in effect is positing a geographical explanation for how the world economy avoids crisis and revolution. This has had a global geographical dimension in so far as the single capitalist world economy has developed into three structural regions: the core, the periphery and the semi-periphery. The core originally emerged around northwest Europe but in the twentieth century can be understood as broadly equivalent to the First World. The core therefore expropriates surplus value not just from labour but also from peripheral areas of the world economy. A third structural region, the semi-periphery, acts as a political balance. If there were no semi-periphery the world economy would be far less politically stable and would not 'run smoothly'. In the twentieth century various world systems theorists have viewed Latin America or South Asia as fulfilling semi-peripheral functions which prevent the upper stratum of world society in the core from being challenged by a unified opposition.

Wallerstein's work is important in that it represents an early attempt to examine the nature of capitalist integration at the global scale. It has been criticized from a variety of angles that are common to many wider criticisms of Marxian theories. These include a tendency to construct global history in a teleological fashion, the problematic extension of Marxist assumptions about the inevitability of capitalist crisis and revolution and also its rather simplistic division of global territory into three functional geographical areas. Yet it remains important as a basis from which a variety of theorists have developed theories of capitalist integration and its relationship to social, political and **cultural globalization**. Rather like Karl Polanyi's work, Wallerstein's work has led subsequent theorists to problematize the economic-centred conception of **globalization** and to view societal integration as a more wide-ranging set of processes.

Further reading
Wallerstein, I. 'The Rise and Future Demise of the World Capitalist System', ch. 8 in Lechner, F. and Boli, J. (eds) *The Globalization Reader* (Oxford: Blackwell, 2004)

WAR
An armed conflict between states or nations (international war) or between factions within a state (civil war) that is prosecuted by force

and aims to compel the defeated side to do the will of the victor. It is a collective form of conflict and cannot meaningfully exist between individuals. Among the causes of war are ideological, political, racial, economic, and religious conflicts. Imperialism, nationalism, and militarism have been called the dynamics of modern war. According to the nineteenth-century military strategist Karl von Clausewitz, war is famously a 'continuation of political intercourse by other means'. As such it often occurs after arbitration and mediation have failed. War has been a feature of history since primitive times but in the context of debates around **globalization** it is the evolution of international war and warfare that is of importance. Over the last century, wars have become more globally extensive and war as a phenomenon more interconnected between different societies. This in combination with the rise of machine-based warfare made possible by industrialization led to the first global-scale wars in the twentieth century (the **First World War** and the **Second World War**). These wars killed more people than any previous conflicts and provoked the organized efforts to develop international institutions aimed at preventing war: the **League of Nations** and then the **United Nations** and **European Union**. Since 1945, the **Cold War** prospect of a nuclear war between the US and Soviet Union shifted the terms of war to an arms race, a succession of regional wars in Asia and Latin America and a proliferation of guerrilla wars and counter-insurgency campaigns. In the post-Cold War world, however, the so-called 'war on terror' has shifted the scope of war to conflict between new actors – namely states and collections of states versus globalized terrorists and other organizations. Commentators such as Mary **Kaldor** thus argue that war has been transformed in the contemporary era and that state-based conflict is being replaced by new forms of war.

Further reading
Barkawi, T. *Globalization and War* (London: Rowman & Littlefield, 2005)

WASHINGTON CONSENSUS
A set of policies that were argued to offer a formula for promoting **economic growth** in Latin America in the late 1980s. It was first presented by the economist John Williamson from the Institute for International Economics in 1989 and consists of ten major areas of national economic reform. These are: fiscal policy discipline; the

redirection of public spending towards education, health and infrastructure; tax reform which flattens the tax curve to reduce the burden on high tax brackets and increase it on lower brackets; the market determination of interest rates; competitive exchange rates; trade liberalization; openness to FDI; privatization of state enterprises; deregulation to encourage competition; and legal security for property rights.

Since the early 1990s, a number of proponents of neo-liberal **economic globalization** have argued for the applicability of the consensus in a wider context and the concept has extended beyond its original remit. It has thus taken a centre-stage role in discussions about the nature of national economic policies in the wider context of economic globalization. A number of commentators such as Dani **Rodrik** have argued there now exists an 'augmented' Washington Consensus that has been propagated through supranational institutions. This extends the scope to issues including corporate governance, corruption, labour markets, **World Trade Organization** agreements and financial standards.

For many, both Williamson's original proposals and subsequent developments have become synonymous with neo-liberal economic globalization and a major target for critiques from the **anti-globalization movement**. From an academic perspective, theorists have criticized the consensus from a post-Keynesian standpoint, arguing that a number of the areas of reform (notably fiscal discipline and liberalization) are in conflict and work against **economic growth** in certain contexts. There is thus an ongoing academic debate about whether all of the Washington Consensus reforms can be and need to be taken as one 'package'. This presents a more complex development in the polarized debate that engagements with the anti-globalization movement have produced as to whether the consensus is simply 'good' or 'bad'. Many supranational bodies such as the **World Bank** or **World Health Organization** now refer to the post-Washington Consensus to denote a reformulated project of managed economic growth that takes account of the global **environment** and the need to address poverty in the **global South**.

Further reading
Fine, B. 'Neither the Washington nor the Post-Washington Consensus: An Introduction' in Fine, B., Pincus, J. and Lapavitsas, C. (eds) *Development Policy in the Twenty First Century: Beyond the Post-Washington Consens us* (London: Routledge, 2004)

WENT, ROBERT

Adopting a perspective highly critical of **economic globalization**, Went's contribution is to argue that **globalization**, defined as a wider set of processes, is not the exclusive property of neo-liberal architects. Viewing globalization from a historical perspective, he has argued that there can be no period of expansion in future similar to the postwar golden era of the 1960s and 1970s. Like other left-wing progressive commentators, he suggests that unchecked globalization will produce greater social inequality and conflict, as well as ecological disaster. His most distinctive point is that he sees left-wing social movements as already having the basis for offering a viable alternative if they can forge ahead in further developing global civil society.

Further reading
Went, R. 'Globalization Under Fire', ch. 5 in *Globalization: Neoliberal Challenge, Radical Responses* (London: Pluto Press, 2000)

WESTPHALIAN MODEL

Named after the Treaty of Westphalia (1648), in essence, a conception of the **sovereignty** of **nation-state**s as demarcated territorial-political units. The Treaty of Westphalia was a peace treaty which marked the end of the Thirty Years War in Europe under which the European powers agreed in Münster and Osnabrück to stop intruding on one another's domestic politics. The peace formally recognized the territorial sovereignty of the member states of the Holy Roman Empire, leaving about 300 princes in exclusive charge of their pieces of territory. Since that time, the Westphalian model has developed as a premise for the sovereignty of states, and then nation-states, over territory, and in a sense it also marks the birth of the international system. It rests on two principles: territoriality and the exclusion of external actors from domestic authority structures.

The contemporary **globalization** debate has primarily been concerned with the model in so far as commentators have argued that it is breaking down. Factors that are argued to have removed the exclusivity of state sovereignty in recent decades include supranational institutions, **transnational corporation**s, **global financial integration** and **global communications**. Many theorists agree that it is becoming increasingly hard for nation-states in the contemporary world to control everything that occurs within their borders without taking into account external regional or global factors. However, the concept of the Westphalian model has also been criticized within this context by those who argue that the model itself represented an 'ideal' that has never in fact existed. Opinions remain divided also as to whether the Westphalian model is a desirable form for state sovereignty in any case. For example, recent interventions by the **United Nations** in the former Yugoslavia and Africa, along with the US's actions in Iraq and Afghanistan, are based on a philosophical argument that sovereignty should not be an absolute right of states if they violate universal values of **human rights** or **international law.**

Further reading
Keohane, R. 'Sovereignty in International Society', ch. 13 in Held, D. and McGrew, A. (eds) *The Global Transformations Reader* (Cambridge: Polity, 2000)

WHO *see* World Health Organization.

WILLIAMSON, JEFFREY

An economic historian, Williamson has researched and written extensively on mass **migration**, urbanization and the historical integration of economic activity across continents. His work is important to understanding the longer historical processes of global interconnectedness. In analysing historical data on trade, prices and investment flows, his work examines how treaties and international trading relationships developed between countries. In his recent work, with Kevin O'Rourke, *Globalization and History* (2001), Williamson presents a detailed and coherent picture of trade, migration, and international capital flows in the Atlantic economy in the century prior to 1914 – the first great **globalization** boom as the authors term it. His contribution is thus important in providing a comparative basis against which to measure degrees of interconnectedness in the contemporary global economy.

Further reading
O'Rourke, K. and Williamson, J. *Globalization and History: The Evolution of a Nineteenth-century Atlantic Economy* (Cambridge, Mass.: MIT Press, 2001)

WORLD BANK

An international organization set up in December 1945 after the Bretton Woods conference in July that year, with the original mission of financing the reconstruction of nations after the end of the **Second World War**. Called the International Bank for Reconstruction and Development, it is better known as the World Bank, and nowadays its primary task is to fight poverty through financing states and state-run **development** programmes. Its operations and financial resources are maintained through contributions from the wealthier nations.

In the immediate postwar decades, the World Bank's main policy focus was concerned with **economic growth**. It started out making loans for large-scale infrastructure projects such as airports, highways and power plants. As time went by, its initial Western European client states and Japan 'graduated' by achieving certain levels of income per capita, and the World Bank became entirely focused on less developed countries (LDCs) until in the 1990s it also started providing finance to the post-socialist states of Eastern Europe and the former Soviet Union. In the last couple of decades, the focus on **economic growth** has also shifted to a more specific concern with poverty reduction and the World Bank has also increasingly embraced concepts of **sustainable development**.

In the context of the **globalization** debate, the World Bank represents another key supranational institution that can be seen as both symptom and progenitor of greater societal interconnectedness. It has also been the target of much criticism from the **anti-globalization movement** and those opposed to neo-liberal **economic globalization**. A number of major common criticisms can be identified. First, as with the **International Monetary Fund**, the World Bank is argued by some to be an agent of neocolonial globalization. Through its policies it promotes neo-liberal capitalism and undermines the national economic **sovereignty** of recipient countries. In that sense, it represents a joint foe with the IMF in the way it has attached conditions to development financing and structural adjustment programmes that seek economic liberalization, privatization and a restriction on welfare expenditure in less developed countries. Second, and related, recent critics such as former World Bank Chief Economist Joseph **Stiglitz** have argued in effect that the World Bank has been too dogmatic in its faith in markets and free competition, and has favoured foreign investment over local economic growth. Third, it has been argued that the World Bank, like other supranational bodies, is not democratic or accountable and is far too much under the influence of a few wealthy states – most notably the US and other **G8** contributor nations. Its policies have thus been criticized for furthering the vested interests of these states. Fourth, during the earlier part of the 1990s it received considerable criticism for not taking into account the environmental and social impacts of its policies. Even where there might have been a good case for market reform, World Bank projects have been too insensitive to local peoples and the **environment**, which many see as a failing of an organization operating at the global scale but managing local or regional projects.

Overall, therefore, the success of the World Bank in achieving its stated goals remains the subject of heated debate. Undoubtedly the organization has undertaken projects that have tackled poverty and promoted development, but in the twenty-first century there is considerable pressure for it to reform and become more accountable, transparent and sensitive to local peoples and environments.

Further reading
Pincus, J. and Winters, J. *Reinventing the Word Bank* (Ithaca, N.Y.: Cornell University Press, 2002)
Ritzen, J. *A Chance for the World Bank* (London: Anthem Press, 2005)
And see <www.worldbank.org>.

WORLD CITIES
Large cities that play a significant role in the wider global economy and society. Often used (and confused) with the more narrowly defined term **'global cities'**, the term has been criticized for being a 'fuzzy' concept in so far as it has more than one meaning. At least four competing definitions have been suggested: a city with a leadership role at the international scale (whether through emulation or domination); one with an external orientation towards the global economy; one with a high ranking in the world's urban hierarchy; or a major gateway for immigration. Most academic commentators have tended to use economic criteria as the most significant indicator, notably in terms of the presence of **transnational corporation** headquarters, financial markets (especially capital and equity markets) and a broader range of advanced business services, such as credit rating, multi-jurisdictional law and risk management.

Further reading
Newman, P. and Thornley, A. 'Global Transformation and the City: The Debates', ch. 2 in *Planning World Cities: Globalization and Urban Politics* (Basingstoke: Palgrave Macmillan, 2004)

WORLD HEALTH ORGANIZATION (WHO)

A United Nations agency founded in 1948 and based in Geneva, which has the aim of furthering international cooperation in improving health conditions. It has three major constituent parts: the World Health Assembly, which meets annually as the general policy-making body; an Executive Board of health specialists elected for three-year terms by the assembly; and a Secretariat, which has regional offices and field staff throughout the world. The organization is financed primarily from annual contributions made by member governments on the basis of relative ability to pay. Although the WHO inherited specific tasks relating to epidemic control, quarantine measures and drug standardization from the Health Organization of the **League of Nations** (set up in 1923) and from the International Office of Public Health at Paris (1909), the WHO was given a broader mandate under its constitution to promote the attainment of 'the highest possible level of health' by all people. WHO defines health positively as 'a state of complete physical, mental, and social well-being and not merely the absence of disease or infirmity'. Its work focuses on three major areas: health information, disease control and education.

Further reading
See the WHO website at: <www.who.org>.

WORLD MUSIC

In general, music from cultures other than those of Western Europe and English-speaking North America, especially popular music from Latin America, Africa and Asia. World music's propagation as a widely used term is in part a consequence of the development of a transnational record and music industry which has provided the marketing and retailing infrastructure to sell world music at the global scale. As a consequence, some **anti-globalization** commentators have criticized the idea of world music as having been hijacked for commercial gain by large corporations. Theorists of **cultural globali-**

zation also cite world music as a prime example of new hybrid cultural forms arising as a consequence of **globalization**.

Further reading
Bohlman, P. *World Music: A Very Short Introduction* (Oxford: Oxford University Press, 2002)

WORLD SOCIAL FORUM (WSF)

An annual meeting held by left-wing members of the **anti-globalization** or **alter-globalization** movement to coordinate world campaigns, share and refine organizing strategies and inform each other about movements from around the world and around many different issues. It tends to meet in January, timed to coincide with its capitalist rival organization, the World Economic Forum in Switzerland. The first WSF was held from 25 January to 30 January 2001 in Porto Alegre, Brazil, and was attended by around 12,000 people. It was organized by many groups involved in the alter- or anti-globalization movement and was sponsored, in part, by the Porto Alegre government, led at that point by the Brazilian Workers' Party (PT). The second and third WSFs were also held in Porto Alegre in January 2002 and 2004. The event grew larger in 2002 with over 12,000 official delegates representing people from 123 countries. A further 60,000 people attended more than 600 workshops and numerous lectures. The fourth WSF was larger again and held in Mumbai, India, in January 2004. In 2005 the WSF returned to Porto Alegre but it is planned as an event to be held simultaneously in multiple countries in 2006. The WSF has prompted the organizing of many regional social forums, including the European Social Forum, the Asian Social Forum and the Boston Social Forum. All social forums adhere to the WSF's Charter of Principles.

As the key global annual event for critics of contemporary **globalization**, the WSF has sought to try to shift its discussions over the last few years away from pure criticism of global capitalism towards feasible alternative paths that global society can take. Its main slogan is 'Another World is Possible'. Critical commentators, however, remain sceptical as to whether the WSF offers any realistic basis for alternatives and argue that it needs to become yet more focused on amending and modifying the current form of globalization to accommodate its goals.

Further reading
World Social Forum 'Porto Alegre Call for Mobilization', ch. 57 in Lechner, F. and Boli, J. (eds) *The Globalization Reader* (2nd edn; Oxford: Blackwell, 2004)

WORLD SYSTEMS ANALYSIS

A proto-theory for **globalization** proposed by the social historian Immanuel **Wallerstein** in the early 1970s. Conceived within a Marxist framework, world systems analysis is an attempt to understand the integration of human societies into coherent economic and political territorial units from a historical perspective. Wallerstein argues that the modern world system has emerged as a basis for economic organization, centred on capitalist relations, since the late seventeenth century. The capitalist system is thus the basis for a world system that has become global in scope. The system also has a geographical form with the Western 'core' states deriving surplus value from peripheral states. States in a third geographical division – the semi-periphery – enable the successful maintenance of this geographically uneven form that economic activity takes.

Further reading
Wallerstein, I. 'The Rise and Future Demise of the World Capitalist System', ch. 8 in Lechner, F. and Boli, J. (eds) *The Globalization Reader* (2nd edn; Oxford: Blackwell, 2004)

WSF *see* World Social Forum.

WORLD TRADE ORGANIZATION (WTO)

The organization that came into existence on 1 January 1995 to replace the postwar General Agreement on Tariffs and Trade (GATT) framework for international trade negotiations. The GATT was a series of trade treaties agreed since 1945 that were designed to facilitate the freeing up of international trade. The WTO adopted the GATT principles and agreements and represents a more formalized supranational institution charged with administering and extending them. In effect the WTO is therefore the long-delayed successor of the International Trade Organization Charter which was agreed at the UN Conference on Trade and Employment in March 1948. At the time this was blocked by the US Senate, arguably as a consequence of fears within the American business community that the ITO could be used to regulate, rather than liberate, business.

The WTO has two basic functions: as a negotiating forum for discussions of new and existing trade rules and as a trade dispute settlement body. The current 'round' of the WTO negotiations is the '**Doha Development Round**' which was initiated at the Fourth Ministerial Conference in Doha, Qatar, in November 2001. Unlike many supranational institutions that have a one-country, one-vote system, the WTO operates through a process of consensus. This means that decisions such as adopting agreements or revisions to agreements do not require unanimous agreement but simply that no member finds a decision so unacceptable that they insist on an objection. The consensus approach is argued to be advantageous in that it encourages efforts to find the most widely acceptable decision, but it also can take a long time to reach consensus and final agreements often tend to use ambiguous language. It has been argued by some commentators that the consensus process in the WTO, as with the GATT, has tended to favour Western European states and the US. Increasingly, resistance to this process from developing countries has grown within the WTO. The failures at **Seattle** (1999) and **Cancún** (2003) rest on developed countries' refusal to accept proposed decisions. With regard to dispute settlement, the WTO is also different from other supranational institutions in that it has significant powers of enforcement, through the operation of its Dispute Settlement Body. This is in effect an international trade court with the power to authorize sanctions against **nation-state**s that do not comply with its rulings.

In the context of the wider **globalization** debate, the WTO has become a prime focus for criticism aimed at the (neo-liberal) **Washington Consensus** on **economic globalization** and free trade. The **anti-globalization movement** has increasingly targeted WTO negotiations meetings with major protests. The main criticisms levelled at the WTO include its unfair bias in favour of the interests of **transnational corporations** and wealthy nations and the fact that although membership is voluntary, not joining in effect puts a protesting nation-state under embargo. From the perspective of the anti-globalization movement, the WTO is perpetuating and deepening a global economic system that discourages change and experimentation. It is arguably forcing the global economy into a set of institutional arrangements that protect the vested interests of the wealthy few. In future, it seems likely that the WTO will remain a central and highly contentious institution in the development of economic and **political globalization**.

Further reading

Hoekman, B. and Kostecki, M. 'The World Trade Organization', part II in *The Political Economy of the World Trading System: WTO and Beyond* (Oxford: Oxford University Press, 2001)

See also the WTO website at: <www.wto.org>.

ZAPATISTAS

The small force organized as the *Ejército Zapatista de Liberación Nacional* (the EZLN) which, on 1 January 1994, the first day of the **North American Free Trade Agreement**, took control of the main municipalities adjacent to the Lacandon Forest in the southern Mexican state of Chiapas. Most of these 3000 or so lightly armed men and women were Indians from various ethnic groups, although some of them were *mestizos* and some of their leaders and their spokesperson Subcomandante **Marcos** were urban intellectuals. The leaders had their faces hidden behind ski masks and when the Mexican army despatched reinforcements, after a series of skirmishes in which a number of people were killed, the guerrillas withdrew into the rainforest.

In terms of the developing **globalization** debate, the significance of the Zapatista uprising has been considerable for two main sets of reasons. First, what appeared to be a small regional conflict quickly became emblematic for many commentators of a new kind of globalized or postmodern politics. From the outset, the Zapatistas appeared to be a very different kind of new social movement, adopting **global communications** strategies and techniques in order to further their cause. Manuel **Castells** argues that was the key to their success. He terms them the first 'informational guerrilla movement', primarily based around the way they created a media event in order to disseminate their message. Whilst, as **Castells** and other commentators acknowledge, there were real deaths and real weapons, actual warfare was not the main tactic. Rather, the Zapatistas used arms to make a statement in the global media, parlaying the possibility of their sacrifice in front of the world media in order to force the Mexican government into negotiation around a series of well-conceived and reasonable demands which also gained them wide support across Mexican society.

Second, and equally important, is what the Zapatistas were resisting. They represented a direct grassroots challenge in the less developed world to the neo-liberal, or **Washington, Consensus** on international trade and **development**. The uprising was directed explicitly against **NAFTA** and the 'freer trade' it represented. The EZLN pointed out that this liberalization favoured the wealthy elite in Mexican society and in fact was likely to cause economic ruin amongst the rural poor of southern Chiapas, not least also because the commercial interests of large landowners in the aftermath of NAFTA would lead to the progressive disenfranchisement of small farmers. The Zapatistas therefore became the emblematic grassroots resistance movement to the wider consensus on **economic globalization** and during the later 1990s became the impetus behind the wider transnational **anti-globalization movement**.

In that sense, the Zapatista movement is now argued to be a vast transnational network: the archetypal grassroots globalized political organization. Their usage of the **Internet**, media and other **global communications** has been adopted by a wide array of civil society organizations and thus the Zapatistas arguably reside at the centre of the global counter-culture to neo-liberal globalization. Roger Burbach argues that perhaps their most important contribution has been to create the possibility that Castells' informational society also offers the opportunity for new forms of resistance and political practice, rather than just being an appendage to neo-liberal corporate-driven globalization.

Further reading
Burbach, R. *Globalization and Postmodern Politics* (London: Pluto Press, 2001)
Castells, M. *End of Millennium* (Oxford: Blackwell, 2002)
Perez-Bustillo, C. *Zapatistas: An Army of Ideas* (London: Zed Books, 2005)

Additional Readings

The following books and articles provide a series of entry points for further reading and aim to provide additional materials authored by key thinkers cited in the Dictionary. The first group are full-length books and offer a range of overview material on all aspects of the globalization debate. Subsequent sections are lists of more focused selected articles and chapters on specific dimensions of the debate. Where possible, pieces by 'key thinkers' have been included where appropriate. The list is not exhaustive but seeks to represent a range of contributions across the field of discussion.

Readers and Overview Texts
Bauman, Z. *Globalization* (Cambridge: Polity, 1999)
Baylis, J. and Smith, S. *The Globalization of World Politics* (Oxford: Oxford University Press, 2001)
Beck, U. *What is Globalization?* (Cambridge: Polity, 1999)
Castells, M. *The Rise of the Network Society* (2nd edn; Oxford: Blackwell, 2002)
Economist, The. *Globalisation: Making Sense of an Integrating World* (London: Profile Books, 2001)
Greider, W. *One World Ready or Not: The Manic Logic of Global Capitalism* (London: Penguin, 1997)
Held, D. *Debating Globalization* (Cambridge: Polity, 2005)
Held, D. and McGrew, A. *The Global Transformations Reader* (2nd edn; Cambridge: Polity, 2003)
Held, D., McGrew, A., Goldblatt, D. and Perraton, J. *Global Transformations* (Cambridge: Polity, 1999)
Hutton, W. and Giddens, A. (eds) *On the Edge: Living With Global Capitalism* (London: Verso, 2001)
Kofman, E. and Youngs, G. *Globalization: Theory and Practice* (2nd edn; London: Pinter, 2001)
Lechner, F. and Boli (eds) *The Globalization Reader* (2nd edn; Oxford: Blackwell, 2004)

Marcuse, P. and van Kempen, R. (eds) *Globalizing Cities: A New Spatial Order?* (Oxford: Blackwell, 2000)

Mittelman, J. (ed.) *Globalization: Critical Reflections* (New York: Lynne Reiner, 1997)

Mittelman, J. *The Globalization Syndrome: Transformation and Resistance* (Princeton, N.J.: Princeton University Press, 2000)

O'Rourke, K. and Williamson, J. *Globalization and History: The Evolution of a Nineteenth-Century Atlantic Economy* (Cambridge, Mass.: MIT Press, 2001)

Perrons, D. *Globalization and Social Change* (London: Routledge, 2004)

Sassen, S. *The Global City* (2nd edn; Princeton, N.J.: Princeton University Press, 2001)

Scholte, J. *Globalization: A Critical Introduction* (2nd edn; Basingstoke: Palgrave Macmillan, 2005)

Theorizing Globalization

Busch, A. 'Unpacking the Globalization Debate: Approaches, Evidence and Data', ch. 2 in Hay, C. and Marsh, D. (eds) *Demystifying Globalization* (Basingstoke: Palgrave, 2001)

Cox, R. 'A Perspective on Globalization', ch. 2 in Mittelman, J. (ed.) *Globalization: Critical Reflections* (New York: Lynne Reiner, 1997)

Giddens, A. *The Constitution of Society* (Cambridge: Polity, 1990) [see the Introduction]

Harvey, D. 'Contemporary Globalization', ch. 4 in *Spaces of Hope* (Edinburgh: Edinburgh University Press, 2000)

Held, D., McGrew, A., Goldblatt, D. and Perraton, J. 'Conclusion: The Shape of Contemporary Globalization', in *Global Transformations* (Cambridge: Polity, 1999)

Kofman, E. and Youngs, E. (eds) *Globalization: Theory and Practice* (2nd edn; London: Pinter, 2001) [focus on part I]

Langhorne, R. *The Coming of Globalization* (Basingstoke: Palgrave, 2001) [esp. the Introduction]

Robertson, R. 'Globalization as a Problem', ch. 12 in Lechner, F. and Boli, J. (eds) *The Globalization Reader* (2nd edn; Oxford: Blackwell, 2004)

Rosenberg, J. 'Introduction: The Problem of Globalisation Theory', in *The Follies of Globalisation Theory* (London: Verso, 2001) [look at more of this if you can, esp. the chs on Giddens and the Conclusion]

Scholte, J. *Globalization: A Critical Introduction* (Basingstoke: Palgrave, 2005) [esp. Introduction and chs 1, 2 and 4]

Sklair, L. *The Transnational Capitalist Class* (Oxford: Blackwell, 2001) [esp. chs 1, 2 and 9]

Sklair, L. 'Sociology of the Global System', ch. 9 in Lechner, F. and Boli, J. (eds) *The Globalization Reader* (2nd edn; Oxford: Blackwell, 2004)

Urry, J. *Global Complexities* (Cambridge: Polity, 2004) [esp. the Introduction]

The Globalization Debate

Harvey, D. 'Contemporary Globalization', ch. 4 in *Spaces of Hope* (Oxford: Blackwell, 2001)

Hay, C. and Marsh, D. 'Introduction: Demystifying Globalization', ch. 1 in Hay, C. and Marsh, D. (eds) *Demystifying Globalization* (Basingstoke: Palgrave, 2001)

Held, D. and McGrew, A. 'Making Sense of Globalization', ch. 1 in *Globalization/Anti-globalization* (Cambridge: Polity, 2002)

Held, D. and McGrew, A. 'The Great Globalization Debate: An Introduction', in *The Global Transformations Reader* (2nd edn; Cambridge: Polity, 2003)

Hirst, P. and Thompson, G. *Globalization in Question* (2nd edn; Cambridge: Polity, 1998) [esp. ch. 1]

Legrain, P. 'The Poor Profit: Globalisation is the Only Route out of Poverty', ch. 2 in *Open World: The Truth About Globalisation* (London: Abacus, 2002)

Mittelman, J. 'Globalization: An Ascendant Paradigm', ch. 3 in *Whither Globalization? The Vortex of Knowledge and Ideology* (London: Routledge, 2004)

Scholte, J. 'What Causes Globalization?', ch. 4 in *Globalization: A Critical Introduction* (2nd edn; Basingstoke: Palgrave, 2005)

Economic Globalization

Burtless, G. et al. 'Globaphobia: Confronting Fears about Open Trade', ch. 26 in Lechner, F. and Boli, J. (eds) *The Globalization Reader* (Oxford: Blackwell, 2004)

Castells, M. 'Global Informational Capitalism', ch. 27 in Held, D. and McGrew, A. (eds) *The Global Transformations Reader* (2nd edn; Cambridge: Polity, 2003)

Dicken, P. 'The Shifting Contours of the Geo-Economy', part I in *Global Shift: Remapping the Global Economic Map in the 21st Century* (London: Sage, 2004)

Doremus, P., Kellner, W., Pauly, L. and Reich, S. *The Myth of the Global Corporation* (Princeton, N.J.: Princeton University Press, 1998) [esp. ch. 1]

Garett, G. 'Global Markets and National Politics', ch. 33 in Held, D. and McGrew, A. (eds) *The Global Transformations Reader* (2nd edn; Cambridge: Polity, 2003)

Greider, W. 'Wawasan 2020', ch. 21 in Lechner, F. and Boli, J. (eds) *The Globalization Reader* (Oxford: Blackwell, 2000)

Held, D., McGrew, A., Goldblatt, D. and Perraton, J. 'Global Trade, Global Markets', ch. 3 in *Global Transformations* (Cambridge: Polity, 1999)

Held, D., McGrew, A., Goldblatt, D. and Perraton, J. 'Corporate Power and Global Production Networks', ch. 5 in *Global Transformations* (Cambridge: Polity, 1999)

Holton, R. 'The Global Economy: Organizations, Networks and Regulatory Arrangements', ch. 3 in *Globalization and the Nation-State* (Basingstoke: Macmillan, 1998)

Morgan, G., Kristensen, P. and Whitley, R. *The Multinational Firm: Organizing across Institutional and National Divides* (Oxford: Oxford University Press, 2001) [esp. chs 1 and 7]

Rugman, A. 'Strategies for Triad Firms', ch 9 in *The End of Globalization* (London: Random House Business Books, 2001)

Stiglitz, J. 'Globalism's Discontents', ch. 25 in Lechner, F. and Boli, J. (eds) *The Globalization Reader* (2nd edn; Oxford: Blackwell, 2004)

Financial Globalization

Held, D., McGrew, A., Goldblatt, D. and Perraton, J. 'Shifting Patterns of Global Finance', ch. 4 in *Global Transformations* (Cambridge: Polity, 1999)

Isard, P. *Globalization and the International Financial System: What's Wrong and What Can be Done* (Cambridge: Cambridge University Press, 2005) [esp. the Introduction]

James, H. 'Introduction: The End of Globalization and the Problem of the Depression', ch. 1 in *The End of Globalization: Lessons from the Great Depression* (Cambridge, Mass.: Harvard University Press, 2001)

Noble, G. and Ravenhill, J. (eds) *The Asian Financial Crisis and the Architecture of Global Finance* (Cambridge: Cambridge University Press, 2000) [Introduction and esp. the final ch. on the new global financial architecture]

Scholte, J. 'Governing Global Finance', ch. 9 in Held, D. and McGrew, A. (eds) *Governing Globalization* (Cambridge: Polity, 2002)

Strange, S. *Mad Money* (Manchester: Manchester University Press, 1998) [see the Introduction]

Political Globalization, the Nation-State and Global Institutions

Annan, K. 'The Role of the State in the Age of Globalization', ch. 30 in Lechner, F. and Boli, J. (eds) *The Globalization Reader* (2nd edn; Oxford: Blackwell, 2004)

Burbach, R. *Globalization and Postmodern Politics* (London: Pluto Press, 2001)

Cerny, P. 'What Next for the State?', ch. 9 in Kofman, E. and Youngs, G. (eds) *Globalization: Theory and Practice* (London: Pinter, 1996)

Chomsky, N. 'Imperial Grand Strategy', ch. 2 in *Hegemony or Survival: America's Quest for Global Dominance* (London: Penguin, 2003)

Hardt, M. and Negri, A. *Empire* (Cambridge, Mass.: Harvard University Press, 2001) [look at the section 2.2 entitled 'Sovereignty of the Nation-State']

Held, D. 'Cosmopolitanism: Ideas, Realities and Deficits', ch. 15 in Held, D. and McGrew, A. (eds) *Governing Globalization* (Cambridge: Polity, 2002)

Held, D. and McGrew, A. (eds) *Governing Globalization* (Cambridge: Polity, 2002)

Held, D., McGrew, A., Goldblatt, D. and Perraton, J. 'The Territorial State and Global Politics', ch. 1 in *Global Transformations* (Cambridge: Polity, 1999)

Krasner, S. 'Compromising Westphalia', ch. 10 in Held, D. and McGrew, A. (eds) *The Global Transformations Reader* (1st edn; Cambridge: Polity, 2000)

Mann, M. 'Has Globalization Ended the Rise and Rise of the Nation State?', ch. 11 in Held, D. and McGrew, A. (eds) *The Global Transformations Reader* (2nd edn; Cambridge: Polity, 2003)

Ohmae, K. 'The End of the Nation State', ch. 26 in Lechner, J. and Boli, F. (eds) *The Globalization Reader* (2nd edn; Oxford: Blackwell, 2004)

Rosenau, J. 'Governance in a New Global Order', ch. 3 in Held, D. and McGrew, A. (eds) *Governing Globalization* (Cambridge: Polity, 2002)

Scholte, J. 'The Globalization of World Politics', ch. 1 in Baylis, J. and Smith, S. (eds) *The Globalization of World Politics* (Oxford: Oxford University Press, 2001)

Shaw, M. *Theory of the Global State: Globality as an Unfinished Revolution* (Cambridge: Cambridge University Press, 2000)

Strange, S. 'The Declining Authority of States', ch. 27 in Lechner, J. and Boli, F. (eds) *The Globalization Reader* (2nd edn; Oxford: Blackwell, 2004)

Cultural Globalization

Appadurai, A. 'Disjuncture and Difference in the Global Cultural Economy', ch. 13 in Lechner, F. and Boli, J. (eds) *The Globalization Reader* (Oxford: Blackwell, 2004)

Held, D., McGrew, A., Goldblatt, D. and Perraton, J. 'Globalization, Culture and the Fate of Nations', ch. 7 in *Global Transformations* (Cambridge: Polity, 1999)

Huntington, S. 'The Clash of Civilizations?', ch. 5 in Lechner, F. and Boli, J. (eds) *The Globalization Reader* (2nd edn; Oxford: Blackwell, 2004)

Morley, D. and Robins, K. *Spaces of Identity: Global Media, Electronic Landscapes and Cultural Boundaries* (London: Routledge, 1995)

Pieterse, J. 'Globalization as Hybridization' in Featherstone, M., Lash, S. and Robertson, R. (eds) *Global Modernities* (London: Sage, 1996)

Ritzer, G. *The McDonaldization of Society* (London: Sage, 2000)

Ritzer, G. *The Globalization of Nothing* (London: Sage, 2004) [esp. chs 1, 4 and 8]

Robertson, R. *Globalization: Social Theory and Global Culture* (London: Sage, 1992) [esp. chs 1–3]

Robins, K. 'Encountering Globalization', ch. 20 in Held, D. and McGrew, A. (eds) *The Global Transformations Reader* (Cambridge: Polity, 2000)

Tomlinson, J. *Globalization and Culture* (Cambridge: Polity, 1999)

Tomlinson, J. 'Globalization and Cultural Identity', ch. 23 in Held, D. and McGrew, A. (eds) *The Global Transformations Reader* (1st edn; Cambridge: Polity, 2000)

Globalization and the Environment

Elliot, L. *The Global Politics of the Environment* (Basingstoke: Macmillan, 1998)

French, H. *Vanishing Borders – Protecting the Planet in the Age of Globalization* (London: Earthscan, 2000)

Goldsmith, E. and Mander, J. (eds) 'Introduction: Facing the Rising Tide', in *The Case against the Global Economy* (London: Earthscan, 2001)

Held, D., McGrew, A., Goldblatt, D. and Perraton, J. 'Catastrophe in the Making: Globalization and the Environment', ch. 8 in *Global Transformations* (Cambridge: Polity, 1999)

Paterson, M. *Understanding Global Environmental Politics: Domination, Accumulation, Resistance* (Basingstoke: Palgrave, 2001)

Sachs, W. 'Globalization and Sustainability', ch. 52 in Lechner, F. and Boli, J. (eds) *The Globalization Reader* (2nd edn; Oxford: Blackwell, 2004)

Shiva, V. 'Ecological Balance in an Era of Globalization', ch. 55 in Lechner, F. and Boli, J. (eds) *The Globalization Reader* (Oxford: Blackwell, 2004)

United Nations 'Rio Declaration on Environment and Development', ch. 48 in Lechner, F. and Boli, J. (eds) *The Globalization Reader* (2nd edn; Oxford: Blackwell, 2004)

Welsh, I. 'Risk, "Race" and Global Environmental Regulation', ch. 3 in Brah, A., Hickmann, M. and Mac an Ghaill, M. (eds) *Global Futures: Migration, Environment and Globalization* (Basingstoke: Macmillan, 1999)

Yearly, S. 'Environmental Issues and the Compression of the Globe', ch. 36 in Held, D. and McGrew, A. (eds) *The Global Transformations Reader* (1st edn; Cambridge: Polity, 2000)

Critiques, Resistance, Anti-globalization and Alter-globalization

Abrash, A. 'The Amungme, Kamoro & Freeport: How Indigenous Papuans have Resisted the World's Largest Gold and Copper Mine', ch. 51 in Lechner, F. and Boli, J. (eds) *The Globalization Reader* (2nd edn; Oxford: Blackwell, 2004)

Bello, W. 'Introduction: The Multiple Crises of Global Capitalism', ch. 1 in *Deglobalization* (New York: Zed Books, 2002)

Bircham, E. and Charlton, J. *Anti-Capitalism: A Guide to the Movement* (London: Bookmark Publications, 2001)

Bove, J. and Dufour, F. *The World is Not for Sale: Farmers against Junk Food* (London: Verso, 2001)

Castells, M. 'The Other Face of the Earth: Social Movements against the New Global Order', ch. 2 in *The Power of Identity* (2nd edn; Oxford: Blackwell, 2002)

Gray, J. 'What Globalization is Not', ch. 3 in *False Dawn: The Delusions of Global Capitalism* (Cambridge: Granta, 1998)

Ekins, P. *A New World Order: Grassroots Movements for Global Change* (London: Routledge, 1992) [esp. chs 1, 4 and 7)

Esteva, G. and Prakash, M. 'From Global to Local: Beyond Neoliberalism to the International of Hope', ch. 53 in Lechner, F. and Boli, J. (eds) *The Globalization Reader* (2nd edn; Oxford: Blackwell, 2004)

Harding, J. 'Counter-capitalism: Globalization's Children Strike Back', ch. 54 in Lechner, F. and Boli, J. (eds) *The Globalization Reader* (Oxford: Blackwell, 2004)

Harvey, D. 'How America's Power Grew', ch. 2 in *The New Imperialism* (Oxford: Oxford University Press, 2003)

Hayden, T. (ed.) *The Zapatista Reader* (San Francisco: Nation Press, 2000)

Kingsworth, P. 'Part Two: Many Yeses', in *One No, Many Yeses* (London: Free Press, 2003)

Klein, N. *No Logo* (London: HarperCollins, 2000) [esp. Introduction and parts I and III]

Klein, N. *Fences and Windows: Despatches from the Frontline of the Globalization Debate* (London: Flamingo, 2002) [sample from a collection of Klein's articles]

Marcos, Subcomandante 'The Punch Card and the Hour Glass', *New Left Review* 9 (2001): 69–79

Marcos, Subcomandante *Zapatista Stories* (London: Katabasis, 2002)

Marcos, Subcomandante 'Tomorrow Begins Today', ch. 56 in Lechner, F. and Boli, J. (eds) *The Globalization Reader* (2nd edn; Oxford: Blackwell, 2004)

Mittelman, J. and Chin, C. 'Conceptualizing Resistance to Globalization', ch. 9 in Mittelman, J. *The Globalization Syndrome* (Princeton, N.J.: Princeton University Press, 2000)

Monbiot, G. *The Age of Consent* (London: Perennial, 2004) [esp. Introduction]

[One-Off Press] *On Fire: The Battle of Genoa and the Anti-capitalism Movement* (London: One-Off Press, 2001) [not so well written but look esp. at Moore's ch. 16 for an agenda of action]

Scruton, R. 'Globalization', ch. 4 in *The West and the Rest: Globalization and the Terrorist Threat* (New York: Continuum, 2002)

Stiglitz, J. *Globalization and its Discontents* (London: Penguin, 2002) [esp. chs 1, 2, 3, 7 and 9]

Went, R. *Globalization: Neoliberal Challenge, Radical Responses* (London: Pluto Press, 2000) [esp. the Introduction and 'Globalization Under Fire']

Index

Note: Where index headings are followed by more than six page references **bold type** indicates major treatments.